Unraveling
Resident Evil

CONTRIBUTIONS TO ZOMBIE STUDIES

White Zombie: Anatomy of a Horror Film. Gary D. Rhodes. 2001

The Zombie Movie Encyclopedia. Peter Dendle. 2001

*American Zombie Gothic: The Rise and Fall (and Rise)
of the Walking Dead in Popular Culture.* Kyle William Bishop. 2010

*Back from the Dead: Remakes of the Romero
Zombie Films as Markers of Their Times.* Kevin J. Wetmore, Jr. 2011

*Generation Zombie: Essays on the Living Dead
in Modern Culture.* Edited by Stephanie Boluk and Wylie Lenz. 2011

*Race, Oppression and the Zombie: Essays on Cross-Cultural Appropriations
of the Caribbean Tradition.* Edited by Christopher M. Moreman
and Cory James Rushton. 2011

Zombies Are Us: Essays on the Humanity of the Walking Dead.
Edited by Christopher M. Moreman and Cory James Rushton. 2011

The Zombie Movie Encyclopedia, Volume 2: 2000–2010. Peter Dendle. 2012

Great Zombies in History. Edited by Joe Sergi. 2013 (graphic novel)

Unraveling Resident Evil*: Essays on the Complex Universe
of the Games and Films.* Edited by Nadine Farghaly. 2014

"We're All Infected": Essays on AMC's The Walking Dead
and the Fate of the Human. Edited by Dawn Keetley. 2014

Zombies and Sexuality: Essays on Desire and the Walking Dead.
Edited by Shaka McGlotten and Steve Jones. 2014

Unraveling *Resident Evil*

Essays on the Complex Universe of the Games and Films

EDITED BY
NADINE FARGHALY

CONTRIBUTIONS TO ZOMBIE STUDIES

McFarland & Company, Inc., Publishers
Jefferson, North Carolina

Library of Congress Cataloguing-in-Publication Data

    Unraveling Resident Evil : essays on the complex universe of
the games and films / edited by Nadine Farghaly.
      p.   cm. — (Contributions to Zombie Studies)
    Includes bibliographical references and index.

    ISBN 978-0-7864-7291-8 (softcover : acid free paper) ∞

    ISBN 978-1-4766-1440-3 (ebook)

    1. Resident Evil (Game)   2. Resident evil (Motion picture)
3. Video games—Philosophy.   4. Motion pictures—Philosophy.
I. Farghaly, Nadine, 1981– editor of compilation.
GV1469.35.R47U57 2014
793.93'25369—dc23   2014002000

British Library cataloguing data are available

On the cover: Milla Jovovich in *Resident Evil: Retribution,*
2012 (Screen Gems/Photofest)

Printed in the United States of America

McFarland & Company, Inc., Publishers
  Box 611, Jefferson, North Carolina 28640
  www.mcfarlandpub.com

For the families we choose ourselves

Acknowledgments

As a longtime *Resident Evil* fan I could not believe that there have not been multiple books on it. When I first started researching this topic I expected to find various articles and books on the subject. However, I was mistaken. While I am confident that we will do this wonderful universe justice, I hope that there are going to be many more academic works focusing on the *Resident Evil* franchise.

So many people were involved in this project, both through actual work and support in any other needed form. I want to thank all the people who were not only wonderful peer review readers, but also dear friends and who supported me throughout this endeavor and never stopped believing that this project would be a success: Suzan Aiken and James Campbell for being such wonderful reviewers and people. Tom Schaefer, thank you for inspiring the book's title. All my love to my grandparents, my mother, and my sisters for their incredible support and belief in me. Cheers and my love to Iris, Kathi, Simone, Monika, Martina, and all my friends who let me rant and wail to my heart's content before they tried to help me fix whatever crisis I had (whether imagined or real). Last but not least, my friend Leslie Ormandy for doing a spectacular job as manuscript editor. Thank you all so much.

Table of Contents

Introduction: Unraveling the Resident Evil *Universe*

Although *Resident Evil* started out as a video game produced by Capcom in 1996, it has since then become one of the best known zombie franchises. The company surely did not anticipate the huge fan base they would attract with their zombie survival game. However, Capcom has sold 56 million units of these games, and since its debut, seven main video games have been distributed with the latest coming out in May 2013 (http://www.capcom.co.jp). While the games were the starting point for this remarkable series, it is the adaptations into other media that have created the huge appeal *Resident Evil* holds for many of its fans, through graphic novels, sound dramas, novels, various merchandise and action figures, in addition to animated and live action feature films. Notably, the movie series, which started with *Resident Evil* (2002), introduced a character that had not been present in any of the games before: Alice, the former Umbrella Corporation security operative who later becomes infected with the T-virus, the virus that is responsible for animating dead cells and starting the zombie apocalypse. However, Alice manages to bond with the T-virus on a cellular level, which gives her sophisticated and advanced regeneration capabilities as well as increased physical strength and, to a certain extent, extraordinary abilities. Since then Alice has been featured as the main character of five movies, with the sixth one due out in 2014. Despite mixed reactions, these feature movies have generated an income of over 600 million dollars worldwide; with each movie being more successful than the previous one (http://www.the-numbers.com). Consequently, this movie series is featured in *The Guinness World Records Gamer's Edition* 2012 where it holds the place as "the most successful movie series to be based on a video game" (Reeves).

This collection aims to examine *Resident Evil* in literature, games, and other media through the theoretical framework of sexuality, gender, social change and feminism, among others. It will provide an interdisciplinary stage for the development of innovative and creative research and examine the complex world of *Resident Evil* in all of its various manifestations and cultural meanings. Considering that *Resident Evil* is not only one of the best known

1

zombie representations, but also a far from finished project, it seems clear that it should be examined more carefully.

Zombies, or zombie-like creatures, have been around since the *Epic of Gilgamesh* where Ishtar, the goddess of fertility and war, threatens her father if he does not fulfill her wishes:

> I will knock down the Gates of the Netherworld,
> I will smash the door posts, and leave the doors flat down,
> and will let the dead go up to eat the living!
> And the dead will outnumber the living! [*Epic of Gilgamesh*, Tablet VI].

Interestingly, many instances that can be interpreted to be of zombie origin are also found in the Bible. In the Old Testament examples of the undead can be found. In the book of Zachariah certain passages allude to zombie-like occurrences: "And they shall go forth, and look upon the carcases [*sic*] of the men that have transgressed against me: for their worm shall not die, neither shall their fire be quenched; and they shall be an abhorring unto all flesh" (Isa. 66:24). Zombies are therefore arguably even older than vampires, yet zombies have not yet gained as much cultural appreciation. While the reasons for this are manifold and would exceed this introduction by far, I will just demonstrate a few of their differences. However, before that can be done a short definition of the zombie is needed.

The meaning of the word zombie, as well as its characteristics, does not only differ from culture to culture, but also from franchise to franchise. However, most zombies share common traits: they are dead beings—formerly human—that retain basic motor function after they are reactivated; they are not coherent, they sustain themselves be feasting on human flesh, and they are able to increase their numbers by infecting living beings through biting, scratching, etc. Sometimes zombies are fast ... sometimes they are not. But they all used to be living human beings. Allin Cottrell claims that a zombie "is a being that is physically (and hence also functionally) exactly like an ordinary human being, but which has no conscious experiences" (4). Cottrell's claim is true for most zombies; they are usually unable to comprehend written or verbal communication. As the Red Queen would say: "They are driven by the basest of impulses, the most basic of needs. [...] The need to feed" (*Resident Evil*). Conversely, while vampires certainly also feel the need to feed, most vampires differ from zombies as day does night.

A friend of mine once told me that the main difference between zombies and vampires is that vampires are actively dead while zombies are passively dead. On first glance this might not be such a paradigm shifting observation, however, the distinction (made by Martina Kress) very simply states the difference between the these two undead monsters. While most vampires are able to articulate themselves and pass as humans, zombies are not so lucky. Zombies decay. Inexorably. However, the recent trend in zombie romances has been trying to shift the zombie image; nonetheless, the cuddly-live-happily-ever-after zombie is still a minority. Nevertheless, they are neither as sophisticated nor as suave as most vampires, nor do zombies generate the same revenue. While the zombie industry created revenue of six billion dollars in the last thirteen years (http://de.sodahead.com), vampires have generated seven billion dollars since 2008 (http://encoremag.com) (numbers from 2011 and 2010 respectively). Nowadays, the zombie and his close relatives can be found almost everywhere in popular culture; whether it is the success of the *Resident Evil* movies; the adaptation of classics with a twist, such as *Pride and Prejudice and Zombies*; the TV phenomenon *The Walking Dead*; *Warm Bodies*, the first zombie romance that was adapted to the big screen; or the multitude of video games that flood the market such as *Left for Dead* and *Doom*. Zombies are everywhere, and with the recent shift in image they are also conquering new grounds. Although this collection focuses entirely on the *Resident Evil* franchise and universes, it will help to facilitate discussions of the genre on a broad scale, since so many academics have contributed to this collection with their unique perspectives and theories on the *Resident Evil* universe.

Tanya Carinae Pell Jones tracks the evolution of the zombie genre in her essay "From Necromancy to the Necrotrophic: *Resident Evil*'s Influence on the Zombie Origin Shift from Supernatural to Science." Here she takes the reader on a journey through zombie history, carefully explaining how they arrived at this new zombie stage and how its characteristics have changed.

In "Survival and System in *Resident Evil* (2002): Remembering, Repeating and Working-Through" Daniel Müller argues that *Resident Evil* endeavors to exceed the symptomatic deadlock and tries to converse with as well as shape answers to the loss of historical and chronological continuity that is articulated in Alice's loss of memory, concluding that Alice ultimately needs to adhere to, and is limited by, the fictional world that created her.

Adam M. Crowley discusses how "the vanishing dead are emblematic of a corporatist desire to conceptualize progress as a force that redeems its own call to violence by erasing its expenditure" in "Why They Keep Coming Back: The Allure of Incongruity." Utilizing Slavoj Žižek as well as Gérard Genette, among others, he paints a vivid picture of the *Resident Evil* games and their possible interpretations.

In "Opening Doors: Art-Horror and Agency," Stephen Cadwell discusses the differences between the *Resident Evil* games and the movies. Through lively analyzes and a unique style Cadwell debates different points of view and concludes that, for him, the games "should be considered a text, or work of fiction, equivalent to any movie, novel, or comic."

Broc Holmquest takes a different approach when he applies video gaming theory to perceptions of field and formula in "Survival Horror, Metaculture and the Fluidity of Video Game Genres." Here he thoroughly discusses gaming theory and how it can be applied, as well how it needs to be adjusted, in connection to the *Resident Evil* games.

"The Strong, Silent Type: Alice's Use of Rhetorical Silence as Feminist Strategy" by Suzan E. Aiken discusses Alice's rhetorical silence in the first movie as a positive feminist strategy through which she sheds the image of the supposed victim and triumphs as not only a survivor but also as the hero and warrior.

In "'My name is Alice and I remember everything!' Surviving Sexual Abuse in the Films," James Stone focuses on the connection between sexual assault and the idea that Alice is often rendered childlike while facing domineering patriarchs. He concludes that *Resident Evil*, unlike real life, offers the audience a place where the demons of carnal violence can be defeated.

Jenny Platz focuses her attention on a different female character in "The Woman in the Red Dress: Sexuality, Femmes Fatales, the Gaze and Ada Wong." Here she discusses femmes fatales as well as film noir in connection to this outstanding female character. Praising her as "the true celebration of unchecked power," Platz thoroughly discusses this warrior and her importance to the *Resident Evil* universe.

Nicolas J. Lalone takes a look at the masculine side of this universe in "Chris Redfield and the Curious Case of Wesker's Sunglasses." Lalone states that Redfield and Wesker can be used to thoroughly critique American culture. Focusing on *Resident Evil 5* he concludes that the final message found in this particular game is "that all the people in the stable countries of the world are worth the mass murder of a victimized people."

Discussing Alice's connection to her fairy tale namesake is Hannah Priest in "Through the Looking-Glass: Interrogating the 'Alice-ness' of Alice." Priest meticulously draws connection between these two characters and asks the all-important question: to what extent, then, can we read Alice alongside Alice? Her chapter will answer this interestingly unique approach to the *Resident Evil* universe.

A completely different approach is undertaken by Kristine Larsen in "Thank You for Making Me Human Again: Alice and the Teaching of Scientific Ethics." Using ELSI—the ethical, legal, and social implications of science—she claims that *Resident Evil* can be used to engage with, and debate about, controversial issues in 20th century science.

JL Schatz argues in "Zombies, Cyborgs and Wheelchairs: The Question of Normalcy Within Diseased and Disabled Bodies" that through Alice's interactions with other characters her own dichotomic identity as well as the importance and interpretation of her character are being brought to the surface.

In "'I barely feel human anymore': Project Alice and the Posthuman in the Films" Margo Collins stipulates that the various posthuman choices presented to the audience in *Resident Evil* are all eliminated since "Project ALICE—must become all of these: cyborg, corporation, clone, mutation, revenant. In doing so, she becomes the answer to the question of what it means to be humane in a posthuman world."

The final essay was crafted by Simon Bacon. In "'Six Impossible Things Before Breakfast': Living Memory and Undead History" Bacon concentrates on the assembly of the undead zombie as the corporeal personification of undead memory. Using existing theories on memory he thoroughly discusses how identity, cloning, and evolution all factor into the *Resident Evil* universe.

While there are many more venues that need to be addressed when discussing such a lively, ongoing, and diverse universe as *Resident Evil*, this collection offers an interesting and detailed starting point for various themes. During the 17 years of its existence *Resident Evil* has become the best known zombie franchise and we hope that readers enjoy the journey we are taking them on.

Works Cited

"Box Office History for Resident Evil Movies." www.the-numbers.com/movies/franchise/Resident-Evil, Web. 22 May 2013.

"CAPCOM | Total Sales Units Data." www.capcom.co.jp/ir/english/business/salesdata.html, 31 March 2012. Web. Accessed 22 May 2013.

Cottrell, Allin. "Sniffing the Camembert: On the Conceivability of Zombies." *Journal of Consciousness Studies* 6 (1999): 4–12. Print.

Epic of Gilgamesh: Tablet VI. Academy for Ancient Texts, Ancient Texts Library. www.ancienttexts.org, N.p., n.d. Web. 20 May 2013.

King James Bible. Cambridge, Eng.: Proquest LLC, 1996. Print.

Reeves, Ben. "*Guinness World Records 2012 Gamer's Edition* Preview," www.gameinformer.com, 30 Dec. 2011, accessed 22 May 2013.

From Necromancy to the Necrotrophic: Resident Evil's Influence on the Zombie Origin Shift from Supernatural to Science

Tanya Carinae Pell Jones

"I don't want to be one of those things. Walking around without a soul."—Rain, *Resident Evil* (2002)

Soulless. Whether a zombie is a human puppet without strings carrying out the nefarious schemes of a deranged puppet-master or a rotting corpse tearing into the flesh and muscle of the living with their teeth, the idea of a soulless being driven by impulse is what comes to mind when considering such a creature. Originally, zombies were the product of Vodou/Voodoo or necromancy, spawned by ritual to serve a master. That zombie is—for all intents and purposes—as good as dead and buried in popular culture. Instead, a cultural shift has been seen from the living-dead puppet to a biologically or genetically manipulated creature driven not by a need to serve, but by the instinct to feed. Yet, regardless of their origins, both the supernatural and the biological zombie remain empty shells of what they once were: human.

It would be a challenge to pinpoint the exact moment when zombies saw their mythology shift from a supernatural origin to a scientific theory. Some zombie scholars (and they are out there), argue the shift began with George A. Romero's *Night of the Living Dead* (1968). Others would argue that it truly began with Richard Matheson's *I Am Legend* (1954), the novel from which Romero claims to have gleaned inspiration, though Matheson's hero battles creatures more akin to vampires rather than Romero's ghouls. Some would point fingers at Wade Davis, the world's leading authority on the zombification process in Haitian culture. It may very well be impossible to determine only one prime mover, but we have certainly seen an evolution of the zombie through the years.

Regardless of the catalyst, it suddenly seems far too simple to blame black magic for the reanimation of a corpse, especially as more and more films and literature start to utilize the zombie figure. With information being more readily available as the years progress, more people begin to question the why of things. Our society demands explanation and necromancy no longer cuts it.

Just as evolution began saturating society and pushing against the common creation myths and theories of a prime mover, so too did folklore have to adapt. This was especially easy to do with the zombie, as zombie mythology has no definitive literature. In fact, zombies are essentially "the only creature to pass directly from folklore to the screen, without first having an established literary tradition" (Dendle 2–3). Without a mythological canon firmly in place, the modern zombie saw its voodoo creators or "gods" pushed to the side by a new Big Bang. Only, this time, science gave man credit for partial creation: the modern day zombie is a product of human science gone horribly wrong.

The *Resident Evil* franchise has been an integral part of modern day zombification. Taking into account new technology, new social fears and anxieties, and the cinematic appeal of zombies, the *Resident Evil* teams have helped solidify the scientific theory of a modern day zombie's origin. Through film, games, comics, and more, they have created entirely new species of zombies through the use of biological weaponry, genetic manipulation, and parasitic/symbiotic relationships. Retaining the popular Gothic and horror feel of zombie folklore, the *Resident Evil* creators and contributors have adapted the myths to accommodate reality, which is truly terrifying. However, before one can begin to truly appreciate the variety of zombie-like creatures developed by the *Resident Evil* franchise, it is important to understand the origins of such monsters. This means tracking the progression of the zombie evolution from the island country of Haiti to the undead cannibals of modern film and literature to the science born monsters of *Resident Evil* fame.

Dark Origins: Haiti and the Science of the Supernatural

The zombie myth originated in the depths of Haiti, but the image of "a corpse in tattered rags, trailing remnants of necrotic flesh as it rises from the cemetery," is a far cry from the zombies of Haitian lore (Davis, *Passage* 56). The Haitian zombie is a product of Haitian Vodoun (or Vodou), though the practice of the zombification ritual is not a necessity of the religion. The common misconception of Vodoun practices being akin to Satanic worship has likely added to the mythology of the zombie. Regardless, the Haitian *zombi* is unlike the rotting corpses of pop culture.

The Haitian *zombi* is the child of both supernatural faith and the science of pharmacology. In the Vodoun faith, individuals of untold spiritual power may possess the ability to manipulate the line between life and death. These sorcerers in the Vodoun faith, known as the *bokor*, are capable of the magic required to spawn a *zombi* with their ability to "strike people down to a death-like state and revive them later from the grave to become virtually mindless servants" (Bishop 197). Upon their rising, the *zombis* are little more than automatons, serving a specific master—usually the man or woman that commissioned a *bokor* to create the creature in the first place. These beings are not so unlike the villagers that serve *Los Illuminados* in *Resident Evil 4*.

Yet, the Haitian *zombi* is not so much the spawned creation of necromancy as it is the product of careful pharmacological procedure. Wade Davis, the world's leading authority on the process of zombification, traveled to Haiti in 1982 on an expedition to understand and explain the mystical phenomenon of bringing the dead back to life. What Davis found in the remote villages of Haiti, where the veil between the physical and the spiritual seems precariously thin, was a rather impressive understanding of botany and chemistry by the *bokor*. Using local influence and foreign currency, Davis convinced a *houngan* (a *bokor* priest) to prepare a sample of the zombie powder. As he observed the ritual, Davis realized that "the Vodounist believes emically that the preparation is only a support of the magical force of the sorcerers and it is the power, not a poison, that creates the zombie" (Davis, *Passage* 5). Thus, the necromancer is far more inclined to put his or her faith in the ritual itself as opposed to the product of the ritual.

Davis, a Harvard ethnobotanist at the time of his expedition, carefully and methodically recorded both the ingredients he had observed during the ritual and those that he discovered through chemical analysis. Among the ingredients were the tetrodotoxins found within puffer fish; *Datura stramonium*; and the skull of a small child, ground into a fine powder (Davis, *Passage* 124). Of all the ingredients, it is of course the skull that seems to be the most reconcilable with the zombie mythology and Vodou stereotypes regarding necromancy. Though lacking any pharmacological usefulness, the bones of the dead are not omitted from any region of Haiti in the creation of the zombie powder and, Davis, horrified and yet unabashedly curious of the procedure, brought such practices international attention, fueling society's association of zombies with the dead.

But it is the other two ingredients that truly made Davis believe in the possibility of the existence of zombies. The puffer fish contains a distinctly potent nerve agent called tetrodotoxin. This agent, of which there are several varieties, "induces a state of profound paralysis, marked by complete immobility during which time the border between life and death is not at all certain, even to trained physicians" (Davis, *Serpent* 2037). It is this ingredient that allows the individual being targeted to become a zombi, but it is *Datura stramonium* that maintains the master's control over the "undead." *Datura stramonium*, or "the zombi cucumber," is a powerful psychoactive plant that, when administered, is what truly makes the Haitian zombi: [I]ts intoxication has been characterized as an induced state of psychotic delirium, marked by disorientation, pronounced confusion, and complete amnesia. Administered to an individual who has ... already passed through the ground, the devastating psychological results are difficult to imagine (Davis, *Serpent* 2801). Through the intoxication of the zombi cucumber, the zombi master can enact total control over his new zombi slave. It is this image of a human rising from the grave in a trance-like state that has led to whole new "species" of zombies.

"They're coming to get you, Barbara": Modern Zombification

Though the Haitian zombi is documented long before American cinema, "in many respects it looks as though the Haitian zombie is a thing of the past, permanently eclipsed by the success of Romero's cannibals" (Moreman 5). George A. Romero, nicknamed the "Godfather of Zombies," took the idea of the zombie from the mystified puppet to the cannibalistic ghoul of modern mythology. It was Romero who turned America and the world onto the rotting corpse, staggering after the living, driven to gorge itself upon human flesh and brains and, as Dendle acknowledges, "Romero liberated the zombie from the shackles of a master, and invested his zombies not with a function ... but with a drive (eating flesh)" (6).

Prior to Romero's *magnum opus*—and the first modern zombie film—*Night of the Living Dead* (1968), zombies had little staying power in the media and were certainly not the monsters we now envision. Zombie films were second, third, and fourth rate entertainment ventures, lagging far behind the cinematic monsters of Dracula, Frankenstein, the Mummy, and the Wolf Man. Romero not only *gave* zombies staying power, he effectively revolutionized the monsters themselves and, by necessity, their creation myths. Suddenly, zombies were terrifying as they were not limited to archaic European landscapes or tropical wildernesses like so many other movie monsters. Zombies were the potential horror next door; the "what if?" that kept you up at night. To make it more horrifying, the zombies no longer had to be created one at a time through careful ritual and mysticism. Instead, mass hordes of walking dead were suddenly being spawned by events such as viral outbreaks or chemical catastrophes.

Regardless of the catalyst, zombies were suddenly able to spawn on a mass scale. Popular zombie trends tend to disregard any mention of a "patient zero," and instead focus on the zombie pandemic once it has already spread to the masses. Thus, the birth of a zombie was suddenly explained through things like bites or scratches or bodily fluid exchange, all but turning zombification into a sexually transmitted disease or plague. Again, it was Romero who introduced us to this phenomenon in *Night of the Living Dead* (1968). Though his monsters were never once referred to as zombies in the film, they became the character sketch that all other zombies would mimic in both their origins and their appetites: "[D]ead bodies will continue to be transformed into flesh-eating ghouls. All persons who die during this crisis—from whatever cause—will come back to life to seek human victims unless their bodies are disposed of by cremation" (*Night of the Living Dead*). Romero's ghouls were no longer loved ones bodies resurrected and possessed by dark magic. Instead, they were soulless, mindless scavengers. As far from sentient beings as one can get, the id-driven zombies of Romero's making are the stuff of our nightmares and a media franchiser's wet dream.

Resident Evil *"Zombies": The Science of Horror*

The zombie makeover from occult born drone to cannibal corpse may have begun with Romero and those who have followed in his footsteps, but it seems no entertainment venue has come close to the success of the *Resident Evil* franchise. But it is not their success as zombie peddlers that has this author so intrigued. Instead, it is their focus on the "whys" of the zombie that is intriguing. Rather than begin in the middle of a crisis as so many other zombie authors do (including Romero), the creators of *Resident Evil* chose instead to consider *how* the zombie outbreak occurred and what the effects would be given that particular scenario. Though they continue to give their products a horror/supernatural feel, the authors of *Resident Evil* storylines—for both films and games—are devoted to understanding the evolution of the zombie through scientific means. Truly, of all zombie focused film, games, and literature, *Resident Evil* is the most focused on the science of the walking dead and their science has changed with the times, showcasing a sophisticated understanding of modern science instead of only focusing on horror and gore. As such, we have seen the franchise focus on the origin of the zombie through biological weaponry, genetic manipulation, and even parasitic symbiotic relationships.

The real life horror of biological weaponry has been the driving force behind the *Resident Evil* franchise since its birth in 1996 with the first installment of the video game series. In Capcom's original horror survival game *Resident Evil*, the protagonist takes refuge inside a mansion with his/her comrades in arms. While progressing through the game, the player comes across several documents littered around the mansion. These documents help the player piece together what happened in Raccoon City: the notorious Umbrella Corporation had been exposing both human and animal subjects to biological testing before something went wrong. This testing revolves around the viral compound known as the T-virus, a Bio Organic Weapon (B.O.W.). A similar scenario takes place in the 2002 film of the same name, though it is Umbrella Corporation's sentient computer that explains the virus and its terrible implications. During a conversation between the Red Queen (Umbrella's master computer) and the STARS team, the Red Queen explains:

> "The T-virus was a major medical breakthrough, although it clearly also possessed highly profitable military applications.... Even in death, the human body still remains active.... The T-virus provides a massive jolt, both to cellular growth and to those trace electrical impulses. Put quite simply, it reanimates the body."
> "It brings the dead back to life?"
> "Not fully. The subjects have the simplest of motor functions; perhaps a little memory; virtually no intelligence. They are driven by the basest of impulses. The most basic needs.... The need to feed" [*Resident Evil*].

It seems the T-virus has much more ominous side effects than bargained for, resulting in unchecked zombie hordes attacking anything with a pulse.

Here, Capcom has recreated the zombie horde, making it more sympathetic with modern day horrors. Author Kyle Bishop explains humanity's fear of the zombie by making a direct correlation to our fear of doomsday: "The end of the world is the ultimate societal fear, made all the more real by current weapons of mass destruction" (Bishop 22). The T-virus is the perfect weapon of mass destruction: a military grade weapon of biological warfare, inflicting damage on both the living and the dead. The zombies of *Resident Evil* fame who are spawned from technology and chemistry perverting biology are a much more disturbing image than those of Haitian lore. Whereas the Haitian zombie is created through careful ritual, focusing on only one individual at a time, the birth of the *Resident Evil* zombie is seemingly random, created through an extremely contagious, protean chemical. And, as later game and films were released, the threat of the T-virus only grew until, finally, in *Resident Evil: Extinction* (2007), Alice explains how the world had succumbed to the walking dead, with survivors depicted like war refugees struggling day to day: "Within weeks, the T-virus had consumed the United States. Within months? The world. The virus didn't just wipe out human life. Lakes and rivers dried up, forests became deserts and whole continents were reduced to nothing more than barren wastelands. Slowly but surely, the Earth began to wither and die."

Equally disturbing is that infection with a zombie virus is not limited to humans as is the Haitian zombification ritual. It seems that any living organism is susceptible to the infection caused by the T-virus in the *Resident Evil* world, destroying not only humans, but animals and plant life. Among such creatures are the zombie–Dobermans in both the *Resident Evil* (1996) game and the film *Resident Evil* (2002) and the mutated, homicidal murder of crows in *Resident Evil: Extinction* (2007). By shifting the zombie origin mythology to include biological weaponry instead of supernatural necromancy, the *Resident Evil* creators considered the effects it would have beyond the human species. The zombie–Dobermans, with their exposed muscles, milky eyes, and bloody fangs, and the mutated crows with their insatiable desire for flesh bring to light the monstrous possibilities of a biological outbreak.

Though debatable as a zombie creating serum, a second B.O.W. found in the *Resident Evil* universe is that of the Uroboros virus, a mutagen Wesker intended to use in order to create an entirely new race of superhumans. It was Wesker's intent to expose the populations of the world to the Uroboros virus which, when absorbed into the body, would perform a type of genetic cleansing, ridding the world of "inferior" hosts and ensuring that only the strong would survive. With Uroboros, Wesker hoped to take his place as the prime mover of a new world: "The right to be a god.... Only one truly capable of being a god deserves that right.... With Uroboros, I have that right" (*Resident Evil 5*). Unfortunately for Wesker, through both flashback sequences and gameplay in *Resident Evil 5*, one learns that the Uroboros virus is far too powerful and that few infected actually survive. Those that do survive undergo incredible mutations, most resulting in the sprouting of tentacle-like appendages. Creatures infected with Uroboros are not necessarily zombies, but still play a huge part in the zombie universe created by Capcom and may suggest an evolutionary strain of zombies.

Yet, a distinct correlation between *Resident Evil*'s biological zombie and the Haitian zombie can still be made, despite the obvious differences in origin. During his expedition, Wade Davis was able to identify two distinctly different types of zombis: *zombi astral* and *zombi corps cadavre*. The *zombi cadavre* is the type most recognizable in Haiti as it is "a zombie of the flesh that can be made to work" (Davis, *Passage* 301). It is this zombie that is made to be a slave, often on plantations in outlying Haitian districts. It is this same creature that Dr. Isaacs is trying to create via science in *Resident Evil: Extinction* (2007). Through various injections of the modified T-virus, Dr. Isaacs hopes to turn the zombie hordes into a viable, submissive work-force, making the T-virus not only a biological weapon, but a replica of the slave producing potion of Haitian *bokers*. It is with Dr. Isaacs that *Resident Evil* actually blurs the line between mad scientist and necromancer.

However, biological weaponry is not *Resident Evil*'s only source of "zombification." Alice, the main character in the *Resident Evil* film series, is a product of both infection with the T-virus and genetic manipulation. Though certainly nothing like the rotting corpses she battles in film after film, she is still far from human, having been infected with the very serum that has spawned the zombie scavengers. Through careful genetic manipulation, Alice has been engineered to be an incredible fighting force with psychic/telekinetic abilities, making her a target and a possible liability.

Alice is a being most comparable to a *zombi astral*, also identified by Davis in Haiti. A *zombie astral* is a creature missing "an aspect of the soul that may be transmuted at the will of the one who possesses it" (Davis, *Passage* 301). In *Resident Evil: Apocalypse* (2004), Alice awakens with the knowledge that she was genetically altered and subsequently infected with the T-virus during experiments under Dr. Isaacs and the Umbrella Corporation. At the end of the film, as she "escapes" captivity yet again, Dr. Isaacs orders his scientists to boot up a program called "Project Alice." This program allows Dr. Isaacs to manipulate Alice at will until she overrides the system with her telekinesis in *Resident Evil: Extinction* (2007). Again, we can see a direct correlation between the modern zombie and the Haitian zombi: one has their soul taken from them by dark magic while the other loses their free-will (soul) to science.

A second genetically altered character, Matt Addison—the only other survivor of *Resident Evil* (2002) alongside Alice—is another vain attempt to get the zombie serum right. Though not necessarily a zombie, Matt is both engineered and mutated into the creature known as Nemesis in *Resident Evil: Apocalypse* (2004). However, with his lack of free will and self control, Nemesis is, like Alice, a candidate for the title of *zombi astral*. As we are never privy to the exact terms of the experiments done on Matt, we can only guess at his true place in the zombification process. Matt, like Alice, is a puppet for Dr. Isaacs to control like any *boker* manipulating Vodoun magic for their own purposes.

While biological weaponry and genetic manipulation are terrifying in their potential, *Resident Evil* creators went above and beyond the science of zombification when they actually began using parasitic symbiosis to explain the birth of particular zombies. Parasitic symbiosis is a biological relationship where one entity benefits from the relationship (the parasite) and the other is harmed and, in some cases, destroyed (the host). In circumstances where the host is actually destroyed, the parasite is known as necrotrophic. It is this type of parasite that is so interesting when considering the zombification process both in the real world and in the alternate reality found in *Resident Evil* as it is the most sympathetic with our perceptions of the walking dead as an instinct-driven entity that is no longer what it once was.

The most prolific of the necrotrophic parasites is likely the vast number of fungi species known as *Cordyceps*. The *Cordyceps* fungi release spores that, once attached to a host (usually an insect), will eventually take it over, feed off its tissue, and sprout from its body (Holliday). Seeming more akin to science fiction that science, the *Cordyceps* fungi varies in its form and function. For this chapter, I shall focus on the *Cordyceps* fungi which actively infiltrate not only the host's body, but its brain, controlling major functions like a puppet-master or Haitian *boker* necromancer.

Creatures infected with particular types of *Cordyceps* become little more than zombie slaves to the parasite. This necrotrophic parasite has given rise to the term "zombie ants." Usually infecting insects, the fungus begins to immediately break down the cells of the host for food, but, more importantly, ensures its continual survival by forcing the host to "help" it achieve maximum prolificacy. In "zombie ants," this is done by manipulating the host into climbing vegetation and then latching on to a stem with their mandibles: "Infected ants bite onto vegetation (leaves, bark, stems) in tropical forests just before being killed by the fungus. The parasite then grows a spore-dispersal structure from the base of the ant's head" (Anderson 424). This necrotrophic parasitic relationship is terrifying in its reality and even more horrifying given the possibilities. It was these possibilities that the creators behind the *Resident Evil* games turned to during some of the later installments to the series.

In 2005, *Resident Evil 4* introduced players to an entirely new type of zombie horror with *Los Illuminados*. The Illuminados, a vicious cult that worships the *"Las Plagas,"* were no longer the walking dead engineered by biological weaponry or genetic alterations. Instead, they were zombies much akin to the "zombie ant": hosts for Las Plagas, the necrotrophic endoparasites that fed on and manipulated their hosts to serve the higher power of the dominant strain of Plaga. Through gameplay, the player learns in *Resident Evil 4* (2005) that the modern strain of the Plaga was actually due to a mining incident. Fossilized remains of the Plagas, thought to be dead, actually survived as spores which were inhaled by village miners, resulting in infection.

Here, we find yet another new origin of zombification. Just like the *Cordyceps* infecting the "zombie ants," the Plagas take over their hosts, robbing them of cellular nutrients and true sentience, till they become little more than walking dead puppets. This is an interesting combination of both the Haitian zombi and the modern zombie. Though the villagers infected with the Plaga are, at first, little more than submissive slaves, once a major part of their form is destroyed (usually the head), the Plaga may take over even more effectively, resulting in a parasitic corpse. This explains certain circumstances in gameplay when, upon exploding the head of an infected opponent, the Plaga erupts from the spinal column, forcing the corpse to continue the attack.

A more terrifying marriage of zombification and Plaga infection is in the creation of the *Regeneradores* or Iron Maidens (a Regenerador prototype) of *Resident Evil 4* (2005) fame. Considered by many fans to be the most horrifying creation of the *Resident Evil* franchise—with their hitched, erratic breathing, twitchy limbs, and slow gait—the Regeneradores are monsters a player must battle in the laboratory facilities found on The Island site in *Resident Evil 4* (2005). Interestingly, the Regeneradores seem to be an attempt by the creators to merge genetic manipulation with a necrotrophic parasite. To that effect, the Regeneradores are creatures resulting from genetic testing of the Plagas. As such, they are among the more difficult enemies to kill, since they are not only parasite dwelling hosts, but they are in an in-between state, much like the zombie we are familiar with. Very little is left of the human host once the engineered Plagas have infested the body, and they seem driven to destroy and consume the living, driven by the "need to feed" instinct. However, unlike the more traditional *Resident Evil* zombies, these particular manifestations of science can regenerate rapidly (thus their namesake).

Resident Evil creators actually extended the use of Las Plagas into *Resident Evil 5* (2009). However, the Plaga used to create the mindless zombie hordes in the 2009 installment of the game were significantly more destructive, as they were genetically engineered. The new strains of Plaga were used to infect African tribes, wreaking mass havoc on the victims and spawning "Majini." As a result of being exposed to advanced strains of genetically enhanced Plaga, the Majini in *Resident Evil 5* seemed to be much more dangerous hunters, able to communicate with each other and even operate both land and water vehicles. Though not necessarily self-aware, they functioned as more of a unit instead of relying on chaotic, berserker rages.

Oddly, a distinct difference between the zombies created with the T-virus and those infected with the Plaga parasites is their driving force. Whereas creatures like Los Illuminados and the Majini are following the call of a master (the dominant strain of Plaga) in order to ensure the parasites continued survival, the zombies spawned from the T-virus are driven by the instinct to feed alone. It is curious to see this shift in, not only the zombie origin, but in the zombie intent. Neither creature is focused on self-preservation, because though the flesh-eating zombie is driven to feed, it is not driven to ensure its safety. And while the Plaga is *more* focused on its safety, seeking to destroy threats, it is for the good of the higher strain and not for itself, much like an ant colony protecting its queen. Accordingly, as they changed the zombie origin, *Resident Evil* contributors had to start altering the zombie purpose.

Stealing Souls

Regardless of their "divine" origin, most zombies and zombie-inspired creatures found in both myth and pop culture are seemingly soulless. It is this very condition that seems to spark the greatest fear both in Haitian societies, where Vodou is prevalent, and *Resident Evil* installments. The separation of the soul from the flesh is the true horror of zombification, regardless of the means. Those who have their soul extracted through supernatural rituals are hounded from society in Haitian culture, doomed to live as outcasts even if they manage a "cure." The victims in *Resident Evil* have their souls severed by scientists playing God; hoping to create the perfect lifeforms while actually damning humanity.

When Rain recognizes the inevitable, she is determined not to share the fate of the others. Barely self-aware, she begs Alice to end things as she cannot bear to be a zombie and doomed to live after death, "[w]alking around without a soul" (*Resident Evil*). The creators of such creatures, whether *boker* or scientist, have little pity for their creations and even less for those that will be affected—or infected. In most mythologies, the creator is usually one to be respected and the creation is something to be held sacred. The processes of zombification, through either means (supernatural or science), is a perversion of such rites. Nothing is truly created, only destroyed and altered to fit a purpose. The zombie origin may have shifted with the times, moving beyond the hut of the necromancer, to the lab of a scientist, to the spores of a necrotrophic parasite, but the loss of the soul will always be the end result of that evil.

Works Cited

Anderson, S.B., S. Gerritsma, K.M. Yusah, D. Mayntz, N.L. Hywel-Jones, J. Billen, J.J. Boomsman, and D.P. Hughes. "The Life of a Dead Ant: The Expression of an Adaptive Extended Phenotype." *The American Naturalist* 174.3 (2009): 424–33.

Bishop, Kyle. "Raising the Dead: Unearthing the Nonliterary Origins of Zombie Cinema." *Journal of Popular Film and Television* 33.4 (2006): 196–205. Print.

Davis, Wade. *Passage of Darkness: The Ethnobiology of the Haitian Zombie.* Chapel Hill: The University of North Carolina Press, 1988. Print.

_____. *The Serpent and the Rainbow: A Harvard Scientist's Astonishing Journey into the Secret Societies of Haitian Voodoo, Zombis, and Magic.* New York: Touchstone, 1997. Kindle ebook file.

Dawn of the Dead. Dir. George A. Romero. Perf. David Emge, Ken Foree, Scott H. Reinger, Gaylen Ross. 1978. Anchor Bay Home Entertainment, 2004. DVD-ROM.

Dendle, Peter. *The Zombie Movie Encyclopedia.* Jefferson, NC: McFarland, 2001. Print.

Holliday, J., and M. Cleaver. "On the Trail of the Yak: Ancient *Cordyceps* in the Modern World." Online posting. June 2004. June 2012. www.alohamedicinals.ca/Cordy_Article.pdf.

Moreman, Christopher M., and Cory James Rushton, eds. *Race, Oppression and the Zombie: Essays on Cross-Cultural Appropriations of the Caribbean Tradition.* Jefferson, NC: McFarland, 2011. 1–13. Print.

Resident Evil. Dir. Paul W.S. Anderson. Perf. Milla Jovovich, Michelle Rodriguez, Eric Mabius, and James Purefoy. 2002. Resident Evil Trilogy, Sony Pictures Home Entertainment, 2008. DVD-ROM.

Resident Evil: Apocalypse. Dir. Alexander Witt. Perf. Milla Jovovich, Sienna Guillory, Oded Fehr, and Sophie Vavasseur. 2004. Resident Evil Trilogy, Sony Pictures Home Entertainment, 2008. DVD-ROM.

Resident Evil: Extinction. Dir. Russell Mulcahy. Perf. Milla Jovovich, Oded Fehr, Ali Larter, and Iain Glen. 2007. Resident Evil Trilogy, Sony Pictures Home Entertainment, 2008. DVD-ROM.

"Resident Evil 4." Wii. V 1.8. June 19, 2007. Capcom.

"Resident Evil 5." Xbox 360. V 1.3. March 13, 2009. Capcom.

Survival and System in Resident Evil (2002): Remembering, Repeating and Working-Through

Daniel Müller

While the games of the *Resident Evil* series are frequently labeled as "survival horror," there is no such clarity in the generic affiliation of the *Resident Evil* movies. In this essay, I will argue that the first entry in the *Resident Evil* movie series also focuses on survival, and I will discuss the distinctive narrative and filmic devices it uses to this end. The movie's thematic preoccupation with survival makes it adequate to use psychoanalytic thought and terminology to grasp the psychological consequences of surviving. The first *Resident Evil* movie foregrounds the story of Alice's survival. She wakes up in an abandoned mansion after a catastrophe in a subterranean research facility and suffers from amnesia. Even though she is—in the course of the film—threatened by the effects of the initial catastrophe, the story of her survival can be read as a narrative of her recovery as it tells of her attempt to remember the initial and forgotten traumatic moment. The narrative lends itself to being read as the story of a therapeutic travel or, as it were, *travail*.

Alice's amnesia is key to translating the concept of survival into the context of narrative film: For one, her amnesia triggers the necessity of exploration, creating an intra-diegetic excuse for the initial lack of knowledge about the narrative universe and the premise for a central aspect of every narration, namely the (re)construction of knowledge about the diegetic world.[1] Moreover, such amnesia of the main protagonist has become a common starting point for movies and games alike since the mid–90s,[2] and can thus quite conveniently be described as a narrative device in its own right. Thus, the construction of a narrative from the vantage point of a protagonist unable to remember both satisfies the classical need for a movement towards knowledge and a more contemporary interest in the effects of trauma.³ In its use of this narrative device, then, *Resident Evil* is a symptom of our cultural moment. I will argue, however, that it attempts to transcend the symptomatic deadlock and tries to discuss as well as construct answers to the loss of historical and temporal continuity that is expressed in Alice's amnesia.

Interestingly, *Resident Evil* starts out with a segment that is seemingly unrelated to what follows. In the first minutes, a catastrophe unfolds in the subterranean Hive: Somebody unleashes the T-virus, an aggressive biological weapon that is meant to turn people into undead super soldiers. To contain this virus the artificial intelligence reigning over the Hive, the "Red Queen" closes all doors and terminates all life in its realm.⁴ After the last of the Hive workers dies, the camera fades to black, and Alice awakens. Only a few things indicate the connection between the mansion where Alice finds herself and the Hive of the previous scenes: Set design, lighting, and the colors used all clearly demarcate the mansion as a distinctly separate space. The presence of surveillance cameras similar to those in the Hive is the first obvious connection between both spaces, and the intrusion of a group of soldiers finally destroys the distinction that made the mansion feel securely removed from the horrors unleashed in the Hive. The soldiers connect both spaces: They are on a mission to go through the mansion's hidden door into the underworld of the Hive. This act reveals the hidden architecture (the train station below the mansion) and the hidden connection between both spaces.

With its idea of a subconscious, psychoanalysis constructs a landscape similar to that of *Resident Evil* with its subterranean connection between mansion and Hive, the journey into that underworld and persistent allusions to dreaming.⁵ The two spaces, Hive and mansion, seem to reflect different degrees of symbolization: The mansion, set above the earth, is home to Alice, and part of her everyday world. The Hive, in contrast, is buried underground and unknown to the public (a fact communicated at the beginning of the film). The movement from one to the other, then, is also the gradual and uncanny realization that what we think we know is inextricably linked to the unknown, that our conscious everyday life is related to and, indeed, framed by the unconscious. Alice's story, in this light, is a story of reconstructing, or resymbolizing, the buried place and the lost memory it contains. The gradual realization of what happened in the Hive and how Alice is involved in that catastrophe coincides with the return of Alice's powers.

The aim of psychoanalysis, too, is overcoming the neurotic symptoms through the integration or (re)construction of suppressed memories. This ultimate goal of the analytic process is most clearly formulated by Sigmund Freud in his technical essays *Remembering, Repeating and Working Through* and *Constructions in Analysis*:

It is well known that the object of analytical work is to bring the patient to the point of removing the repressions—in the widest sense of the term—of his early development, to replace them with reactions more in keeping with a state of psychological maturity. To do this he has to recall certain experiences and the emotional impulses they gave rise to, which he has now forgotten. We know that his present symptoms and inhibitions are the result of such repressions; in other words, they operate as surrogates for what he has forgotten [*Constructions* 77–8].

In shorter words, the aim of psychoanalytic technique is "[d]escriptively speaking, [...] to fill in gaps in memory; dynamically speaking, it is to overcome resistances due to repression" (*Remembering* 147–8).

Surrogates and resistances prevent the patient from confronting repressed experiences, and memories that cannot easily be integrated into the biographical narrative. There is an instance of such use of surrogates in the movie when, in the course of exploration, the original conflict, or, in more plot-related terms, the *true* enemy is revealed: both the Red Queen that sealed the Hive and the zombies are only surrogates for the evil Umbrella Corporation (that will take center stage as the villain in the later films of the series). Psychoanalysis describes how such repressed elements return as traces in the behavior of the patient from which the psychoanalyst recovers the true experience. For Freud, these suppressed memories are not yet fully understood, and the work of the psychoanalyst is aimed at integrating them into a coherent self-narrative. The most important step on that route is the construction of the past by the analyst that

should end in the patient's recall; but it does not always take us that far. Often enough it fails to lead the patient to recall what has been repressed. In lieu of that, through the correct conduct of the analysis, we succeed in firmly convincing him of the truth of the construction, and therapeutically this achieves the same result as regaining a memory [*Constructions* 85].

The reconstruction of a forgotten memory or, in post-structuralist terms: the integration of a traumatic experience into the symbolic universe (of language), is not necessarily based on the reality of that memory. The representation of that memory may differ strongly from the real experience:

Thus, key theoretical positions on trauma reinforce the postmodernist position that lived experience, and especially traumatic experience, resists linguistic representation and in doing so, separates the writer from lived experience. We are left with the sense that narrative and experience can have little, if anything, to do with each other [Robinett 290].

In psychoanalysis, the memory is constructed ex post, in analysis. Freud does not admit any problem with such constructed memories,[6] even if the reaction to an analysts' construction does not lead to a recognition, or understanding, of the forgotten past but instead to something quite different:

I have noticed in a few analyses that being presented with what was obviously an accurate construction had a surprising and at first incomprehensible effect on the person undergoing analysis. They experienced vivid memories, which they themselves described as "unusually clear," but what they recalled was not so much the event itself that formed the content of the construction, but details closely related to this content, for example, the unnaturally sharp features of the people who appeared in it, or the rooms in which something of that sort could have happened, or—a little less immediate—the furnishings of these rooms, of which the construction naturally could know nothing. This happened both in dreams immediately after the presentation, and in waking states, in a condition of heightened imagination. Nothing else followed in the wake of these memories; so it seemed reasonable to see them as the result of a compromise. An "upsurge" of the repressed, activated by the narrating of the construction, wished to bring these important traces of memory up to the level of consciousness, but a resistance had succeeded, if not in blocking this movement, then in diverting it on to nearby, secondary objects.

You might have been able to call these memories hallucinations, if, in addition to their clarity, the patient also believed in their actual reality. But this analogy increased in significance for me when I noticed the occasional occurrence of true hallucinations in other cases that were definitely not psychotic in nature [*Constructions* 85–6].

The clarity of the therapeutic process is undermined by Freud's observation. Uncannily, the effect of the cure in these cases is a transition from the neurotic to the psychotic state. What is achieved is not the understanding and reintegration of a real occurrence, but the construction of an alternative, hallucinatory "reality" that, however, replaces the suffering. Such is the power of the narrative construed in analysis that it is able to trigger false, hallucinatory memories. In any way, the closure achieved in the psychoanalytic cure is a construction through persuasion. The "real" of the suppressed memory can only be accessed belatedly, and as such it is necessarily infused with traces of wish-fulfillment. Closure is a delusion, if of a different order. Or, as Gilles Deleuze has put it with regard to closure in the fiction film: "[E]verything which is closed is artificially closed" (10).

The talking cure is a narrative cure; the improvement of the patient's condition is achieved through the construction of a coherent narrative. *Resident Evil*, too, tries to develop its narrative as an answer to the initial catastrophe, severed as it is from the film's "body." The narrative aims at incorporating this separate and not fully understood episode in which the Hive is depopulated into a coherent and understandable plot structure, or symbolic order. Also, *Resident Evil* directly engages the question of the truth of its narrative construct by frequently alluding to sleeping and dreaming. I will come back to this point towards the end of my argument.

The way in which such symbolic order is created is strongly standardized in narrative, or classical film, and it is against this set of rules that *Resident Evil* develops its narrative. Classical film creates stability through a tight symmetric framework. The most obvious expression of this symmetry is found in the relation between beginning and ending. According to Bellour, "The principle of classical film is well known: the end must reply to the beginning; between one and the other something must be set in order; the last scene frequently recalls the first and constitutes its resolution"(238).

Stephen Heath has described the underlying symmetry of the classical film as the succession of situation and action, a structure that can be found both at macroscopic level of szyuzhet construction and in microscopic segments or episodes:

> In short, a narrative action is a series of elements held in a relation of transformation such that their consecution determines a state S' different to an initial state S; thus: S-x-x-x-x-x-x-x-x-S'. Evidently, the action includes S and S' (they are defined by it); and equally evidently, the elements articulating—"carrying"—the transformation are themselves "little actions" with their own beginnings and endings [48–9].

Symmetry, in the case of *Resident Evil*, is created through catastrophe: The film begins with a catastrophic incident and ends with outright apocalypse. Such use of catastrophe illustrates the ambivalent role the disturbance, or action, plays in the context of narrative: apart from its disruptive and potentially traumatizing quality, catastrophe and danger suture and stabilize the narrative fabric. Without it, Alice would not be able to (re)construct her identity, and the narrative movement towards meaning and knowledge would not be possible. Thus, the film stages what Stephen Heath described as violence inherent in classical narration: "[I]f there is symmetry, there is dissymmetry, if there is resolution, there is violence" (49).

In terms of its overall structure, the movie falls into three parts, the longest of which is the descent and subsequent flight from the Hive, framed by the initial catastrophe and the ensuing apocalypse. In the central part, the film relies heavily on symmetrical structures and embraces a fundamental adherence to the classical canon of film-making. The movement through the topography of the Hive is organized by spatial continuity and symmetry: The group enters and later leaves the Hive along the same landmarks: train station, laboratory, and server room. The temporality of this longest segment, too, is constructed along the lines of the classical standard, as it utilizes "a device highly characteristic of classical narration—the deadline" (Bordwell 157). This deadline is repeatedly highlighted both in the dialogue and in recurrent computer screens as "mission time." David Bordwell stresses the structural power of this device, stating "That the climax of a classical film is often a deadline shows the structural power of defining dramatic duration as the time it takes to achieve or fail to achieve a goal" (157). However, the end of the countdown does not end the film, nor does it lead to a climactic confrontation. The symmetric order of the movement into and out of the Hive, too, is discarded in the last part of the movie. The closed and stable segment with its strong adherence to classical film-making proves to be ineffective in the context of *Resident Evil*. When Matt and Alice emerge from the Hive, its doors are safely sealed behind them. Just as they are about to leave the mansion, though, they are overpowered by agents of the Umbrella Corporation who open the Hive again. The final minutes see Alice exploring an abandoned hospital and finally facing a post-apocalyptic Raccoon City alone.

Resident Evil's aberration from classical stability, and of the coherence of the successful analysis, lies in the structural surplus of its form: The initial catastrophe is given beforehand, but only understood belatedly, and the ending literally falls out of place in that it explores a place otherwise unrelated to the story. The Hive episode is constructed as a film within the film, framed by segments that show local and global catastrophe, respectively. Stability itself is thus framed as a constructed and ultimately impossible condition.

Despite this bleak commentary on the possibility of coherence and stability, one element of classical narration remains intact: The narrative movement towards "full and adequate knowledge" (Bordwell 158) remains the single effective element that is able to move towards a conclusion. The process of remembering can be completed, but it does not have the anticipated effect.

The First Sequences

The ultimate inability to use classical symmetry and continuity as a means to achieve closure is already inherent in the initial moments of the movie. A title text offers information otherwise inaccessible through filmic representation about the power and secrecy of Umbrella Corporation, their pervasive business segments, and their hidden agenda. This information about the superstructure of the diegetic world could not have been achieved through a classical establishing shot, which otherwise shares its function of placing the spectator in a relative and superior distance to diegesis. Classically, the establishing shot positions the camera as an omniscient narrator and outside of the frame of immediate narrative. It is "[a] shot, usually involving a distant framing, that shows the spatial relations among the important figures, objects and setting in a scene" (Bordwell and Thompson 504). Instead of being introduced into diegesis from such a safe vantage point, the spectator is kept outside of the diegetic world.

Similarly, the following sequence fails to convey any safe vantage point for the spectator. While it seems to show a zoom from black space towards the image of a person whose face is hidden behind a Hazmat suit, it really is only the digital enlargement of a detail (a medium close-up, in this case) that creates the illusion of a movement of either projector or screen. The approximation of the image out of the darkness of cinematic space thus challenges the fixed position of these cinematic devices and is as such an attack on the totality of the cinematic apparatus and its pre-conditions. Apart from such speculation, this movement explains the function of the earlier title text, replacing the impossible establishing shot that was able in classical cinema to demonstrate its inherent power to show. The scenes in their arrangement draw on the classical movement from abstraction and totality to concreteness, but they travesty their model by bereaving them of their intrinsic power.

Consequently, both introductory scenes fail to create the possibility of immersion, and further the distance between spectator and diegesis. This is indeed the strongest contrast between the first and second segment. In the first segment, there is no empathetic relationship between audience and protagonists: The man in the Hazmat suit remains invisible and unknown. His suit reflects the camera's gaze; he is undifferentiated from the technical apparatus he operates. After he leaves the laboratory, four different locations within the Hive and the effects of his initial act are shown. No single person in the Hive, however, is able to act up against the apparatus. The unlucky man whose coffee is spilled turns out to be a powerless victim. The two women who try to control the situation are equally unable to resist the technical apparatus of the Hive and die. The woman who tries to escape from the lift is maybe closest to becoming a point of identification: After a number of close-ups of her face in the lift (after she emerges from the background of the group in 0:04:25), and a medium close-up from the perspective of a surveillance camera (0:04:36), she finally tries to climb out of the lift and the camera takes on her position (0:07:48) as she is nearly smashed against the ground. A reverse shot shows her face in a 180 degree cut. This succession of shot and reverse shot is repeated as she is ultimately smashed against the ceiling. The final reverse shot, however, is substituted by a black screen. The impact is only heard, not seen.

The sequence described above constitutes the first instance of such classical continuity editing. Continuity editing "creates a spatially consistent visual field and single diegesis by means of the following editing conventions: the 180 degree rule, the shot/reverse shot pattern, staging in depth, eyeline matches, cutting only within a 180/30 degree radius, match on action cuts" (Buckland and Elsaesser 37). Those rules of continuity editing "ensure smooth, invisible (because either expected or retrospectively explicable) transitions from shot to shot and from segment to segment" (ibid.). "The 180 degree system ensures that relative positions in the frame remain consistent" (Bordwell and Thompson 233) and "[t]hanks to the shot/reverse-shot pattern and the eyeline match, we understand the characters' locations even when they aren't in the same frame" (ibid. 236).

The main function of continuity is thus to create stability of the diegetic space and, consequently, stability of the spectator's position. Rather than fortifying such stability and spatial clarity, the singular use of such composition in the above sequence undermines such them: The scene ends before any stable positioning is achieved. Ultimately, this first segment defies tendencies towards an immersive film experience. There are only few cues for emotional connection to what is happening on screen. In many ways, *Resident Evil*'s first segment is a representation of a modern working place—a place that is lost in the course of catastrophe.

While the Hive employees fail to develop any kind of personality,[7] Alice is at the center of the representation as soon as she is introduced. First of all, she is not introduced in a narrative context. Her slow awakening is not visibly motivated by the narrative of the film but rather another beginning. Lying naked and bruised in a shower cubicle, the first encounter with Alice is most intimate and opens the possibility of empathetic identification. This strategy towards identification with Alice is underlined by the next scene that shows her standing in front of a mirror: The first shot establishes her position by showing her shoulder in the foreground. In the next shot, though, her real body is no longer in the frame; the camera takes her position as she is looking into the mirror.

The Belated Return of Catastrophe

The stark contrast between the first and second segment is obvious in so many respects that it strongly conveys the sense of a different status of diegetic reality of the respective scenes, and of the experience thereof. These very tangible differences in the form of representation can, as I will argue, best be explained by taking into account the concept of traumatic experience and the mechanisms of coping and coming to terms with such experiences. Introducing the concept of latency in his *Moses and Monotheism*, Freud famously stated that:

> It may happen that someone gets away, apparently unharmed, from the spot where he suffered a shocking accident, for instance a train collision. In the course of the following weeks, however, he develops a series of grave physical and motor symptoms, which can be ascribed only to his shock or whatever else happened at the time of the accident. [...] The time that elapsed between the accident and the first

appearance of the symptoms is called the "incubation period," a transparent allusion to the pathology of infectious disease [qtd. in Caruth 16–7].

There is a latency to the emotional processing of the traumatic event that severs the immediate experience from its effects. For survival, this latency is essential: when someone is confronted with overwhelming experiences, this mechanism allows him or her to react as if it were a normal experience. It is only after having survived that the latent traumatic experience belatedly returns to haunt its victim. This means that the confrontation with the traumatic incident is repeated after the incident (a repetition that can in itself be re-traumatizing), and understood belatedly.

While the return of the traumatic incident is enacted in Alice's confrontation with the zombies, the concept of latency is illustrated in *Resident Evil* by the T-virus and its antidote. The virus is the agent of catastrophe (and it openly addresses the discourse of "infectious diseases" that Freud draws on). The very first scene shows the manipulation of the two substances in careful detail, thus highlighting their importance for the plot. Their function, however, is only revealed indirectly: when a vial breaks, an ominous gas emerges and moves into the air duct, while elsewhere dogs suddenly start barking, and the surveillance footage registers the rise of T-virus levels in the Hive's atmosphere. All this points to a threat that does not immediately materialize, that remains invisible. Rather than the virus, the Red Queen is the (immediate) agent of the Hive's demise.

The existence of the virus is forgotten after the catastrophe is complete. The descent into the Hive, in this light, is the struggle for the recognition of the virus' existence and of its function.

Despite being constructed as the object of desire and the ultimate cause that sets the narrative apparatus as well as the catastrophe in the Hive in motion, the virus is lost and forgotten. It takes Alice a full (movie) hour to finally remember that there might be a cure for the T-virus. She states, "There is a cure. The process can be reversed." Only then does the group realize that the remedy was stolen, and when the suitcase is finally retrieved, it proves to be inefficient: Spencer is killed by a monstrous "Licker" before the antidote could possibly have any effect, and Rain's treatment comes too late to save her from death and turning into a zombie. Matt, too, can't be healed because he is abducted by Umbrella agents and only returns in the sequel *Resident Evil: Apocalypse* as a giant mutant called "Nemesis."

The suitcase and the antidote it contains, then, are another insufficient goal, unable to move the narrative towards closure. Nevertheless, it implies the promise of a cure. In its portrayal of the antidote, the movie's problematic relationship to closure becomes manifest again. Rather than working through to the traumatic experience and thereby neutralizing its effects, the movie sets up a bait that is ultimately inefficient.

The Return of Memories

Ultimately, the movie succeeds in its motion towards full and adequate knowledge—in the end, both Alice and the audience know about the origins of the catastrophe, about her motives and about Spencer's betrayal. These insights are the product of a single revelatory scene in the last third of the movie. While the movie is frequently intercut with short flashback sequences in which Alice's backstory is presented, they fail to present details that would allow an assessment of Alice and Spencer's motives and their respective character traits. These facets are only revealed in the later scene in which all revelations concerning the character's backstory cumulate.

Fleeing from the zombies with a group that has been reduced to four, Alice, Matt, Rain, and Spencer pass through a laboratory tract. This is the same place where the substances were stolen in the very first scene, that was subsequently flooded by a false and fatal fire alarm, and where the first undead appeared (the lady in the water). After the Red Queen was shut down and all doors opened, the water has gone and the labs are accessible again. However, as the group passes through the floor between the labs, Alice suddenly pauses. Now she recalls what happened in the Hive before the catastrophe. This memory, unlike earlier flashbacks, reveals what really happened in the Hive. While Alice is standing in the derelict hallway, transparent apparitions of Hive workers appear, gaining substance as the hallway itself is transformed back into its original state. The ghosts appear as the camera moves from Alice's face to a vantage point above her in the beginning of the scene (taking a position similar to those of the surveillance cameras and thus one of power and distance to diegesis). Through a window, Alice now witnesses for a second time the animal experiments in the labs. Confronted with the past, Alice is no longer able to differentiate between past and present. The ghosts do not interact with the present scene (and with Alice), they are just apparitions of a past moment. There remains a sense of unreality, distancing the ghosts and the change of appearances in the hallway from the narrative present of the movie. Nevertheless, this short sequence strongly alienates the spectator from the diegetic action. Through the incorporation of the past in the present, the temporal categories themselves are blurred, thus making any narrative progress seem irrelevant.

The intrusion of these ghosts also allows an understanding of the function of the undead: Both ghostlike apparitions and the undead originate in the same moment, namely the Hive before or during the catastrophe. They are the return, so to speak, of that repressed moment, of the traumatic experience. This insight is hardly original; Slavoj Žižek describes the return of the living dead in a similar way:

> Why do the dead return? The answer offered by Lacan is the same as that found in popular culture—because they were not properly buried, i.e, because something went wrong with their obsequies. The return of the dead is a sign of a disturbance in the symbolic rite, in the process of symbolization, the dead return as collectors of some unpaid symbolic debt. This is the basic lesson drawn by Lacan from Antigone and Hamlet. The plots of both plays involve improper funeral rites, and the "living dead"—Antigone and the ghost of Hamlet's father—return to settle symbolic accounts. The return of the living dead, then, materializes a certain symbolic debt persisting beyond physical expiration.
>
>   It is commonplace to state that symbolization as such equates to symbolic murder: when we speak about a thing, we suspend, place in parentheses, its reality. It is precisely for this reason that the funeral rite exemplifies symbolization at its purest: through it, the dead are inscribed in the text of symbolic tradition, they are assured that, in spite of their death, they will "continue to live" in the memory of the community. The "return of the living dead" is, on the other hand, the reverse of the proper funeral rite. While the latter implies a certain reconciliation, an acceptance of loss, the return of the dead signifies that they cannot find their proper place in the text of tradition [*Looking Awry* 23].

The dead return because they have not been integrated into a closed narrative. Freud has argued that the integration of a traumatic, forgotten event into the self-narrative is the crucial point of the talking cure. Traumatizing events forestall the possibility of understanding and incorporating said event into a coherent narrative. A gap opens between the Real and what is realized in the narratives of the victim. The ghosts and the undead of *Resident Evil* both originate in what Žižek describes in the *Sublime Object of Ideology* as the place between two deaths. They embody the "difference between real (biological) death and its symbolization, the 'settling of accounts,' the accomplishment of symbolic destiny" (*Sublime Object* 150).

   The difference between ghosts and the undead in *Resident Evil*, however, is rather less subtle than Žižek's argument, and it is to be found in the immediate plot context: Unlike the undead, the ghosts do not interact with the survivors. This observation allows us to see the undead as manifest memories of the traumatic event that have direct consequences for the presence. In this, they are embodiments of Cathy Caruth's theory of trauma: "What returns to haunt the victim is not only the reality of the violent event but also the reality of the way that its violence has not yet been fully known" (6). The undead are embodiments of the tendency in Post-Traumatic Stress Disorder to repeat traumatizing experiences.[8] They are a return of the repressed insofar as they renew the suffering, in the same way as the symptoms of neuroses are surrogates for an immediate confrontation with the original conflict. Consequently, the undead become obsolete as soon as the memory of what happened is reconstructed: The last zombie of the Hive is killed just after Spencer is exposed as the villain,[9] and it sinks back into the water from which it had emerged.

While the undead thus stand for the failure to symbolize, the apparitions point Alice towards remembering. The hallucinatory memory triggers the process of Alice's recognition and understanding of the catastrophic event, leading to full and adequate knowledge—and to apocalypse. This is the movie's disturbing commentary on the possibility of a cure: The abrupt ending of the flight from the Hive gives way to the final segment in which Alice faces outright apocalypse. While the narrative quite coherently aims at containment both in terms of its structure (the classical narrative form) as with regard to its plot (containment of the spreading disease), the last segment questions the possibility of human agency in the face of corporate capitalism. After all they went through, neither Alice nor Matt can prevent the disease from spreading due to the interference of the Umbrella Corporation. The same is true with regard to narrative form: the classical system, though effectively displayed, can no longer contain the disruptive threat that lies at its center.

The vantage point of psychoanalysis allows a further interpretation: As a story of survival, *Resident Evil* shows Alice's confrontation with her traumatic memories. Scenes of waking up, metaphors of dreaming, and most importantly the hallucinatory memory described above, question the reality of what Alice lives through. Her second awakening answers to the problem that the socially sanctioned coping mechanism of containment and classical continuity which is portrayed extensively in the long middle segment no longer works. Having found it impossible to effectively work through all resistances and integrate the past event into a coherently closed symbolic order, Alice takes the symbolization to another level. Where society and community in both the context of formal system of film and on the diegetic level of group interaction failed to create coherence and rather lead to a repetition of loss, she empowers herself as the center of her own symbolic universe.

Now, Alice indeed becomes the only protagonist of the film. The final apocalyptic scenario elevates her value and meaning as the last survivor. Writing about paranoia, a delusion marked by a high degree of abstraction,[10] David Trotter argues that "the paranoiac's ultimate vindication is the ending of the world which had for so long remained indifferent towards him, refusing to recognize his true worth. The best man (the only valuable man) has survived. And there is nobody left to persecute him" (73f.).

Such idiosyncratic delusion finally severs its ties to socially sanctioned forms of symbolization (such as the classical model of causality and continuity) and leaves the individual without the normative corrective of a group. Hallu-cination, dream, and reality can no longer be differentiated. Earlier, Matt was able to contain Alice's hallucinatory vision of the past by stepping into the transformed space; but now, there is no one left to correct what Alice sees. In this light, the alternative ending does indeed make sense: There, Alice takes the fight into the headquarters of Umbrella Corporation. This solution to the film is too rash, and too unsuspected in the context of the exploration of the Hive. As an expression of a delusion of grandeur, however, the image of Alice fighting back is a stronger stance on how her character has developed in the course of the movie. Importantly, this alternative sequence is finally realized in *Resident Evil: Afterlife*, stressing the development of Alice's character to contain the larger story arks.

The final image of *Resident Evil* is not so much a bleak vision of a post-apocalyptic city, it is also a grandiose image of Alice's self-empowerment against all odds: Standing amidst the smoking ruins of Raccoon City, Alice is finally able to face all threats. While Alice's grandiosity is not as important an issue in *Resident Evil: Apocalypse*, the second movie of the series, it returns with a vengeance in *Resident Evil: Extinction*. In *Extinction*'s last scene, Alice discovers an army of clones. The whole subterranean world of another of Umbrella Cor-poration's underground facilities is populated by numerous versions of Alice. The inherent grandiosity of this image can hardly be surpassed. In this third movie, Alice is literally constructed as the world's savior: her blood can save the world because it contains the antidote to the T-virus.

Surviving in Fiction

Alice has traveled a long way in *Resident Evil*. From her beginning as a victim of a catastrophic event to the only savior of mankind she has reclaimed power over her role in the narrative or symbolic order and has shaped it accord-ingly. As a metaphor for the workings of psychoanalysis, the movie discards the idea of constructing closure by confronting, or working through the past. Rather, the movie portrays an idiosyncratic coping strategy that remains trapped in a circle of psychopathologies surrogating each other. The really bleak outlook at the ending of *Resident Evil* is not that there is no cure to the T-virus, it is that there is no cure for surviving.

Implicitly, this is also a critique of the narrative approach to coping with trauma that is proposed by psychoanalysis. *Resident Evil* shows the backside of such narratives in that it highlights their constructedness. Trauma as an experience that defies representation and that is marked by the loss of coherent language and narrative is mastered in the movie through a generic narration that offers a way of coping with that loss, of lending a surrogate narrative voice to an otherwise inexpressible experience. In other words: the only way for Alice to survive the traumatic experience lies in the construction of a different, narrativized and ultimately fictional experience. The reality of the original experience is thereby eradicated and overwritten according to the rules of fiction, leaving its protagonist limited to the fictional realm.

Notes

1. David Bordwell argues that "[t]he mystery film, with its resolved enigma at the end, is only the most apparent instance of the tendency of the classical syuzhet to develop toward full and adequate knowledge. Whether a protagonist learns a moral lesson or only the spectator knows the whole story, the classical film moves steadily toward a growing awareness of absolute truth" (158–9).

2. *The Bourne Identity* (Doug Liman: 2002), *Source Code* (Duncan Jones: 2011), *The Long Kiss Goodnight* (Renny Harlin: 1996), *Resident Evil* (Paul W.S. Anderson: 2002), *Memento, Sixth Sense*.

3. The rise in interest of academia in trauma theory since the early 90's is another expression of the same tendency. The books of Cathy Caruth (1995, 1996) and Judith Herman (1992) are still among the most-quoted books in the context of cultural explorations of trauma, and they are among the early examples of a still growing corpus of texts on that matter.

4. The movie is rife with references to Carroll's *Alice in Wonderland*: The heroines name, the movement through the mansion's looking glass into the underworld of the Hive, the white rabbit who is injected with the antidote.

5. Not least among those allusions is the intertextual reference to Carroll's Alice. The film, however, addresses this issue on a number of levels: By showing Alice opening her eyes, introducing a textual reference to dreaming ("Tonight all your dreams will come true," and by a dreamlike sequence, in which past and present are intertwined.

6. It should be noted in this context that Freud was strongly criticized for abandoning his early theory on the etiology of hysteria in which he traced the symptoms back to an early and traumatic sexual encounter, cp. e.g., Judith Herman: "Freud's subsequent retreat from the study of psychological trauma has come to be viewed as a matter of scandal." (Herman 1992). It is at this early point in both Freud's career and the history of psychoanalysis that the Real is considered to be relatively irrelevant with regard to psychic processes and functioning.

7. An early draft version of the film script highlights this representative function of the Hive workers: "Typists type. Assistants assist. Busy worker bees." (http://www.daily script.com/scripts/resevil.html, accessed 06/22/2012)

8. A tendency which Caruth highlights. For a critical assessment, cp. Ruth Leys, *Trauma: A Genealogy*.

9. There are two more zombies afterwards: Both Spencer and Rain, however, are "turned" into zombies and do not fall into the same category as those that come from that traumatic place in the Hive.

10. Paranoiac delusion exceeds the more commonly used meaning of paranoia as a persecution anxiety. Persecution in paranoia is connected to the delusion of grandeur in the patient, or as Trotter writes: "[P]aranoid symmetry requires that the degree of fantasized grandeur should match as closely as possible the degree of fantasized persecution" (79).

Works Cited

Anderson, Paul W. S., dir. *Resident Evil*. Perf. Milla Jovovich, Michelle Rodriguez, and Colin Salmon. 2002. Constantin Film. DVD.

_____, *Resident Evil: Afterlife*. Perf. Milla Jovovich, Ali Larter, and Kim Coates. 2010. Constantin Film. DVD.

Bordwell, David. *Narration in the Fiction Film*. Madison: University of Wisconsin Press, 1985. Print.

_____, and Kristin Thompson. *Film Art: An Introduction*. New York: McGraw-Hill, 2008. Print.

Buckland, Warren, and Thomas Elsaesser. *Studying Contemporary American Film: A Guide to Movie Analysis*. London: Arnold, 2002. Print.

Caruth, Cathy. *Unclaimed Experience: Trauma, Narrative, and History*. Baltimore, MD: Johns Hopkins University Press, 1996. Print.

Deleuze, Gilles. *Cinema 1: The Movement-Image*. New York, London: Continuum International, 2005. Print.

Freud, Sigmund. *Constructions in Analysis*. Ed. Adam Phillips. The Penguin Freud Reader ed. London: Penguin, 2006. 77–89. Print.

_____. *Remembering, Repeating and Working-Through (Further Recommendations on the Technique of Psycho-Analysis II)*. Trans. Joan Riviere. 1914. *The Standard Edition of the Complete Psychological Works of Sigmund Freud*, Volume XII (1911–1913): *The Case of Schreber, Papers on Technique and Other Works*. Ed. James Strachey. London: Hogarth Press, 1958. 145–156. Print.

Heath, Stephen. "Film and System: Terms of Analysis Part I." *Screen* 16.1 (1975): 7–77. Web.

Metz, Christian. "The Imaginary Signifier." *Screen* 16.2 (1975): 14–76. Web.

Mulcahy, Russell, dir. *Resident Evil: Extinction*. Perf. Milla Jovovich, Ali Larter, and Odid Fehr. 2007. Constantin Film. DVD.

Robinett, Jane. "The Narrative Shape of Traumatic Experience." *Literature and Medicine* 26. 2 (2007): 290–312. Web.

Trotter, David. *Paranoid Modernism: Literary Experiment, Psychosis and the Professionalization of English Society*. Oxford: Oxford University Press, 2001. Print.

Witt, Alexander, dir. *Resident Evil: Apocalypse*. Perf. Milla Jovovich, Sienna Guillory, and Odid Fehr. 2004. Constantin Film. DVD.

Žižek, Slavoj. *Looking Awry: An Introduction to Jacques Lacan Through Popular Culture*. Cambridge, MA: MIT Press, 1991. Print.

_____. *The Sublime Object of Ideology*. London: Verso, 2008. Print.

Why They Keep Coming Back:
The Allure of Incongruity

Adam M. Crowley

"I think a lot of what people want now is to have Chris and Jill in a game, or they want it to look like Resident Evil *used to look like. That's what makes the game work for them."*—Masachika Kawata 01/31/13

In a recent interview with IGN.com, *American Mary* (2013) directors Jen and Sylvia Soska—a.k.a. "The Twisted Twins"—allude to *Resident Evil's* (1996) memorable juxtaposition of "chintzy" transitional sequences with genuinely frightening atmospherics. The twins attribute the dramatic failures of the "corny" transitions to their stilted and often poorly-delivered dialogue: e.g., Jen Soska, quoting *Resident Evil's* Barry Burton in a mocking tone, "'Blood. Hope that this is not Chris's blood'" and Sylvia Soska, also quoting Burton, "'Here is a lock pick. It might be handy if you, *the master of unlocking*, take it with you.'" Their incredulity echoes complaints that are voiced in the game's reviews. For example, the editorial staff of Gamespot.com notes that the game is "filled to the vomit-line with some of the most hokey, badly-translated, drama-killing, god-awful voice acting ever burned onto a disc." Similarly, Edge.com complains that the dialogue and delivery are so poorly executed that they could "make the cast of the [mawkish English sitcom] *Hollyoaks* blush." However—and despite these hyperbolic reactions—it is also true that these commentators endorse the game as being singularly magnificent. *Resident Evil* is variously described as a "classic horror" ("Twins"), as "gorgeous" (Gamespot.com), and as an experience that cannot be done justice by "words alone" (Edge.com).

The commentary's unanimity regarding these divergent facets of the player's experience raise practical questions about how *Resident Evil* succeeds with audiences despite its glaring flaws. A solution to such questions can be found in Slavoj Žižek's holistic scheme for video game analysis, which regards even divergent components in digital entertainments as elements that work in concert to achieve a singular effect. Žižek presents this theory in *Plague of Fantasies*, under his commentary on "cyber-liberation" (154). He indicates that the structural components of video games constitute a discourse of submission between the player and the game, characterized by the relentless limitation of the player's experiences by the programming's "God-like technical presence." Žižek's logic suggests that *Resident Evil*'s "chintzy" transitions and celebrated atmospherics would contribute—like all other features of the game—to a common effect: to an evidencing of the programming's unwavering "prospect of control" over the player and her decision-making processes. It is a novel theory, though certainly reductive in its approach and interpretive possibilities. Nevertheless, its application to a work like *Resident Evil* is somewhat irresistible, insofar as it promises a common rationale for what have long been regarded as experientially distinct and significant features of this popular entertainment. Moreover, the audacity of Žižek's hypothesis makes the prospect of such analysis tempting, as it is difficult to imagine two gameplay features that are more divergent and difficult to bring under the concept of a common experience than *Resident Evil*'s expository exchanges and atmospherics.

However, such analysis should begin with the sobering recognition that Žižek does not detail the particular discursive conventions that assumedly inform the experience of "cyber-liberation." Consequently, his work must be supplemented with more specific theories of discourse and rhetoric before it is practical for analysis. The field of classical narratology—defined here by the mid– to late–twentieth-century structuralist considerations of narrative by critics as diverse as Tzvetan Torodov, Roland Barthes, and Gérard Genette, is relevant to this concern. In works such as *Grammaire du Décaméron* (1969), *Introduction to the Structural Analysis of Narrative* (1975), and *Narrative Discourse: An Essay on Method* (1980), these scholars advance the notion that narratives have key discursive components that can be isolated and examined for their intertextual significance. Within this body of work, Genette's *Narrative Discourse* is arguably the most relevant to Žižek's theory, as it provides schemes for adjudicating the significance of such components to dialectical structures— in particular, to dialectical structures that indicate perceptional imbalances between narrators.

Genette advances the theory that narratives can be conceptualized as the "expansion of a verb," and that a text's various voices—i.e., its first-, second-, or third-person narratorial structures—can be defined by their relationship to that verb in its stages of transformation. His primary examples are drawn from Proust's experimental representations of the act of "remembering" in *A Remembrance of Things Past* (*Narrative* 30). Žižek's identification of "control" as the central experience of gameplay presents an opportunity to consider the significance of a game like *Resident Evil*'s evident voices to the development of that verb as it arises from their interactions. In this instance, the relevant voices would be the voice of the "game," as defined by the experiential possibilities for play, and the voice of "the player" as it emerges through an individual's interactions with those possibilities. Genette's theories enable the analyst to characterize such discourse as being representative of a particular dialectical structure, one with characteristics that detail the nature of the player's subordination to the game. In its findings, this scheme presents an explanation for *Resident Evil*'s widespread and continuing popularity with its audience. The significance of this explanation to the game and game players is that it illuminates what it is that player's "want" from their *Resident Evil* experience. In a recent interview, Masachika Kawata, a producer of the now-failing *Resident Evil* franchise, indicates that the series's next iteration will return players to the gameplay dynamics of the original *Resident Evil*. If this is indeed the case, then gamers can expect to once again enjoy the experience of "control" that is outlined in this argument.

Resident Evil opens with a cinematic concerned with the misadventures of STARS (Special Tactics and Rescue Services) agents Chris Redfield and Jill Valentine. Redfield, Valentine, and the other members of STARS Alpha Team search for the organization's Bravo Team, which vanished while on assignment researching a series of savage murders on the outskirts of Raccoon City. Alpha Team's mission is disrupted by a pack of ferocious dogs that—inexplicably—chase away the team's helicopter, prompting Redfield to clench his fists and scream his infamous appeal "NOO! DON'T GO!" into the nighttime sky. The rescuers, now turned victims, are then chased into a seemingly abandoned mansion "where they thought it was safe." The game unfolds within this space, with the player's choice of either Redfield or Valentine working to overcome a series of challenges: e.g., deadly puzzles, diabolical traps, and a creeping hoard of genetically modified horrors. This dark journey plunges the player into the research of the Umbrella Corporation, which has developed a deadly virus—the T-virus—that is poised to infiltrate civilization. In the concluding action, the survivors battle the twisted fruit of that research, the Tyrant, before escaping into a now-doomed world. Depending upon which character the player selects—and other gameplay choices—*Resident Evil* concludes with one of three possible endings, all of which show the survivors flying away in a helicopter.

The game's creepy atmospherics and their associated mad scientist narrative are informed by early twentieth-century pulp-horror: the writings of authors like H.P. Lovecraft (e.g., "Herbert West—Reanimator" [1922]) and other luminaries from the pages of *Weird Tales*, who were themselves influenced by the literary, stage, and film traditions surrounding Mary Shelley's *Frankenstein*. However, within the field of digital entertainments, the game borrows schemes for its relevant scenarios from a number of works from the 1980s and early 1990s, many of which unfold within the confines of a haunted or merely haunting abode. A list of such works would include, but would not be limited to, *Haunted House* (1982), *Terror House* (1982), *Monster Bash* (1982), *Ghost House* (1986), *Ant Attack* (1983), *Shiryou Sensen: War of the Dead* (1987), *Sweet Home* (1989), and *Alone in the Dark* (1992). This context is useful to an understanding of the game's early reviews, which are unified in their celebration of the mansion's creepy atmospherics, which are technological marvels from the perspective of these earlier works. For example, Edge.com claims that "[W]ords alone fail to do justice to the fanatical richness of *Resident Evil*'s art design, where even the wallpaper and carpets warrant admiring scrutiny." Gamespot.com explains that players should go to the game not only to "use shotguns and rocket launchers to blast mutant dogs" but, first and foremost, to "prowl gorgeous, photorealistic, dilapidated rooms and abomination-filled corridors." The notion that the atmospherics in a horror-themed video game could be aesthetically pleasing is remarkable in the context of *Resident Evil*'s period of production, and part of a much broader multi-genre renaissance in the industry that can be traced back at least as far as the original *Myst* (1993).

While these visuals appear to be less than remarkable today, their significance to the game's original audience should not be overlooked, primarily because these experiences are the proper context for the universally derided "drama-killing ... voice acting" (Gamespot.com). As Patrick Crogan points out, numerous survival-themed games from the early 1990s—including the *Tomb Raider* and *Metal Gear Solid* franchises—contained such "scene settings"—or "transitional sequences"—between isolated play spaces, and that the function of these settings is to convey notions of "character development, relationships with supporting cast, and ... backstory" (651).

A broader consideration of *Resident Evil*'s essential gameplay mechanics reveals that the game's playable scenes and scene settings contribute to the development of a common verb: control. Here, control is understood to be the control of the game over the player, expressed and managed through the game's subjugation of the player to a series of events that are essentially incongruous with the narrative frame established in the game's opening exposition: i.e., the escape from the mystery mansion. The player's experience of incongruity can be associated with three facets of gameplay. It is manifested in the game's numerous puzzle challenges for the player, virtually all of which adhere to an internal logic that has no—or only limited—relevance to the general gameplay scenario. It also informs the player's movement through the mansion, which is marked by the peculiar—and seemingly nonsensical—elisions of the evidence of her actions: i.e., dispatched zombies and other enemies vanish from sight when the player returns to the scenes of her violent confrontations. Finally, the scene settings themselves can be associated with the player's experience of incongruity, insofar as the involved characters express actions and concerns that—quite literally—suspend the fantasy of survival-horror the player constructs through her white-knuckle navigation of the mystery mansion. Each of these facets works to make meaning—i.e., develop—the operative verb, control, through a common dialectical structure. As a consequence, at any and all points in the game, the player's understanding and agency is limited to her navigation or experience of a particular manifestation of the mansion: to one of its puzzles, to one of its corridors, or to one of the game's disruptive scene settings, many of which evince their own logical peculiarities and eccentricities.

With regards to the game's numerous puzzles, *Resident Evil*'s primary gameplay is characterized by the player's discovery of key objects—e.g., guns, maps, and other totems—that enable the player to resolve or otherwise avoid various challenges. Consequently, at every turn the player is literally coming to know the Umbrella Corporation's mad research agenda through an adjudicating technical presence that delimits her liberty—the player can only advance through the mansion through her adherence to the logic of the mansion's mazes and monsters. It is noteworthy that the logic that is required of the player to solve many of these puzzles is alien to the setting. For example, the player must locate a typewriter to save her game, the player must destroy a random statue to find a stone to unlock another statue, and the player must activate a series of switches to answer a riddle to reveal a secret passage. Individually, the premises of these puzzles and their possible solutions do not find an explanation within the gamespace—not because the game fails to explain their presence, but because they indicate a logic that has no source in the story itself: i.e., why does the game include the typewriter conceit, why does the statue for the hidden stone have to be that particular statue, and why would someone construct a switch-riddle to hide something like a key from the player? Certainly, this type of gameplay is not unique to *Resident Evil*, and it is evident in various forms in many of the games discussed so far. However, this reality does not change the fact that the player's experience of play can be described in terms of her management of a series of puzzles that are incongruous in the context of the mystery mansion. As a consequence of this reality, the player is never allowed to feel that she has any control over the game itself—rather, at best, she feels a momentary sense of control and accomplishment through her mastery of puzzles that are, ultimately, only significant unto themselves.

The mad technical presence that curtails the player's advancement also works to make meaning in the game by modifying the significance of that very advancement to the player's past. For example, *Resident Evil* is a game of many doors and stairways, as well as other thresholds that delimit the mansion's numerous rooms and venues. The player's passage through all such spaces coincides with a transitional sequence that involves a cut-away to the door (or other marker) and the player's movement across the barrier. Sometimes, the movements involve the player's return to an area where she dispatched a zombie or some other horror. However, when the player returns to these spaces, she inevitably finds herself in a sanitized space—any bodies that she may have left at the location previously have been removed from the game. It is reasonable to regard such vanishings as a practical manifestation of certain technological limitations of interactive digital entertainments: i.e., there is simply not enough computing power behind the game for the save feature to retain data on such variables. However, the technological explanation does not obviate the significance of the vanishing dead to the gameplay. With their presence, the dead contribute to the atmosphere of suspense that permeates the terror mansion. In their absence, that value is modified—a bloody corpse is transformed into a clean carpet, a skinless horror is replaced by an undisturbed curtain or window. Consequently, these transformations are not meaningless, or—to be more precise—they are no more meaningless than any other aspect of the game that can be ascribed to a programming scheme, such as the removal of incongruous objects from the player's inventory after she uses them to resolve the riddles and traps that facilitate her movement through the gamespace.

Productive and related questions bearing on multiple levels of gameplay can be asked about such removals. For example, what is the significance of these purified spaces to the game's unfolding narrative of horror and violence, and what are the logical implications of these vanishings to the narrative itself—e.g., where do the bodies "go"? However—and without dismissing these concerns—a more fundamental observation can be made: the player must relinquish her "prospect of control" over each of the mansion's individual spaces as she moves about (Žižek 154). In terms of the vanishing dead, this relinquishing reveals a significant narrative incongruity that distinguishes the player's act of play from the game's representation of that same act: the player never has any more control over her experience of play than the control she can achieve within the confines of an isolated space, outside of which a dominate pattern of narrative absurdity dictates the significance of her future experiences (more puzzles) and past experiences (the selective erasure of the evidence of her accomplishments).

The issue of incongruity that emerges from object gathering and the disappearance of the dead extends into many of the game's scene settings. A representative example of this effect can be located in one of the game's three possible closing cinematic sequences. It involves Redfield and Rebecca Chambers's helicopter escape. This scene follows the climactic battle with the Tyrant, which functions as the culmination of the player's experience of suspense. Throughout the cinematic, Redfield and Chamber's discourse is entirely inconsistent with the seriousness of their situation and the nature of their triumph over the Umbrella Corporation:

REBECCA: [Yawns]
REDFIELD: Are you tired, Rebecca?
REBECCA: Sorry, Chris, I am.
REDFIELD: You did a really good job. This case was just too weird.

Here, Chris's "chintzy" paternalism, coupled with his cornball assessment of "the case," is striking—like so much of what he says elsewhere—because it diverges so dramatically from the narrative's atmospherics at the time of the cinematic's appearance: i.e., the experiential qualities that define gameplay—which, in the universe of the game, have (assumedly) common significance for the character of Redfield as he is realized in the cinematic sequences and for the character of Redfield as he is realized under the player's direction. Only—they do not. An effect of the cinematic is to recast Redfield as an exponent of silly and superficial concerns that are not germane to the player's decision-making processes: the hero in the helicopter is not only physically distinct in the sense that he is an actor instead of a cartoon, but he is also perceptionally and emotionally divorced from the qualities of that cartoon character as it was advanced by the player to this point in the narrative. In this way, the game's programming renders one final—and devastating—blow to the player's act of play: the concluding image of Chris is one that contravenes the experience of playing Chris to this final moment.

Throughout the game, then, the significance of player action is arrested at every level and subjugated to incongruities that evidence the game's dominance of the player and her experiences in the game space. To the question of what the larger purpose of this relationship between game and player might be, one could turn toward the reviews. For example, Edge.com observes, "Everything in *Resident Evil* is geared towards suspense: the skewed camera angles, the haunting strains of the soundtrack, the fact that you can run forwards but only retreat in painfully slow steps." Though this approach is limited, it is productive to discuss the qualitative differences between the game's scene settings and playable scenes with comments bearing on *Resident Evil*'s aesthetic practices for establishing suspense. This is because these otherwise divergent facets of the game are informed by these same practices. For instance, some of the identified qualities—the camera angles and haunting soundtrack—are descriptive of both facets of the game. This linkage makes it possible for the analyst to express his or her disappointment (or, perhaps, enjoyment) of the scene settings in terms of the dialogue's expression of suspense and how that expression compares to the experience of suspense as it is manifested in the relevant framing scenes. For example, regarding the atmospherics of gameplay, this approach illuminates the peculiar construction and beautiful realization of the mystery mansion as evidence of the game's investment in suspense—hallways turn off at unexpected angles, gothic wallpaper and moody lighting heighten the sense of foreboding in select rooms. This same standard can bring added context to the stilted dialogue that characters exchange in the transitions, which are not merely bad in a subjective sense, but affective to the extent that it distracts from the experience of suspense.

However, as an aesthetic agenda, the concept of "suspense"—like the concept of the game's "God-like technical presence"—is essentially abstract, and is not an explanation for the fundamental gameplay realities that facilitate the experience of the concept itself: i.e., though it is reasonable to argue that the game's technical aspects work in concert to convey a sense of suspense, that argument raises—but does not answer—practical questions about the general quality of suspense as it might be attributed to any individual or constellation of suspense-building mechanics. This general observation points towards the practical limitations of Žižek's theory, as well. For example, while digital landscapes may indeed evidence "radical closure" through the prospect of control attributed to a technical presence, pragmatic assessments of such closure would assumedly rest on an even more fundamental scheme, one capable of characterizing with some specificity the player, the programming, and interactions between these subjects that contribute to the power-politics implied under cyber-liberation (Žižek 154). For either analytical frame, then, the missing concept is one that would be informative of the rhetorical forces that are in play in *Resident Evil*: i.e., what is the evident discursive art that is used to curtail the player's liberation, or to ironically infuse that liberation with a sense of dread and foreboding?

Frank J. D'Angelo observes that video games, like many popular forms of entertainment, share narrative features that can be associated with the concept of "intertextuality." D'Angelo draws from Julia Kristeva's definition for the term, which is "the transportation of one (or several) sign system(s) into another" (33). D'Angelo uses the concept to illustrate the interconnectedness of various narrative formats: e.g., films, comic books, and video games. The notion that video games are, first and foremost, sign systems with rhetorical characteristics that place them in conversation with other sign systems (which may or may not themselves be video games), creates a basal position for judging the essential divide between a game like *Resident Evil*'s scene settings and playable scenes. For example, the amateur exchanges that characterize the transitional scenes are recognizable as such precisely because they evidence fallacies the player is already familiar with from other poorly acted dramas. Similarly, the powerful sense of foreboding and suspense that is generated in the course of gameplay can be associated with the player's extratextual experiences. However, when considering a general concept like cyber-liberation, the significance of intertextuality to the player's experience is itself too general a concept to be practical for analysis, as they player's subjective extratextual experiences of domination are in no way quantifiable. However, the concept of intertextuality has been associated with critical schemes that are attentive to the kinds of power dynamics that are implied by the phenomenon of cyber-liberation as it appears in this game: e.g., the player's subjection to the totalizing gaze of the programming's God-like perspective through the experience of incongruity. In terms of *Resident Evil*, the value of one such scheme—produced by Genette—is that it illuminates the discursive convention that unites the game's transitional sequences with its gameplay mechanics.

Genette's commentary on intertextuality emerges as part of his broader theorizing on narrative, which is detailed in works including but not limited to *Narrative Discourse: An Essay on Method*, *Palimpsests* (1997), and *Fiction and Diction* (1993). In *Palimpsests*, he addresses the term as an act of allusion to other narrative forms—either implicitly or through plagiarism. Intertextual references, for Genette, emerge as a function of "voice," which Genette uses to address the grammatical qualities of personhood as they bear on discourse: i.e., first-, second-, or third-person rhetoric. In *Fiction and Diction*, he approaches these qualities with a five-part scheme of identity relations that exist between an author, a narrator, and the characters associated with the narrative (represented as A, N, and C, respectively in *Fiction and Diction*). Two of the five categories that emerge from this logic—and the essential conceptual divide that distinguishes these categories from each other—can be used to contextualize the programming/player dialectic in *Resident Evil*: "heterodiegetic fiction," $A \neq N \neq C \neq A$—the voice of the programming, and "historical narrative," $A = N \neq C \neq A$, the voice of the player.

Heterodiegetic fiction is defined by the narrator's dissociation from both the author and the characters: consequently the narrator's evident discursive qualities are only representative of the narrator. The term foregrounds questions—but not necessarily answers—about the key features of the narrator's disposition, which Genette reasons can be pursued through critical attention to the "enunciated subjects" that emerge from the narrator's various "enunciations" (*Narrative* 31). Without being unnecessarily reductive, it is reasonable to assert that the manifold enunciated subjects of *Resident Evil* find their articulation in the economy of incongruous puzzles that work to make meaning by challenging the player's progress. Such enunciations are descriptive of this subject, though they are not wholly descriptive of it, as the subject is broad enough to be associated with all of the possible representations in the game. However, insofar as such aspects of the game constitute a consistent pattern in terms of the narrative's unfolding, they can be aligned with the concept of narrator.

For her part, the player—to be distinguished from the character the player controls—can be associated with the category of historical narrative, which is predicated on the notion that the voice in question is the author and the narrator of the involved discourse. For Genette, the concept of authorship implies an intentionality that can be tied to a real world subject: i.e., a particular entity is responsible for the decision-making processes that result in or otherwise contribute to various enunciations. This linkage has implications for gameplay insofar as it suggests that the player's discourse is literally the historical record of her time interacting with the heterodiegetic narration. In terms of this argument, this record is significant to the voice of the player insofar as it also engenders a specific question: namely, what does this historical record indicate about the player's practices for navigating the incongruous opportunities and representations that are afforded to her by the narrator?

For Genette, the essential divide between the heterodiegetic and historical voices is the question of authorship. Under his scheme, the gameplay dynamic of *Resident Evil* is illuminated as a structure wherein the player is consistently responsible to her decision-making processes, which are in fact indicative of who she is in the gamespace—while the "God-like" technical presence of the game is not held to any such logical standard. That presence is free to introduce incongruous puzzles, modify its own record of the player's movement through the gamespace, and supplant its own cinematic interpretation of events over the reasoned interpretations of the player at will. A definitive characteristic of this entity, then, is its ability to violate the player's experience of congruity without itself ever being responsible for the broader significance of such violations to the player's history in the gamespace: i.e., no responsibility is ever taken for the implications of the game's efforts to "control" the gamespace with incongruous narrative developments precisely because the narrator is always already introducing a new incongruity into the player's experiences. In this way, the game creates a fantasy of non-judgment for the player, wherein she never needs to consider the implications of the game's evident lack of logic, as the game rewards her investment in the illogical and incongruous with the gameplay experience itself. It is no wonder then that the only real aspect of the game that the reviews find fault with is the "transitional scenes"—these scenes violate that essential relationship: by supplanting the voice of the player with the voice of the narrator, they expose the (deafening) absurdity of that voice—which is always present, but much more tolerable for the player when she has the illusion of benefiting from it—of participating in a discourse wherein the very absurdity of the dialectic frees her from the responsibility of her own madcap choices. The experience of such freedom can be singled out as a source of *Resident Evil*'s popularity—and the absence of such freedom in many of the game's more recent manifestations can be singled out as a cause for their market failures. In his efforts to recapture the "magic" of the franchise, Masachika Kawata might direct his game designers to return to such concerns.

Note

1. See Gérard Genette, *Fiction and Diction*, 68–78.

Works Cited

Alone in the Dark. 1992. Infogames. 3 Jan 2013.

American Mary. Dir. Jen Soska. IndustryWorks, 2012. Film.

Ant Attack. 1983. Quicksilva. 4 Jan 2013.

Barthes, Roland. *New Literary History*. Winter, 1975. Baltimore: John Hopkins University Press, 237–72. Print.

Crogan, Patrick. "Blade Runners: Speculations on Narrative and Interactivity." *The South Atlantic Quarterly*. Summer 2002. Duke University Press. 639–57. Web. 9 Jan. 2013.

D'Angelo, Frank J. "The Rhetoric of Intertextuality." *Rhetoric Review*. 29. 1, 21–47, 2010. Web. 10 Jan. 2013.

Genette, Gérard. *Fiction and Diction*. Trans. Catherine Porter. Ithaca: Cornell University Press, 1993. Print.

_____. *Narrative Discourse: An Essay on Method*. Trans. Jane E. Lewin. Ithaca: Cornell University Press, 1980. Print.

_____. *Palimpsests: Literature in the Second Degree*. Trans. Channa Newman. Lincoln: University of Nebraska Press, 1997. Print.

Ghost House. 1986. Sega. 3 Jan 2013.

Haunted House. 1982. Atari. 3 Jan 2013.

Krupa, Daniel. "*Resident Evil* Will Return to Its Roots." IGNwww. Web. 8 Jan. 2013.

Lovecraft, H.P. "Herbert West—Reanimator." *Zombies! Zombies! Zombies!* Ed. Otto Penzler. New York: Vintage Books, 2011. Print.

Monster Bash. 1982. Sega. 5 Jan 2013.

Myst. 1993. Cylan. 3 Jan 2013.

Resident Evil. 1996. Capcom. 1 Jan 2013.

"*Resident Evil* (Long Box) Review." Gamespot.com. 1 Dec. 1996. Web. 1 Feb 2013.

"*Resident Evil* Review." Edge.com. 3 May. 1996. Web. 1 Feb 2013.

Shiryou Sensen. 1987. Victor Music Industries. 7 Jan 2013.

Shelley, Mary. *Frankenstein*. New York: Signet Classics, 1963. Print.

Sweet Home. 1989 Capcom. 1 Jan 2013.

Terror House. 1982. Bandai. 17 Jan 2013.

Todorov, Tzvetan. *Grammaire du Décaméron*. The Hague: Mouton, 1969. Print.

"The Twisted Twins Talk Horror Games." YouTube.Com. 21 Jan. 2013. Web. 1 Feb 2013.

Žižek, Slavoj. *The Plague of Fantasies*. New York: Verso, 2009. Print.

Opening Doors:
Art-Horror and Agency

Stephen Cadwell

I remember opening the door. I found myself standing in a short corridor, not dissimilar to the corridors I had already seen in this old mansion house. To my left I could see a corner. In three short steps I was there. I heard a noise, a wet rustling. I turned the corner; my gaze froze. A figure in a weathered green jacket kneeled before me; he seemed to be eating something, eating something off the floor. I stood still transfixed; slowly the figure reared up. I saw a pockmarked, bald head, cuts and bruises littering his eyes and nose. One bold, white eye revolved in its socket. It locked me in a deathly stare and groaned. I couldn't contain myself any longer, and against my better judgment; I let out a long and loud curse. My mother looked up from her newspaper. The look she gave me, as I sat in front of the television, right beside the Christmas tree was not one of pride, more of exhaustion. Her son, now 19, would never, it seems, grow out of video games. I noticed none of this as I was far too busy trying to remember which button drew my combat knife, an inventory screen flicked on and off my television. I turned in circles and stabbed the air as the zombie relentlessly bit my neck. A moment later the game told me I had died.

Fast-forward to March 2002, I was sitting in front of the biggest screen at my local Cineplex. As a fan of the *Resident Evil* games series I was excited, perhaps too excited, to see it transfer to movies. The film opened well with some good scares and an interesting take on the "Umbrella Corp." mythology, but after thirty minutes I noticed a distinct lack of zombies. I was eager to see how they would handle the first zombie encounter. Like many fans of the game, I had been enthralled and excited by many tense moments throughout the series but nothing equaled that first encounter, the first moment where the zombie turned its bug eye to me and I flailed around the corridor trying to escape. That moment had not been matched by the games, nor would it be matched by the movie. I watched as Michelle Rodriguez's character stalked through the basement of the strange old mansion, her machine gun locked and loaded. Her brow furrowed as a gas canister rolled in front of her, and she turned the corner. A woman in white scrubs leaned against an upstanding black pipe. Her jaw slack; her skin grey and damaged. She lurched clumsily forward and fell onto Rodriguez. After a brief struggle the zombie was dispatched and with her went my hopes that this film would match the experience of playing the game *Resident Evil*.

In this chapter, I will put forth two strands of argument; one general and one specific. I will also employ two distinct methodologies; one taken from the discourse of analytic philosophy and one anecdotally recounting my own experiences. It is the *Resident Evil* franchise that gives me license to do this. It is a franchise that features movies based on games and games that take so much from movies. As such, I think that my two strands of argument and my two methodological approaches will link together and form a double helix akin to the shifts between action and cut-scene in the original *Resident Evil* game.

My general argument concerns an important difference between computer games and movies. It is my contention that computer games, as a form of fiction, can make their audiences experience emotions at a level inaccessible through the medium of film. This general point underwrites the more specific argument concerning *Resident Evil*. In this strand of my argument I will try to analyze and explain why I found the *Resident Evil* game to be so much more horrifying than the *Resident Evil* film. This argument centers on two issues; firstly the game-maker's use of the "cut-scene,"[1] and secondly the effect that controlling a game has on the gamer's emotional experience.[2] In order to clarify precisely what this emotional experience is, the first section of the chapter will present a definition of Noël Carroll's art-horror. Carroll argues that this term captures most accurately the emotions which are derived from experiences of the cross-art, cross-media horror genre. The second section of the chapter will analyze and examine the first zombie encounter from Paul W. Anderson's 2002 film, *Resident Evil*. This section will explain why my emotional response to the film was weaker than my response to the game under the terms of Carroll's definition of art-horror. The third section will offer a similar examination and analysis of the first zombie encounter from Capcom's 1996 game *Resident Evil*. This section will define the game as an example of a text from "ergodic literature" (literature which requires non-trivial effort to traverse the text) and offer it up as a prime example of the horror genre, again using the terms of Carroll's art-horror definition. The final section will focus on the general strand of my argument asserting that even in an ideal circumstance, *Resident Evil* as a computer game would necessarily be a more efficient catalyst for the art-horror response than its filmic equivalent.

Certain parts of this essay will employ the discourse of analytic philosophy. This technical and occasionally difficult approach is not meant to baffle or bemuse, but rather treats the *Resident Evil* games and films as objects worthy of serious and rigorous philosophical discussion. To this end, nothing will be assumed or taken for granted. In section two I will set out the reasons why the *Resident Evil* film should be considered a mediocre example of a movie in the horror genre. These reasons will go beyond my opinions and judgments and focus instead on precisely how the film failed to satisfy the criteria which define the horror movie genre. Similarly, section three offers a precise and step-by-step explanation of why the *Resident Evil* game should be considered a text, or work of fiction, equivalent to any movie, novel, or comic. Proceeding from this I examine why, as a work of fiction, it should be considered a prime example of the horror genre. Finally I explore why, as an example of the horror genre, it satisfies that genre's governing criteria in a way that the *Resident Evil* film simply does not.

But the methods at the disposal of the analytic philosopher can only account for certain parts of this discussion. The nature of gaming is such that when I play a game, only I can access the particular narrative of that gaming experience. Gaming is, in a philosophical sense, a wholly subjective pursuit. Consequently, those aspects of this discussion which are not suitable to the analytic method are offered up in an anecdotal way. You can never experience the *Resident Evil* game as I experienced the *Resident Evil* game, but perhaps by reading the story I tell about those experiences you can relate them to your own and thus flesh out an important but elusive element of my argument.

* * *

For anyone who has had the pleasure, or certain displeasure, of playing *Resident Evil*, or watching the film *Resident Evil*, they can be left in no doubt that both are works of horror, but the precise sense of horror must be defined. It would be wrong to claim that it is the sense of horror used to describe acts of genocide, animal cruelty, or environmental destruction. These are horrific at a genuine, deep, and real level. The sense needed for the game and film must be some kind of not-really-horrifying-horror. Noël Carroll is very helpful on this point. In his book *The Philosophy of Horror* he coins the term *art-horror* as the emotion ideally elicited from art objects of the horror genre.[3] His definition of art-horror will provide us with the exact sense of horror necessary for the analysis of *Resident Evil* in all its forms.

Carroll begins his description of the art-horror response by outlining the field of fiction that will be subject to its terms.

"Art-horror," by stipulation, is meant to refer to the product of a genre that crystallized, speaking very roughly, around the time of the publication of *Frankenstein*—give or take fifty years—and that has persisted, often cyclically, through the novels and plays of the nineteenth century and the literature, comic books, pulp magazines and films of the twentieth [Carroll 13].

This set enables the clarification of the unifying features or traits from these works and allows the development of a set of necessary and sufficient conditions by which the appropriateness of an object's inclusion into the horror genre[4] can be determined. In an Aristotelian mode,[5] Carroll argues that what unifies the various objects from the horror genre is that they elicit the same emotional response; namely, art-horror. He writes

> The cross-art, cross-media genre of horror takes its title from the emotion it characteristically or rather ideally promotes; this promotion constitutes the identifying mark of horror.... Members of the horror genre will be identified as narratives and/or images (in the case of fine art, film, etc.) predicated on raising the effect of horror in audiences [14–15].

It is now clear that the term applies to the emotional response derived from certain works of art in a variety of media, dating roughly from the publication of *Frankenstein*. This, by stipulation, will exclude historical documents, scientific theories, and real human behavior from our field of objects which can elicit art-horror as an emotional response. Feelings of horror, qua art-horror, can now be discussed in a way that allows the exclusion of responses to genocide, animal-cruelty, and environmental destruction.

Next, Carroll defines precisely what the horror genre should include and exclude on his account. Some of his exclusions, on first glance, can appear confusing. For example, Michael Powell's *Peeping Tom* is, according to Carroll, to be excluded from the horror genre. Carroll argues that the terrifying and infamous film, which depicts a disturbed cameraman murdering women, achieves its frightening effects by drawing on psychological phenomena that are too human, too natural (39). He argues that if the fictional account of a deranged murderer were included in the horror genre then it would be more difficult to exclude real accounts of deranged murders from the terms definition of art-horror, as if one account elicited a certain emotional response then so too would the other. If exclusion of non-fiction accounts could not be maintained then the whole definition of the art-horror response would quickly break down into incoherence. Works of fiction that derive their frightening elements from natural, albeit extreme, human behavior, must be excluded from the horror genre as they lack an element of fantasy which will prove necessary for the definition of art-horror. Carroll accepts that these kinds of fictions may bring about feelings of terror, but terror is not horror, and it is horror, specifically art-horror, which he is trying to analyze.

Carroll adds another element to his definition and that is the necessary presence of monsters in works of fiction from the horror genre. He writes, "Correlating horror with the presence of monsters gives us a neat way of distinguishing it from terror, especially of the sort rooted in tales of abnormal psychologies" (15). This may seem like an unnecessary move to make but its importance will become clear when a certain objection is considered. Carroll writes, "Rather than characterizing art-horror solely on the basis of our own subjective responses, we can ground our conjectures on observations of the way in which characters respond to the monsters in works of horror" (18). By introducing the necessary presence of monsters to his definition of the art-horror response, Carroll has secured art-horror from accusations of subjectivism. Rather than merely arguing that monsters in movies make him experience an emotion like horror, he can now argue that, in most cases, the emotional response felt by the audience mirrors the emotional response of the positive characters in the fiction. To be clear, in an ideal art object from the horror genre, the viewer's emotional response is supposed to match or mirror, in a weak sense, the reactions of positive characters (i.e., the non-monstrous characters). Carroll supports this position by offering a number of solid examples from a broad range of the horror genre where the positive characters react with horror in moments when the audience is being encouraged to respond with horror (Carroll 32–35).

Carroll has created a rubric which allows for the examination of objects from the horror genre and for tracing the moments when the audience are expected to respond with feelings of art-horror. If these intense moments or "scares" are isolated, the successfulness, or "scariness," of an art-object from the horror genre can be developed objectively. For example, if one were to trace five distinct moments in film *x* where the positive characters express horror-like emotions in response to the monstrous characters and yet the audience, or a group of test subjects, only experience three distinct moments of art-horror in response to the film, then it can be said that the film, on Carroll's account, had failed in two of its five attempts at scaring the audience. This rubric for judging the affectivity of an art object from the horror genre is only meant as a starting point for developing a robust critical judgment and as such its importance should not be overstated. But it will prove essential in distinguishing my preference for the *Resident Evil* game over the *Resident Evil* film in more than purely subjective terms.

The last aspect of Carroll's art-horror definition that should be spelled out is the exact nature of the art-horror response as an emotion. Carroll describes the art-horror response as an "occurrent emotional state." He writes, "An occurrent emotional state has both physical and cognitive dimensions" (24). This is to say that it is more like a flash of anger than a dispositional emotional state such as undying envy. Carroll is arguing that the art-horror response affects the gamer or the viewer's body as well as their mind. This makes the relationship between the viewer and the film an active relationship and not the passive relationship that one may naively assume. This is commonly experienced when viewing horror films with a cinema audience. When a monster lunges out of the shadows, the viewers may find themselves jumping in their seat, or widening their eyes or perhaps just sharply drawing a breath. These small, simple bodily actions are mirrored by the positive characters onscreen that generally react more violently, but always in a similar fashion. The film acts on the viewer and the viewer reacts, both physically and cognitively.

Carroll quantifies the cognitive side of this relationship in terms of evaluation and desire. If the horror film viewer sees the monster lunge at the hapless hero, they evaluate the situation as unpleasant or horrific which means they have a related desire to escape the unpleasant or horrific situation, i.e., if they were really in such a situation, they would find it threatening and desire to leave.[6] To sum up, Carroll offers the following definition of art-horror

> I have hypothesized that art-horror is an emotional state wherein, essentially, some nonordinary physical state of agitation is caused by the thought of a monster, in terms of the details presented by a fiction or by an image, which thought also includes the recognition that the monster is threatening and impure. The audience thinking of a monster is prompted in this response by the responses of fictional human characters whose actions they are attending to, and that audience, like said characters, may also wish to avoid physical contact with such types of things as monsters [35].

Carroll dedicates a great deal of his book to defending his definition of the art-horror emotional response and in doing so offers a strong answer to questions about why audiences enjoy this paradoxical unpleasant and yet entertaining emotion. For present concerns, it is not necessary to relay this defense, suffice to say that Carroll argues that it is curiosity, and in particular curiosity about the impossible nature of monsters, that makes the genre so popular. Instead I would like to take his definition and use it as a way of understanding why I found the *Resident Evil* game to be so much more emotionally intense than the film.

* * *

In 2002, Sony pictures released *Resident Evil*, written and directed by Paul W. Anderson. The plot of the film borrows heavily from the first two *Resident Evil* games although it is itself a new take on the games mythology.

As mentioned above, the first encounter with a zombie takes place roughly thirty-eight minutes into the film. This positions the arrival of zombies to the narrative at the beginning of the second act and marks out the sharp turn in the films plot. Having outlined Carroll's definition of art-horror I can use it to explain in a more rational way, why I found the first encounter with a zombie to be so disappointing.

Resident Evil (2002, theatrical release) certainly seems to fit Carroll's necessary requirements for something to be of the horror genre; there are monsters present within the narrative and the positive characters from the narrative react to them with fear and disgust. This means that, unlike *Peeping Tom as* mentioned above, the film does qualify as a horror film by Carroll's standard. But as Carroll defines it, the viewer has an art-horror response when they are triggered to do so by the positive characters on-screen, in the case of a film. But this does not happen with the first zombie encounter in the *Resident Evil* film. At the thirty-eight minute mark, the audience sees Michelle Rodriguez's character, named Rain, stalking through an industrial tunnel with a machine gun pressed to her shoulder. This pose, and the way the character has been set up within the narrative, will make it very difficult for her to appear threatened or frightened. Should anything try to attack her, it seems reasonably clear that she would be able to defend herself. But that is not to say that a strong positive character cannot react in such a way as to encourage a viewer to feel art-horror, it is only to say that the monster would have to appear more threatening than an armed, trained commando. Rain is investigating a noise; she passes a series of black containers being fed by cooling pipes. Her movements are deliberate and slow, they are mirrored in the camera and editing techniques, which is a standard horror-movie trope to build tension. A gas canister rolls out from behind the corner and into our and Rain's view. This is our first little scare. The audience is left wondering what it was that caused the canister to move. Again this is another staple of the horror genre, leading the audience to a reveal, a moment where what we have been expecting, or fearing, will be there and waiting for us. Rain turns the corner and the audience sees what happens from her perspective. A tall woman, dressed in laboratory scrubs is leaning against a pillar. Her skin is grey and mottled and she appears to be in severe need of medical attention. Rain calls out to her fellow commandoes that a survivor has been found. She lowers her weapon and runs to the stricken lab technician's aid. The lab technician bites Rain's hand. They grab each other and scuffle. But again, rather than react with fear to the now obvious threat, Rain reacts, at most, with anger and confusion. Shouting, "Get off of me" and pushing her away, Rain falls to the ground as her fellow commando "J.D." runs to her aid. He throws the attacker off Rain, who is still not displaying any considerable fear, rather, something more akin to general agitation. J.D. then proceeds to warn the attacker to stay down. When she refuses he shoots her in the leg. It is only at this point that something resembling fear is seen from a character on screen. J.D.'s eyes widen and he takes a step back. He shoots the zombie, which seems an appropriate description now, but again she does not stop. He raises his gun and opens fire. Rain suddenly joins in and the zombie is lifted off her feet and propelled across the room, presumably by the force of the gunshots.

This is the totality of the first zombie encounter from the *Resident Evil* film. While it is not as frightening as the first zombie encounters from other zombie films, such as the graveyard scene from George A. Romero's *Night of the Living Dead* or the bedroom scene from Zack Snyder's remake of *Dawn of the Dead*, it is not as ludicrous as many zombie films. In fact, overall, the *Resident Evil* film is an entertaining entry into the zombie canon. I am not striving to offer a general critique of the film here, but instead offer an analysis and comparison of the first zombie encounter from both iterations of the *Resident Evil* story and formally, the game trumps the film. But this is just my opinion and rather than try and convince you of its veracity, I will instead use Carroll's definition of the emotional response of art-horror to ground my critique.

As discussed above, Carroll defines the horror genre as works of fiction that aim to elicit the art-horror response in their audiences. Anderson's *Resident Evil* can quite easily be recognized as a work from this genre. It features the presence of monsters and, for the most part, positive characters who react to these monsters as threatening and impure; however, it is on this very point that the film fails. My point is not that the audience are so passive in relation to film that they can only mimic the reactions of characters on-screen, and that if those reactions are not present then they cannot react. Rather, my argument is that Rain's reaction to one of the central monsters from this narrative is so minimal and so underwhelming, as to remove all sense of threat, fear, or dread from the well-crafted zombie monster. Her lack of reaction deflates the tension that has been rising as she investigated the "noise" and saw the canister mysteriously roll out. The scene plays out more like a "Lewton Tram"[7] except for the fact that the cause of the tension is actually one of the film's prime monster types and not something harmless and ordinary.

To put it in more precise terms; the art-horror response is when the audience is prompted by a work of the horror to react physically and cognitively to the presence of a monster among non-monstrous characters. The physical side of this response can be any number of bodily actions; quickening of breath, widened eyes, jumping, looking away, while the cognitive side of this response is divided into a belief and a desire. The audience must believe the monster to be both disgusting and threatening and they must desire to withdraw from the monster's presence. In the case of the first zombie encounter in Anderson's *Resident Evil* the build-up, as Rain searches out the source of the noise, may offer the viewer sufficient reason to feel a physical tension, the object of their fear being the unknown source of the noise and whatever their imagination can conjure. Once the source of the noise is revealed to be the injured lab technician then the tension should climax with the arrival of a horrific monster. But before the audience has a chance to react to the zombie, to feel the scare as it were, Rodriguez deflates that fear by taking the encounter completely in her stride. Similarly, when Rain is bitten she does not react in the way an ordinary person might, i.e., with horror, instead she rolls with the attack, fighting off her opponent. Even after the zombie is shot and appears impervious to injury, she reacts so minimally that she weakens any perceived threat that the zombie monster may embody. If zombies can be dispatched so easily and if Rain is not threatened by them, then they are of little cause for concern and it would be foolish of me, as an audience member, to feel anything other than mild agitation towards them.

Someone defending Anderson's version against my critique may object on two grounds; firstly, that as a fan of the game I knew the film would feature the presence of zombies, and as such I was expecting them in a way that the character Rain was not, and secondly, that Rain's character was meant to be a tough commando and as such, were she horrified by what she encountered, her character would make no sense. The former shall be referred to as the objection from anticipation and the latter as the objection from toughness.

With regards to the objection from anticipation, I would agree that it is true that if someone went "in cold" to the cinema showing or without any prior knowledge of the *Resident Evil* franchise they may, in fact, share Rain's confused reaction rather than the horrified response I was expecting. But I would only agree if this scene took place much earlier in the film and if the design of the zombie was not so archetypal as to be an iteration of a cultural icon. Given that this scene takes place nearly forty minutes into the film I would imagine even the most naïve viewer would believe themselves to be watching some kind of horror film. In fact, the opening scenes depicting the elevator declare *Resident Evil* to be at least an unpleasant and violent film. Also the fact that the lab technician is so clearly a zombie in the Romero mold, as seen by her shuffling gait, her lurching shoulder and her patchy mottled skin, that the naïve viewer would have to identify some of the lab technician's attributes as being similar to what is culturally recognized as a zombie. For those reasons I would not accept the objection that I was expecting Rain's character to encounter a zombie in any way that is unfair to the film.

As to the objection from toughness, I would not agree that Rain's character is too tough to react with fear or horror to the presence of a monster. I would cite John McTiernan's *Predator* and the performances of his cast as examples of the contrary. In *Predator* Arnold Schwarzenegger, Jessie Ventura, Carl Weathers et al. portray a group of hardened soldiers being hunted by an unknown monster in the deepest jungle. Their performances almost typify the height of 1980's machismo and toughness, and yet they react to the presence and actions of the predator-monster with abject horror and disgust throughout the film. My response to the objection from toughness would be to simply argue that if the cast of *Predator* can react with fear and disgust and maintain their character's integrity then so too should the cast of *Resident Evil*.

In summary, I would argue that the first zombie encounter in the *Resident Evil* film fails to satisfy as a moment designed to elicit an art-horror response because the scene was written, directed, and performed in such a way as to deflate and diminish the threatening components of the zombie-monster type. This weakened the impact of the scene for the audience and the impact of the zombie-monster type for the film as a whole. It is now important to move from the analysis and critique of the film to the comparison with the *Resident Evil* game, but to do so will require a brief explanation of how games and films are comparable and how they are different.

* * *

Although still a relatively new medium for fiction, computer games have received a great deal of rigorous academic attention. One area of particular note and relevance is the debate between, what is termed, the "ergodic" and the narrative. In this context the term "ergodic" refers to ergodic literature which is characterized by Espen Aarseth as literature which requires non trivial effort to traverse the text.[8] In terms of *Resident Evil*, non-trivial effort, i.e., pressing buttons, maneuvering an avatar around a virtual space, and solving problems, is required to traverse the text which recounts the actions of Chris Redfield as he investigates the strange goings-on at Spencer Mansion. For Aarseth, the trivial effort equivalent would be reading a novel which relates the same story, the only effort required being the reading of the words and turning the pages. But the ergodic elements of a game have been compared, contrasted, and compounded with what Aarseth and other computer game theorists would term the "narrative" elements, i.e., the cut-scenes, load screens, in-game maps, in-game texts, etc. These narrative elements are often considered, rightly or wrongly, to draw heavily from other media such as movies, books, and comics. As such the debate revolves around the value or priority of ergodic or narrative elements in the study of computer games. On the one hand, there are ergodic purists who dismiss anything that is not wholly interactive and on the other, there are defenders of narrative who see the game-play as serving the story and thus of no intrinsic value. My own position, and that underwriting my present argument, comes from Douglas Brown who writes "narrative and gameplay are so tightly intertwined around one another that in *medias res* of a game reading they are inextricable, they make up the double helix of a game's DNA" (Brown 59). His argument is that the ergodic and narrative elements of a game occur as *gestalt* figures, where one may come to the fore and the other recedes to the background for any given point but that both figures are unified in the physical and interpretative gameplay process.

In relation to the first zombie encounter in the *Resident Evil* game, the importance of the ergodic/narrative divide can be see through an understanding of the player's experience. The first encounter occurs in one of the first areas available for exploration. Once the opening sequence ends, a player will find themselves controlling Chris Redfield, a S.T.A.R.S. agent sent to investigate Spencer Mansion. After a video and a brief cut-scene to set up the game's narrative, full control of Chris is granted to the player. Chris is in an elaborate dining room where the only sounds are his footfalls and an ominous ticking clock. These stark sounds are a sharp contrast to the exciting video that has just played and the average gamer will find this first room to be rather uneventful, in gameplay terms. Very few objects can be interacted with, with the exception of a mysterious emblem above the fireplace and a single door leading out from the right-hand-side wall. This room is essentially a staging area, a safe space for the player to learn and practice how to run and interact with objects from the games environment. In my first attempt at the game I spent very little time here, confident that I could walk, run, and interact satisfactorily; I exited the room through the right hand door quite quickly. This was my first surprise; the sound of the ticking clock stopped and my control of the game froze out. The screen was filled with a disembodied wooden door, creaking open on an inky-black background. But then, as soon as my control was taken, it was returned. I found myself in a small plain corridor, of the kind that would become commonplace for the game's design. The camera angle, which presented the game environment and Chris's position within it to me, suggested the relevance of the corner but did not emphasize it. I took three steps to my left quite quickly and turned, instantly my control was taken again. They rhythm of the interplay between the ergodic and narrative elements of the game seemed unintuitive and unsettling. As a novice to the game I was unsure about what was normal, or appropriate. The fact that I was now in another cut-scene only minutes after beginning the game disconcerted me. But that was only the beginning, the sight of the zombie kneeling on the floor sent chills down my spine. The gurgling, chomping noise left no doubt in my mind as to what he was doing to the body of the S.T.A.R.S. agent that was prostrate before him. My initial belief was that the game was presenting me with a zombie who was busy, or distracted, thus allowing me to register his presence, find some in-game method that would allow me to kill zombies, and return to this point where I could practice that method. All of which is a fairly standard way of teaching the beginner how to operate the action components of a game successfully. *Resident Evil* was not that kind of game. By the time that comforting thought had formed the zombie's head slowly began to turn, his bulbous white eye stared out of the screen and directly at me. And this point is an important one. In *Resident Evil*, the cut-scenes take place from Chris's perspective, which means that when something happens in a cut-scene it is seen as if it is happening to the player. This subtle shift from third to first person perspective is one of the many reasons why the game is so emotionally evocative. The zombie glared at me, the background music swelled and just as it reached its crescendo, the control of Chris was returned to me. This sudden shift from the narrative mode to the ergodic mode is, for me, the primary reason why this game is so frightening. The cut-scene was horrific enough to distract me from the fact that I was in control of Chris. He would not move, he would not fight or run away unless I made it happen. The brash confidence I showed by leaving the dining room so quickly took its toll in this moment as I could not remember how the controls functioned. My fumbling with the controller gave the zombie time to rise from my fallen colleague and to bite down on my avatar's neck. The spray of blood and the quick check of my health status revealed to me that I could not withstand many more attacks. In fact, in my naivety, I was unable to flee the scene quickly enough and the zombie killed me on its third bite. The Chris avatar was, just like the door, singled out on a black background as the zombie fed and the words "You died" appeared across the screen in tall bloody letters, a twisted innovation on the "Game Over" screens of earlier computer games. Fortunately, within a few moments I had restarted the game and I was back in the same position. I was steeled by my horrific experience and this time I was able to escape the zombie and flee, knowing that soon I would learn how to reap my revenge.

Obviously, this was an emotionally intense experience, but the question still remains as to whether this experience would qualify, on Carroll's terms, as an art-horror response. If the answer to this question is positive, then the *Resident Evil* game must be a work of fiction from the horror genre. Carroll specifies, in a non-exhaustive list, that the horror genre is made up of "the novels and plays of the nineteenth century and the literature, comic books, pulp magazines and films of the twentieth" (Carroll 13). He also further clarifies the genre by writing that "Members of the horror genre will be identified as narratives and/or images (in the case of fine art, film, etc.) predicated on raising the effect of horror in audiences" (14–15). In his 2008 text, *The Philosophy of Motion Pictures*, Carroll defines a motion picture, or more accurately, a moving image as something which meets the following five criteria:

> (1) it is a detached display or a series thereof; (2) it belongs to the class of things from which the production of the impression of movement is technically possible; (3) performance tokens of it are generated by templates which are tokens; (4) performance tokens are not artworks in their own right; and (5) it is a two-dimensional array [78].

Aaron Meskin and Jon Robson argue, in their paper "Video Games and the Moving Image," that Carroll's definition of a moving image can easily incorporate the inclusion of video games. They write, "[O]n a reasonable interpretation of [Carroll's] account of the moving image, videogames belong to that category" (Meskin and Robson 11). Therefore it seems like a legitimate rhetorical move to argue that if on Carroll's account video games qualify as moving images, and if they engender the emotion of art-horror in their audience, then the *Resident Evil* game should qualify as a relevant member of the horror genre. Meskin and Robson's paper seems to positively satisfy the first condition, so now all that needed is to satisfy the second.

As discussed above, the art-horror response is when the audience is prompted by a work of the horror to react physically and cognitively to the presence of a monster among non-monstrous characters. The *Resident Evil* game easily satisfies these conditions. Given that *Resident Evil* is an ergodic text, then by definition some non-trivial effort is required to traverse it. With button pushing and joystick maneuvering there is an obvious physical interaction with the game, and with problem-solving and skill development there is an obvious cognitive connection. But this is not in the spirit of Carroll's requirement. He is not suggesting that any physical or cognitive interaction is what determines the emotional response to art-horror but rather that is an appropriate physical and cognitive reaction, where appropriateness is determined by how well it mirrors the reactions of the positive characters within the fiction. Thus there is a need to physically and cognitively react to the game's ergodic and narrative dimensions.

Within the *Resident Evil* game narrative, prior to the first zombie encounter, the only positive, or non-monstrous characters encountered are the other S.T.A.R.S. agents and the player's own avatar Chris Redfield. I would argue that Chris's character is analogous to the "star" or primary protagonist of a movie, novel, or comic. But what makes him different is that the player cannot mirror his responses as his responses are, causally, also our own. This may seem like a clear reason to exclude the *Resident Evil* video game from the set of horror texts which can elicit an art-horror response, but I would argue the exact opposite. Carroll argues that horror audiences mirror the responses of positive characters from the text due to a curiosity about the fictional circumstance or an "as if we were there" attitude. This brings about an asymmetric identification with the positive character's emotional match. The player does not match their emotions fully, but rather shares in something akin to what the characters feel or should be feeling (Carroll 92–96). So when I, as an audience member, watch Alice, played by Milla Jovovich, react with fear to the onslaught of the Cerberus dogs in the *Resident Evil* movie, I also react with fear, albeit in a weaker sense, because I am wondering what it would be like if I had to encounter blood-thirsty and monstrous dogs. In the case of Chris in the *Resident Evil* game, I would argue that that curiosity and the "as if I were there" attitude is even more pronounced since, due to the ergodic nature of the game, I am taking an active and non-trivial part in the way the text plays out. Chris cannot scream, or draw breath, or run away from the presence of a monster unless the player actively chooses to make him do so by entering the appropriate commands.

For non-ergodic fiction, Carroll cannot argue that the audience has a symmetric identification with the positive characters since, to use his example, they may be merrily swimming in the sea while the audience are aware that a monster lurks beneath, thus they are meant to be feeling a rising tension completely at odds with the merry and unsuspecting swimmer. However, for ergodic texts like the *Resident Evil* game, direct character identification can be achieved since, significantly, the character has no agency beyond the agency provided through the appropriate commands pressed into the controller by the player.

The audience also has a strong response to the narrative elements of the *Resident Evil* game, as would be necessary in order to elicit an art-horror response. This is because much of the *Resident Evil* game's success was due to the way it borrowed from non-ergodic horror fiction, movies in particular, to present satisfying narrative components that enriched the game-play. At the beginning of the game, in the uncontrollable discussion that takes place in Spencer Mansion's foyer, Jill's character clearly responds with some fear and certain trepidation. This combined with the eeriness provided by the careful use of "camera angles" and the stark sound effects of the ticking clock and our own footsteps are good examples of the tropes and methods taken from traditional horror movies which prompt the audience to similarly strong emotional responses. But none of these compare to the skillful way, discussed above, in which the game creators used the cut-scenes of the opening door and the zombie turning its head to instill strong emotional responses in the gamer.

Consequently, I would argue that the *Resident Evil* game should be considered an example of a work of fiction from the horror genre which successfully elicits an art-horror response in its audience. I would also argue that the *Resident Evil* game is more successful than the *Resident Evil* film in eliciting this art-horror response as seen in the first zombie encounters. Finally, I would like to argue that even in an ideal circumstance, where we could experience ideal versions of a *Resident Evil* film and a *Resident Evil* game, the art-horror response would be more intense in reaction to the game than to the film.

* * *

To expand on this thought, I have argued above why the *Resident Evil* film failed to bring about in me an art-horror response when I watched it. I have also explained how and why the game brought about such an intense art-horror response in me when I played it. The question remains as to whether the *Resident Evil* game is just a very good example of a horror game, where goodness is determined by its success at prompting an art-horror response, and that the *Resident Evil* film is just a mediocre example of a horror film, based on the same criterion. I feel that this much is true, but if we were to imagine an ideal *Resident Evil* film, perhaps the version George A. Romero began but never completed, we could make it perfectly satisfying in every way. Since this is an imaginary film and not at actual one we can be very loose with its description. Imagine then, that it succeeds where all other horror films fail, it consistently brings about in its audience just the right amount of art-horror responses leaving them utterly entertained, utterly satisfied and, of course, utterly art-horrified. If this ideal *Resident Evil* film were to be compared with an ideal *Resident Evil* game, it can be imagined in the same way, a totally satisfying game in all respects. I believe that the game would still stand above the film as the superior catalyst for the art-horror response. My reason for this is simple; due to the ergodic nature of games as horror fictions, gamers have to be more actively involved in the fiction's narrative. The gamer determines how and when the next event will occur, obviously within the parameters defined by the games creators. But this level of involvement imbues the gamer's experience of the horror fiction with an agency that simply cannot be present in the audience's experience of the film as a horror fiction.

To be precise, in this ideal circumstance, when a moment of intense art-horror was experienced by a viewer of the film they would share in the positive characters' emotional response, believing the threat the character faced to be possible and disgusting, they would feel it physically, in some appropriately excited way and then they would relax, realizing and believing that the film is just a fiction and that the monster which both threatened and reviled them is not real. In my own experience, this usually results in a long exhale of breath and if I am experiencing the film *en masse* in a nervous round of laughter. We get frightened, we react appropriately, and then we relax.

However, in the ideal game our experience of fear, threat, and disgust is prolonged. When a moment of intense art-horror is experienced by the player of a game they cannot relax, let out a long exhale of breath nor even laugh, because as the active agent of the narrative their continued concentration and control is required for the narrative to keep moving. If they were to stop and relax, the threat that brought about the feelings of fear and disgust would actually, albeit in a fictional sense, be fulfilled; e.g., the zombie would attack them. Therefore in the ergodic narratives of horror games the experience of art-horror is necessarily prolonged due to the player's role as agent of the text. The gamer cannot escape the fictional reality of the monstrous threat with the same ease that the film viewer can; they must endure the art-horror if they wish to survive the horrific realm they have already entered.

Notes

1. A cut-scene is a moment in a game where, traditionally for computational reasons, the interactivity of the game pauses allowing the next sector of the game environment to be read from the disc. However, *Resident Evil* used the cut-scene in an innovative way. Rather than show a counter or display the word 'loading' they used the practical necessity of including cut-scenes as a way not only to advance the game's narrative, a practice which was not uncommon, but also and more importantly to heighten the tension that the player would experience.

2. The incident that I will be focusing on, the first zombie encounter from the game, uses not one but two closely positioned cut-scenes as a way to heighten tension and, as I hope to show, a way of manipulating the agency of the gamer in order to prolong and compound their feelings of displeasure.

3. And as contrary to *natural horror* which describes the sense of horror used in relation to acts of genocide, animal cruelty or environmental destruction (Carroll 1990 p. 12).

4. It is worth noting that games in general, and specifically video games, are absent from this initial list, thus while defining the term art-horror I will also put forward an argument as to why *Resident Evil* should be incorporated into the art-horror set.

5. What Aristotle did for the genre of tragedy in his *Poetics*, Carroll is trying to do for horror (Carroll 1990 p. 15).

6. The make-believe aspect of the threat and disgust are, in some part, what gives rise to the pleasure and entertainment that can be derived from the horror genre, but that topic is not our present concern.

7. A "Lewton Tram" is a term used in describing tense moments in horror films where the audience is led to believe something horrific will appear only to have their fears dismissed by the appearance of something harmless. It derives from Lewton's film *The Cat People* where the apparent noise of an approaching wild animal is revealed to be merely the noise of an approaching tram.

8. For a full definition see Espen Aarseth, *Cybertext: Perspectives on Ergodic Literature* 1997 pp. 1–2.

Works Cited

Aarseth, Espen. *Cybertext: Perspectives on Ergodic Literature.* Baltimore: John Hopkins University Press, 1997. Print.

Brown, Douglas. "Gaming DNA—On Narrative and Gameplay Gestalts." DiGRA 2007. Web.

Carroll, Noël. *The Philosophy of Horror.* New York: Routledge, 1990. Print.

_____. *The Philosophy of Motion Pictures* Oxford: Blackwell, 2008. Print.

Meskin, Aaron, and Jon Robson. "Video Games and the Moving Image." *Revue Internationale de Philosophie*, 2011. Web.

Resident Evil. Dir. Paul W. Anderson, Sony Pictures, Theatrical release, 2002. DVD.

_____, v. 1.0. Capcom 1996: Playstation One.

Survival Horror, Metaculture and the Fluidity of Video Game Genres

Broc Holmquest

Applying traditional theoretical approaches to the study of new media, such as video games, can often be problematic. While conventional approaches to the study of video games can be helpful, they do not fully acknowledge or compensate for the many unique qualities present in the medium of video games, particularly the rapidly evolving nature of gaming technology, advances in the artistic sophistication of games, and the burgeoning video game industry as a whole. Using traditional theories or concepts is appropriate, but they must be modified in such a way that they take these and other considerations into account; by neglecting to do so, cultural scholars run the risk of overlooking key components crucial to the understanding of the medium. In order to illustrate this concept of medium-specific analysis as it applies to video games, an application of pre-existing theoretical research to the medium is essential; by analyzing the ways in which traditional approaches to a given topic must be modified in order to suit the medium being studied, one can extrapolate several qualities and characteristics unique to the medium itself. For these purposes, I will be applying to the medium of video games a pre-existing concept with an extensive catalog of applied research: the interrelated concepts of genre and formula.

Genre theory can certainly be applied to video games; however, genre theory and the corresponding study of formula, as they are traditionally understood, must be modified when applying them to video games to acknowledge the unique properties of the medium. Video game genres, after all, can be created and categorized in two distinct ways: through narrative and aesthetic conventions similar to those found in film, and through conventions of gameplay, interactivity, and user input. The distinction between these two ways of understanding video game genres is summarized by Thomas Apperley in his analysis of representational and non-representational generic elements:

[C]onventional video game genres rely overmuch on games representational characteristics. Representational in this case refers to the visual aesthetics of the games. Contra to conventional genres ... the nonrepresentational, specifically interactive, characteristics of video games should be deployed by game scholars to create a more nuanced, meaningful, and critical vocabulary for discussing video games; one that can perceive the underlying common characteristics of games that might otherwise be regarded as entirely dissimilar if judged solely on representation [7].

Often these two modes of genre categorization go hand in hand; after all, a game that follows the aesthetic and narrative conventions of the action-adventure genre must surely allow its players to engage in tense shootouts, thrilling car chases, and other suitably action-oriented gameplay styles. Other times, however, there does not exist a clear connection between gameplay and narrative conventions; the first-person shooter genre, for example, incorporates narrative and aesthetic conventions of a variety of different genres, including (but not limited to) science fiction (the *Halo* series), horror (the *F.E.A.R.* series), and military action (the *Call of Duty* series). Thus, the study of video game genres must analyze not just aesthetic and narrative conventions, but gameplay conventions as well; the answer to *how* players are interacting with and in virtual spaces is just as important as *why* they are doing it from a narrative standpoint. Apperley points out that this method of understanding video game genres is frequently overlooked in favor of pre-existing notions of narrative-based genre classifications: "The primary problem with conventional video games genres is that rather than being a general description of the style of ergodic interaction that takes place within the game, it is instead loose aesthetic clusters based around video games' aesthetic linkages to prior media forms" (7). Incorporating game mechanics into an understanding of game genres can be difficult, however, given the rapidly evolving state of video game technology; gameplay conventions can change quickly over the course of a few short years. Often, these changes come as the result of user feedback, either through commercial success, critical reception, or the thoughts and opinions of the outspoken community of video game players. The study of genre in video games, then, must take into account the fact that the conventions of any given genre are largely dictated by the technological limitations of the specific time-period in which that genre is situated, and are informed by the metacultural relationship between game producers and game consumers.

This relationship between media producers and media consumers has been explored previously by David Paul Nord: "[Formulas] emerge in the contention between consumers and producers, whose interests and whose preferences are not the same" (224). Nord feels that formulas are a compromise between consumers wanting individual works of art and producers wanting to "sell the exact same product to everyone" (218), but there are two factors that must be considered when applying Nord's theories on formula to the medium of video games: One, that consumers, through both buying habits and metacultural communication with media producers, do have the ability to influence the formulas of popular culture. Secondly, that video game formulas as dictated by media producers are the creation of not just economic factors, but also of technological and creative limitations. In other words, the formulas of video game genres are dictated, at least in part, by what is possible given the state of the medium at the time. To more clearly illustrate this argument, I will be closely examining one genre which was once wildly successful and clearly defined, and has since fallen in popularity due, at least in part, to technological innovations that have rendered the traditional conventions of the genre outdated and unwanted: the survival horror genre.

This analysis of the survival horror genre is best accomplished through a study of the evolution of the *Resident Evil* game series. Since its inception in 1996, *Resident Evil* and its myriad sequels and spin-off titles have stood as the benchmark for the survival horror genre as a whole. The series' first two entries helped define the formula of survival horror that would be replicated in other horror franchises, such as Konami's *Silent Hill* and Tecmo's *Fatal Frame*, while the evolution of the series in later titles, such as *Resident Evil 4,* signaled a sea-change in the ways in which horror games were made by developers and interacted with by players. In addition to its pedigree as the (arguable) progenitor and most successful example of the survival horror genre, *Resident Evil* has achieved sixteen years of success spanning three generations of home video game consoles. Thus, charting the evolution of the survival horror genre throughout the entirety of the *Resident Evil* franchise (in addition to others) allows us to also examine the ways in which gaming technology has developed over the past fifteen years, and how those developments affect the ways in which players interact with, and ultimately influence, the construction of video game genres.

Alongside this analysis of the mutating conventions of the survival horror genre as seen in the *Resident Evil* franchise, I will also examine the metacultural community surrounding video games. This examination will be primarily focused on two avenues: critical reviews and analysis made by video game critics and journalists, and the comments made by game developers concerning the creation and reception of their own games. The purpose of this metacultural analysis is two-fold: One, it will allow us to examine the ways in which the genre has evolved from the eyes of the subculture that has been formed around video games as a medium. These comments will be useful in explaining why certain conventions have become outdated and subsequently expelled or transformed. Much of this analysis will draw from reviews of applicable games from gaming website *IGN*, whose long-running history and status as a reliable source of information and opinions makes them an ideal source for critical analysis. In fact, many of the reviews were written by the same group of game critics, eliminating the potential for conflicting points of view and thereby offering a more comprehensive assessment of the gradual shift in the expectations of video game players.

The second use for this analysis of critical and consumer feedback is to examine the ways in which game development is influenced by metacultural response before, during, and after the development process. As Nord suggests in his theories on the impact of economics on the use of formula in popular culture, the relationship between consumers and producers is pivotal to understanding the use of formulaic approaches in popular entertainment: "What we require is a more sophisticated understanding of the interaction between consumers and producers in the creation of popular literature and art. This creation is a complex process of communication..." (Nord 224). Using Greg Urban's conception of metaculture, particularly as it influences the creation of new cultural products, will help us identify how the relationship between game development and metacultural responses fuels the fluidity of formula in video game genres:

> The culture of the object moves into the response, which in turn determines—if the response is that of the filmmakers, for example, or is circulated and taken up by them—what new objects will be produced. Culture here travels from the original object to the new one via the response. In other words, the pathway of the motion is: cultural object + metacultural response + new cultural object [Urban 240].

The video gaming subculture is relatively small, though constantly growing (an analysis by the NPD Group showed an increase in video game software sales from $5.5 billion in 1998 to $9.5 billion in 2007 [Hruska], with the industry as a whole expected to be worth $70 billion by 2015 [Takahashi]). Many dedicated gamers are exceedingly loyal and boisterously opinionated; these qualities allow for metacultural input to dictate, at least in part, the design choices made by gaming developers attempting to deliver a critically and commercially successful product. Examining this metacultural influence will allow us to explore how the expectations of gamers, both those looking for more modern design sensibilities and those loyal to the traditional conventions of the genre, have influenced the evolution and constantly changing definition of the survival horror genre.

As with any genre, there are certain conventions, both thematic and technical, that define survival horror. While the thematic conventions do deserve consideration, for the purposes of this essay I will be focusing on the technical conventions: those that dictate the mechanics of game design and presentation. It is these conventions, I am arguing, that are subject to revision in the face of the evolution of gaming technology, and as such they are crucial to understanding why video game genres are constantly being redefined. As John Cawelti points out, the relationship between convention and invention, which in this case takes on the form of a fluid approach to gameplay mechanics, is essential to understanding both the concepts of genre and their widespread appeal in all forms of popular media: "Conventions help maintain a culture's stability while inventions help it respond to changing circumstances and provide new information about the world" (Cawelti 286). The relationship between convention and invention as it pertains to survival horror, however, is often blurry and indistinct; often the very conventions of survival horror game design must be re-invented, with the changing circumstances in this example being the evolution of video game technology. In addition to identifying, describing, and giving examples of the conventions of the genre, the technical limitations and/or outdated elements of traditional game design that influenced them must be identified if the fluidity of genre in video games is to be fully understood.

If there is one cue survival horror games have taken from horror cinema, it is the effective use of atmosphere. Elements of lighting, setting, sound, and mise-en-scène are all compiled to produce an atmosphere befitting of the terrifying themes being explored in survival horror games. As *IGN*'s Rick Sanchez pointed out in his review of *Resident Evil 2*, "One area where Capcom is dead on is atmosphere. The graphics, sound effects, music and level design all work together to create a spooky, horror-filled world, that really keeps you on the edge of your seat" (Sanchez). One technique utilized in the early entries in the *Resident Evil* series was the use of pre-rendered backgrounds through which the player character would move. While these backgrounds did not provide the kind of interactivity one would expect from a three-dimensional game, they did allow for a higher level of graphical clarity and dramatic lighting effects necessary to create an appropriate atmosphere of dramatic tension.

In addition to the use of pre-rendered backgrounds, many survival horror games limited the ability of the player to control the camera angle through which they were viewing the action. Ostensibly a cinematic technique, this use of fixed angles was used along with dramatic sound cues to develop tension within the player. This cinematic approach to player viewpoints was praised in Matt Casamassina's review of the 2002 remake of the original *Resident Evil*: "Odd camera angles shoot the action from eerie spots, as characters walk down long hallways, shadows stretching onto the flooring and tunneling about the environment" (2002). Often, this reliance on fixed camera angles and audio cues allowed for an increase in dramatic tension and atmosphere; for example, after traveling through a door, the player's view could be centered on the character from the front, showing only the player character and the door through which they had just travelled. Sound cues indicating the presence of an enemy could then be played, giving the player a feeling of tension developed by the assured confrontation they are about to become engaged in. This use of fixed camera angles and pre-rendered backgrounds to allow for greater graphical detail and increased atmosphere was, according to IGN's Matt Casamassina in his review of the Nintendo 64 version of *Resident Evil 2*, "a huge success, delivering scare after scare in a cinematic, movie-esque gaming environment made possible, at least in part, thanks to realistic pre-rendered backgrounds and a fixed camera system" (1999).

Interestingly enough, many of these atmospheric design choices were predicated on the limitations of the technology which game developers had to work with. The use of pre-rendered backgrounds in *Resident Evil* was a design decision that had much to do with the lack of graphical processing power at the time; the detail level on fully-rendered backgrounds left much to be desired, so pre-rendered backgrounds were used instead. This allowed for greater graphical clarity and the use of fixed lighting, which contributed to the overall atmosphere. Furthermore, the tension-filled door-opening transitions found in *Resident Evil* were, in actuality, a trick used by the developers to disguise the brief loading periods in between areas; rather than simply showing players a black screen (or, even worse, the words "Now Loading"), Capcom used the burden of frequent loading screens to their advantage by employing them to build tension in the player.

The use of cinematic camera angles seems to have been a conscious decision, but it also seems to be one that was made to work around the limited control options of the time. The first *Resident Evil* was one of the original PlayStation's first games, and as such it predated the invention of analog control—the use of two thumbsticks to give the player the ability to control his or her avatar with the left stick and manipulate the camera with the right. The developers of the first *Resident Evil* did not have the option to easily manipulate the camera, so fixed angles were used instead. This has since become a trademark of the genre, but it has also been criticized heavily. Many games that were able to utilize analog controller technology continued to use preset camera angles (as per the conventions established by *Resident Evil*), but they also gave the player the ability to manipulate the camera to better view their surroundings; *Silent Hill* is one example of this.

Further helping to establish a sense of dread in survival horror games was the complete isolation in which players often found themselves; there were no companion characters, non-playable or otherwise, for the majority (or even the entirety) of survival horror games. The player could not rely on either a computer-controlled companion or a fellow player to ensure their safety, a key component in creating an element of atmospheric tension. This kind of isolation was normal during what is commonly considered the genre's golden era (around 1996 through 2002), given the lack of widespread cooperative multiplayer in video games at the time. With no online multiplayer yet, and few games offering simultaneous cooperative play (most games either had a take-turns approach to local multiplayer, or were based on competition, as in fighting or racing games), the emphasis on single player was a natural decision to make. Artificial intelligence (AI) technology was also rather primitive; as such, it was a near impossibility to have the player character be accompanied by a computer-controlled teammate. What non-player characters (NPCs) did exist were often portrayed only in pre-rendered cut-scenes, and even then were used sparingly.

One of the other conventions necessary to consider when making a survival horror game is the genre's tendency to minimize the combat effectiveness of the player character. Compared to the characters seen in most other action games, the protagonists of survival horror are slower, weaker, clumsier, and frailer. Characters move slowly and awkwardly; often, this makes trying to run away from an overwhelming threat difficult, thereby increasing the tension of the encounter. Maneuvering around a large number of enemies becomes a near-impossibility, and turning around to retreat takes an excruciatingly long time. This limiting of control was, at least in part, a conscious decision by developers, as was the choice to weaken the player in terms of combat with enemy creatures. Even the weaker enemies in survival horror games are threatening figures; this keeps the player wary of danger, as death (and a subsequent "game over") is terrifyingly imminent at any given moment. In order to limit the player character's combat effectiveness, games like *Resident Evil* made it impossible to move and attack at the same time; firing a gun, for example, requires the character to plant their feet into an immovable position. Thus, the player is forced to choose between fighting or fleeing in every enemy encounter.

This can be a particularly difficult decision for the player to make given the relative lack of necessary resources offered in the game, another convention of the genre. While the player does come across an increasingly powerful array of weaponry throughout the course of the game (as the threat levels of the enemies increase), ammunition for these firearms is scarce; the player frequently finds himself facing an enemy monster in a small space with nothing but a knife to defend herself. This limiting of resources is compounded by the relative weakness of the provided weaponry; in *Resident Evil*, even the basic zombie enemy takes several handgun rounds to kill. Not only are ammunition and weapons limited in survival horror games, but life recovery items are similarly scarce. It takes only a few enemy attacks to kill a player character, and the items that keep death at bay are hard to come by; this again creates suspense for the player.

This limiting of resources was closely tied to the convoluted and strictly linear design of the progression of the game, itself a cornerstone of the survival horror genre. *Resident Evil*, for example, takes place in a large mansion that the player gradually explores as they unlock new doors and find items granting them access to new areas. Often, these items are laughably arbitrary; numerous keys, each in the shape of a different symbol (a shield, a suit of armor, etc.) are needed to open different doors. Often the player would find a key to open a door on the other side of the mansion, which would grant them access to a room that contained a key for a door that was located on the opposite side of the mansion from which they had just traveled. There were also frequent puzzles that required one or more items to successfully solve; these items first had to be located, then their uses had to be deduced by the player before being used to solve the puzzle. By lighting the wood in a fireplace in *Resident Evil 2*, for example, an oil painting is burned, which reveals a hidden gem. That gem must then be fitted into an empty slot in the fountain in the lobby of the police station which serves as that game's interior setting. This convoluted level design forced the player to backtrack constantly, as they found items that granted them access to new areas. This emphasis on re-exploration was enhanced by the limited inventory size of the player character; only a few items could be carried at a time, and since a player was never certain which items they would need, constant trips to the storage chests which are scattered throughout the mansion in *Resident Evil* were necessary to procure the required items.

Like the design choices which created a sense of atmosphere, this limiting of player control and combat effectiveness is a combination of conscious design choices and technological limitations. The "tank-like" controls seen in many survival horror games (particularly *Resident Evil*), for example, are again the product of an age without analog control. Players have to use the less precise directional pad (or d-pad) to move their characters. This clashed with the use of pre-set camera angles, however; the sense of direction could conceivably change at any moment, so which direction was forward was rarely consistent from scene to scene. Because of this, *Resident Evil* dedicated forward movement to the up button on the d-pad; while this allowed players to continue moving forward through changing angles without changing buttons, it also enhanced the confusion experienced when trying to direct a character out of harm's way in a tense situation.

The limiting of resources was similarly influenced by the limits of game design technology: while the expectations for game length were growing, the available disc space with which most PlayStation games had to work were limited. While using multiple discs became a common practice later in the system's life-cycle (large RPG games like *Final Fantasy VII*, for example, were played across four different discs, while *Resident Evil 2* used two), when the first *Res-*

ident Evil was released in 1996 it was an unheard-of practice. As such, the game had to create artificial restrictions that increased the length of the game. This is one reason for the limiting of in-game resources; it forced the player to explore, and also made death a much more tangible threat; combined with the archaic save system of typewriters and ink ribbons, this could potentially force the player to replay large sections of the game that they had already completed before dying without having saved their game. This also explains the convoluted nature of the level design of many survival horror games; the game world could actually be quite small, but by forcing the player to gradually unlock more areas and by requiring constant backtracking, the length of the game was padded considerably, as pointed out by Matt Casamassina's review of the 2002 remake of the original *Resident Evil*: "These puzzles are generally satisfying, but there are a few that go above and beyond their call of duty to extend replay value, and these sometimes become frustrating as it's quite obvious that there's really no point to them other than to prolong the length of the game"(2002). This was a source of criticism even during the genre's golden age, but was a tactic used by nearly every survival horror game of the time so that they could more closely resemble the mechanics made famous by *Resident Evil*.

At the dawn of the genre, critical response to the mechanics of the survival horror genre were overwhelmingly positive, and even acknowledged as essential to the feeling of suspense and tension that the games were attempting to deliver. Francesca Reyes' IGN review of 1998's *Silent Hill*, for example, praised the limited combat effectiveness of the player character (a convention established two years earlier in the first *Resident Evil*) as a representation of realism:

> Harry's plain appearance translates seamlessly into how he actually plays through the game. His aim is awful and his running pace, though quicker than most enemies, still keeps him only a heartbeat away from being mowed down by the demons running amok on the streets of Silent Hill. In fact, because of the limited amount of ammunition available in the game and Harry's inexperience with firearms, you'll find yourself evading enemies more often than confronting them. And this is one of the finest features in the game. Not only does this strengthen the adventure element in Silent Hill, but it also draws the player into the world of the game by mixing in enough realism into the madness [Reyes].

Even after the newness of the survival horror formula had worn off, critics such as Douglas Perry were still quick to praise the core conventions of the genre, as seen in his IGN review for 1999's *Resident Evil 3*: "In all of the essential ways, *Resident Evil 3: Nemesis* plays exactly like *Resident Evil* and *Resident Evil 2*. The movement formula is still intact, and it's still a good one" (1999). This review further validates the sluggish control choices made by most survival horror games, though future games would be subject to criticism regarding this point, as can be seen in a review for *Resident Evil: Code Veronica*, released in 2000: "The fact is, the control is pointlessly over done, and simplifying it would do this game a world of good in terms of dragging you into the adventure ... it could be improved upon, and I hope Capcom has the courage to move on if they can make it work, as opposed to being content with this" (Justice). That *Code Veronica* was released at a time when analog control was the norm and a new generation of video game systems were available should be obvious given the more tepid response to the control scheme (in fact, as a game for Sega's Dreamcast console, *Code Veronica* was the first *Resident Evil* game to appear on the generation of systems following the first PlayStation upon which *Resident Evil* debuted). Douglas Perry's review of *Silent Hill 3* comments on the survival horror genre's now trite and outdated formula, pointing out the growing tension between traditional survival horror mechanics and shifting expectations in modern game design:

> The most interesting and frustrating thing in every survival horror game is their control systems. They're deliberately meant to be slow paced, rendering them, in a sense, *anti-action* games.... These time-consuming elements help to create all the good things we like about the genre—shock, horror, fright, tension, and in the case of *Silent Hill*, disturbing surreal horror—but they also in turn create a sense of exasperation in gamers who like faster paced games [2003].

The noticeable shift in the critical reception of survival horror games, as seen in the reviews above, is indicative of the metaculture of video games, critics and players alike, turning away from the once highly praised gameplay mechanics of the survival horror genre in the face of an evolving medium. Video game developers, aware of this receptive shift, would adjust their approaches accordingly.

Survival horror games did not disappear following this negative shift in critical reception, but they certainly did begin to decline in both popularity and number of games being developed. Simply put, the gameplay mechanics that defined the conventions of the survival horror genre were quickly becoming outdated, and thus the genre as it was traditionally defined was in decline. A new approach to survival horror was slowly being developed, but it was not until *Resident Evil 4* in 2005 that the genre would be completely reinvented. In order to understand the fluidity of video game genres, I will examine the ways in which traditional survival horror conventions were transformed or removed, as well as how and why new conventions were created to replace outdated ones.

While many of the atmospheric conventions of the genre have become so commonplace that they still exist to this day, the ways in which they are presented have been altered considerably due to advances in game development technology. The pre-rendered backgrounds found in the early *Resident Evil* titles, an early trademark of that series, were replaced by the release of *Resident Evil: Code Veronica* in 2000. Since then, increases in graphics technology have allowed for higher-detailed environments which are fully interactive, while dynamic lighting has become the norm instead of the fixed lighting seen in those pre-rendered backgrounds; flickering light bulbs and realistic shadows are now commonplace. One needs look no further than 2010's *Alan Wake* to see the effect this advance in technology has had on the genre; characters journey through fully-rendered environments, including forests, using flashlights to view their surroundings and battle enemies comprised of living darkness.

The use of fixed camera angles has similarly been discarded; while golden age survival horror games such as *Silent Hill* compromised by offering predetermined angles that could be manipulated by the player, most modern games instead offer a fully-controllable camera that is situated behind the player character. The advent of dual-analog controllers allowed for full manipulation of the camera, and even the cinematic use of fixed angles were not enough to convince players to abandon that level of manipulation. As such, survival horror game designers have had to focus more on the use of lighting, graphical clarity, and sound to provide the necessary amount of tension within the player.

The sense of isolation which was at one time a staple of the genre has been reconsidered in many modern iterations: *Resident Evil 5* offers a constant companion who can either be controlled by computer AI or another human player, either locally or online. *Left 4 Dead* is a squad-based shooter with many survival horror elements that is built for four people to play together online. Going solo in either of these games is an impossibility: even without humans controlling them, the companion characters are present. This was made possible by advancements in artificial intelligence technology, as well as the widespread implementation of online multiplayer modes in video games as a whole. Popular games such as *Halo* and *Call of Duty* made linking gamers from different parts of the world together an expected experience, and survival horror was modified to meet those expectations. Ryan Geddes' review of *Resident Evil 5* points out (and highly praises) the franchise's shift to this multiplayer-focused style of gameplay: "The combat is truly the focus here, and the fight is at its best when you're tackling the baddies with a buddy."

The gameplay mechanics which limit the combat abilities of the player character and require excessive exploration have also been transformed. The "tank-like" controls of *Resident Evil* are now (largely) non-existent, thanks to the prevalence of dual-analog control. Players now expect a certain minimum level of character control that exceeds the cumbersome movement that once defined the survival horror genre; this is reflected in Matt Casamassina's review of the 2002 remake of the original *Resident Evil*:

The basic [control] setup has, unfortunately or not, remained largely intact with Capcom's GameCube remake, offering no true analog sensitivity.... There is no real precision—it's impossible to tiptoe by an enemy, or to aim at a specific body part, in other words. One wonders why, when Capcom could overcome so many technical feats visually, it couldn't address some of the control problems inherent to the series itself [2002].

The ability to easily and accurately maneuver a character out of danger has been developed alongside a greater emphasis on action in modern survival horror games. Weaponry and crucial supplies, such as ammunition and health recovery items, are much more abundant in games like *Resident Evil 4* than they were in earlier entries. In fact, *Resident Evil 4* changes the emphasis of the series from the atmospheric exploration of the first three games in the franchise to a more action-driven, adrenaline-fueled formula clearly influenced by popular action and shooter games. Again, expectations of player control and fluidity of motion have been dramatically increased, and survival horror games have had to change their design elements to meet those expectations, often resulting in the modification of the conventions that once defined the genre.

The excessive backtracking and exploration of early survival horror titles has also been largely erased from the genre; series like *Resident Evil* have eschewed these conventions entirely, opting instead for a more natural system of player progression. Backtracking is almost non-existent in *Resident Evil 4*, and the arbitrary items that needed to be collected in order to proceed are all but eliminated. This de-emphasizing of item-based progression has also eliminated the severely limited inventory system of past survival horror games; modern inventory systems are either unrestricted or large enough to accommodate anything a player may need. Checkpoints and automatic game save systems have also replaced the once prevalent usage of in-game save items such as typewriters and ink ribbons, allowing a player's progress to constantly be noted by the game. While this is undoubtedly more convenient, and arguably less frustrating, than the use of typewriters as seen in *Resident Evil*, it also minimizes the danger of death; the player no longer fears failure since dying only requires continuing from the last automatic checkpoint. Still, it is obvious when analyzing the criticism of more recent survival horror games (such as the 2002 remake of the original *Resident Evil*) that the convoluted level design and restrictive inventory systems are acknowledged as out-of-date attempts to lengthen a game artificially: "There is an inventory system that must be balanced, items used and stored carefully by players depending upon the situation.[...] It extends the length of the game greatly—but let's face it, it's a cheesy ploy to do so, and it does sometimes become tedious" (Casamassina, 2002).

Resident Evil 4, released on the Nintendo Gamecube in 2005, marked a complete reformulation of the survival horror genre. Discarding outdated camera systems, control layouts, and backtrack-heavy level design, *Resident Evil 4* was received by critics and audiences as a much-needed rebirth for both the series and the genre, as evidenced in Matt Casamassina's review:

> Instead of recycling a formula that Capcom itself conceded was growing tired, the development team behind the ambitious project opted to create a striking new *Resident Evil* experience minus some of the ingredients that spiced up previous franchise games ... [with] some remarkably compelling and rewarding new gameplay dynamics.... When you add in the new camera and action systems, as well as Leon's excellent new analog targeting function, you have a completely transformed survival horror experience [2005].

The over-the-shoulder view that *Resident Evil 4* introduced, along with the heavier emphasis on action-oriented gameplay, would become the new formula upon which future survival horror games would be based. Games that tried to cling to the traditional conventions of the genre, such as *Fatal Frame III*, were viewed as outdated and irrelevant. Jeremy Dunham of IGN states that it is "pretty much a carbon copy of most other survival horror titles over the past ten years.... With games such as *Resident Evil 4* ... offering true forward-thinking control elements, it's hard to be as forgiving with *Fatal Frame III*'s refusal to move on." On the other hand, games that stuck closely to the new formula introduced by *Resident Evil 4* such as *Dead Space* (which utilized the same over-the-shoulder view, control mechanics, and action-heavy approach) were praised as promising new entries in a genre once thought dead and buried: "*Dead Space* does the genre proud with an engaging story; action that's tense, fast-paced and extremely violent; as well as atmospheric qualities that will get under your skin and make you jump.... If you like survival horror ... *Dead Space* needs to be on your radar" (Haynes).

It is clear that, by examining the critical response to survival horror games throughout the genre's life-cycle, changes to the formula were introduced as technological advancements increased the gaming audience's expectations of the medium. Sluggish control schemes and reduced emphasis on combat, though acknowledged as key conventions of the genre, were discarded in the face of modern analog technology and the greater demand for precise action that that level of player control made possible; this emphasis on action is also responsible for the loss of the genre's cinematic but frequently obstructive pre-set fixed camera angles. The convoluted level design and esoteric puzzles, both of which required an immense amount of backtracking, were discarded as disc-space technology allowed for longer, more varied experiences, switching the emphasis of survival horror from exploration to action in the process. While this approach to the genre brought the *Resident Evil* series (and others) more in line with the expectations of modern game design, it was acknowledged that a fundamental shift in the ways in which players experienced the horror genre through video games had occurred as a result. A review of *Resident Evil 5*, for example, stated:

> The resulting experience is an intense, action-packed adventure replete with satisfying combat, tight gameplay and gorgeous, well-crafted environments. Resident Evil 5 offers all those things and then some, but it doesn't do many of the things longtime fans of the series expect. It won't scare you. It won't fill you with creeping desperation. It won't have you collecting and counting bullets like they're precious stones. It won't, in essence, make you feel like you're playing a traditional Resident Evil game [Geddes].

This desire on the part of many players for experiences that were more in line with those offered by traditional survival horror titles such as the early *Resident Evil* and *Silent Hill* games, led to the emergence of several independently-produced titles that captured if not the gameplay conventions of the traditional survival horror genre, at least the aesthetic and narrative ones. Games such as *Amnesia: The Dark Descent*; *Lone Survivor*; and *Slender* all offered players ways of interacting with horror-based games that emphasized the isolation and vulnerability that major-studio produced survival horror games had abandoned in an attempt to remain technologically pertinent. While some players opted for the more horrific experiences of these independently-produced games, mass audiences and major game publishers such as Capcom and Konami adjusted their expectations of the survival horror genre alongside an evolution of video game technology.

Of course, none of this metacultural analysis would be helpful to understand the fluidity of the survival horror genre if video game developers were not aware of, and influenced by, the reception of video games in the gaming community. Greg Urban notes that metacultural response is necessary to guide the creation of new cultural products: "Responses are also forward looking. The production of new cultural objects is guided by responses to them, even as they are being produced. Those responses—the result, in part, of inertial habituation, but also of mass-circulated metaculture that has been taken up—allow the passage of culture extracted from earlier objects into new ones" (241). Developer responses to comments and criticism directed at their games is an invaluable tool in examining the ways in which a given formula, and the medium as a whole, have evolved. Video games, in fact, are uniquely suited to benefit from this metacultual response for a couple of key reasons: One, the medium as a whole is dedicated to the continuation of key franchises that are supported with direct sequels, spin-off games, and multiple versions of the same title, often supported by additional downloadable content (DLC) made available through online marketplaces. Secondly, the development cycle between games is often quite long, and critics and fans are updated constantly on the progress of the game's development; in fact, a large majority of the metacultural focus of video games is on discussions of upcoming games as opposed to the discussion of current or past titles. This allows game developers to constantly reassess their design choices by evaluating feedback from critics and consumers. Finally, the close level of interactivity between the creators of video games and the community that plays them allows for a constant exchange of opinions and information that can, when combined with the previous two points, allow for a relatively significant level of fan impact on the decisions made by video game developers.

One particular franchise which has developed a very loyal and vocal following is the *Silent Hill* series. This following has allowed the developers of those games, none of which were landmark commercial successes like the *Resident Evil* games, to essentially cater to that specific market (though this has become a point of contention given the ever-increasing cost of video game production). *Silent Hill 3*, for example, was developed as a more direct sequel to the first game of the series after complaints that the second entry failed to answer many of the questions left unanswered by the inaugural outing: "The reason for *Silent Hill 3* going back to the themes of the original was in response to criticisms of part 2 being 'too psychological'" (Blaustein). This response to fan complaints was not limited to the narrative structure of the games; developers also re-tooled the formula of survival horror after the genre became over-saturated and unoriginal, leading to the complete re-imaging of the first *Silent Hill* in *Silent Hill: Shattered Memories* as described by producer Tomm Hulett: "One thing we knew was that everyone (including the fans) was tired of seeing the same game template. For a series that was so different when it first appeared, Silent Hill had become too predictable, too formulaic" (Schilling). The positive response to *Shattered Memories* allowed the developers to rethink the very foundations upon which that series was based: "Given the positive fan response, it's clear that everyone is on-board with *Silent Hill* having all these new things in it.... This gives us a lot more room in the future to allow *Silent Hill* to be unique" ("Shattered Secrets: Shared"). That this statement was given as a response to an on-line interview composed of questions from fans delivered via message boards is a testament to the influence that video game metaculture has on the creative direction of the medium.

Fan response can often be conflicting, and some series such as *Resident Evil* have decided to expand the scope of the franchise, allowing for several different approaches to the core themes of the franchise across several different design formulas:

> There's been a lot of feedback from core fans, people who've played *Resident Evil* all their lives, since the PlayStation days, saying they want us to go even more towards the core, very deliberate pacing of those games. On the other hand, there's been a lot of feedback saying, "We want to see an even more shooter and action-

focused experience." And there's really no way to answer all of those requests in one game [Nutt].

This multi-pronged approach to a popular franchise seems to be a direct result of differing fan expectations, particularly following the shift in the formula of survival horror that followed in the wake of *Resident Evil 4*; this would lead to the varied approaches seen in more recent entries in the franchise, such as *Resident Evil: Revelations* and *Resident Evil: Operation Raccoon City*. Developers also correspond with fans while working on games, and often their choices are dictated by fan reaction, as commented upon by the developers of 2012's *Silent Hill: Downpour*: "It's been very useful in validating certain design decisions along the way ... we have actually made a few course corrections along the way based on fan suggestions and comments, so we do listen when the fans have suggestions that make sense" (Whitney). Tsukasa Takenaka, assistant producer on *Resident Evil: Revelations*, echoed this sentiment by acknowledging the ways in which consumer response influences that franchise: "Certainly user feedback and what our fans and consumers want is very important to us.... We're always listening to that feedback and making use of it " (Yin-Poole). While the formula of a given genre is largely dictated by technological limitations, the metacultural response is instrumental in indicating a shift in the expectations of players as a result of evolving technology; this is particularly important given the reciprocal relationship between game developers and video game players.

By closely examining the history, evolution, and shifting formula of survival horror video games, two important considerations reveal themselves: One, that genre theory as it applies to video games must acknowledge the time period in which the genre was created and popularized in order to accommodate the effect that technological availability has on the creation of formula and the representation of genre conventions. Secondly, that video game metaculture, particularly as represented by critical reviews and developer comments, reveals a close relationship between video game developers and consumers that can help reveal and even influence the shifting formulas of video game genres as brought about by consumer tastes and technological innovations. What was once understood to be "survival horror" has been redefined; one can only assume that, as video game technology evolves even further (perhaps with the increased integration of immersion and motion controls), the ways in which audiences define and understand it will again need to be reconsidered; if so, the relationship between video game developers and video game consumers will be essential to creating and formalizing the new definition of survival horror video games.

Ultimately, recognizing the impact of technological advances and the relationship between consumers and producers may affect the ways in which scholars and audiences analyze genre and formula, particularly in a new medium such as video games. Genre is not merely a recurring set of themes that reflect cultural values, nor is it strictly a compromise between producers wanting to deliver the same product and consumers constantly seeking new experiences. While these things still hold true to some extent, the study of video game genres allows us to understand the ways in which critical and consumer feedback directly shape the growth of a genre; as *Resident Evil* fans began to feel limited by the franchise's conventional presentation and control systems, they urged Capcom and other survival horror game developers to embrace more modern technologies and approaches to game design. What resulted was a completely new way of experiencing the horror genre, one which emphasized player control over player helplessness; conquering fears over succumbing to them. If the narrative and aesthetic elements of a genre do in fact reflect cultural values, then the ways in which audiences expect to interact with a genre must do so as well; it is because of this that the analysis of video game genres is so worthwhile. In a medium where interactivity and producer-consumer communication is so important, the evolution of a medium's approach to genre and formula can reveal much about the video game industry, video game players, and the cultural systems in which they both operate.

Works Cited

Apperley, Thomas H. "Genre and game studies: Toward a critical approach to video game genres." *Simulation and Gaming* 37.1 (2006): 6–23. Web. 19 Dec. 2012.

Casamassina, Matt. "Review: Resident Evil 2." *IGN*. N.p., 24 Nov. 1999. Web. 16 Nov. 2011.

_____. "Review: Resident Evil." *IGN*. N.p., 26 Apr. 2002. Web. 17 Nov. 2011.

_____. "Review: Resident Evil 4." *IGN*. N.p., 7 Jan. 2005. Web. 17 Nov. 2011.

Cawelti, John G. "The Concept of Formula in the Study of Popular Culture." *Popular Culture Theory and Methodology: A Basic Introduction*. Ed. Harold E. Hinds, Jr., Marilyn F. Motz, and Angela M.S. Nelson. Madison: University of Wisconsin Press, 2006. 183–91. Print.

Dunham, Jeremy. "Review: Fatal Frame III: The Tormented." *IGN*. N.p., 3 Nov. 2005. Web. 20 Nov. 2011.

Geddes, Ryan. "Review: Resident Evil 5: Gold Edition." *IGN*. N.p., 17 Mar. 2010. Web. 19 Nov. 2011.

Haynes, Jeff. "Review: Dead Space." *IGN*. N.p., 10 Oct. 2008. Web. 18 Nov. 2011.

Hruska, Joel. "Dell XPS Phase-Out Symptomatic of Declining PC Game Sector." *arstechnica*. N.p., 13 May 2008. Web. 27 Nov. 2011.

"Interview with Jeremy Blaustein." *Alchemilla Hospital*. N.p., 24 Nov. 2010. Web. 21 Nov. 2011.

Justice, Brandon. "Review: Resident Evil: Code Veronica." *IGN*. N.p., 30 Mar. 2000. Web. 19 Nov. 2011.

Nord, David Paul. "An Economic Perspective on Formula in Popular Culture." *Popular*

Culture Theory and Methodology: A Basic Introduction. Ed. Harold E. Hinds, Jr., Marilyn F. Motz, and Angela M.S. Nelson. Madison: University of Wisconsin Press, 2006. 214–28. Print.

Nutt, Christian, and Brandon Sheffield. "Two Tendrils of *Resident Evil*'s Evolution." *Gameasutra*. N.p., 7 Oct. 2011. Web. 20 Nov. 2011.

Perry, Doug. "Review: Resident Evil 3." *IGN*. N.p., 11 Nov. 1999. Web. 19 Nov. 2011.

_____. "Review: Silent Hill 3." *IGN*. N.p., 5 Aug. 2003. Web. 21 Nov. 2011.

_____. "Review: Silent Hill 4." *IGN*. N.p., 7 Sept. 2004. Web. 21 Nov. 2011.

Reyes, Francesca. "Review: Silent Hill." *IGN*. N.p., 24 Feb. 1999. Web. 21 Nov. 2011.

Sanchez, Rick. "Review: Resident Evil 2." *IGN*. N.p., 21 Jan. 1998. Web. 19 Nov. 2011.

Schilling, Chris. "Silent Hill: Shattered Memories Developer Interview." *The Guardian*. N.p., 5 Feb. 2010. Web. 24 Nov. 2011.

"Shattered Secrets: Shared. Exclusive Post-Mortem Interview with Tomm Hulett." *Silent Hill Heaven*. N.p., n.d. Web. 25 Nov. 2011.

"Silent Hill Experienced Exclusive Interview with Devin Shatsky and Tomm Hulett." *Silent Hill Experienced*. N.p., 20 Sept. 2011. Web. 21 Nov. 2011.

Takahashi, Dean. "Video Game Industry to Hit $70 Billion by 2015, but Growth Will Slow." *Venturebeat*. N.p., 25 May 2010. Web. 27 Nov. 2011.

Urban, Greg. *Metaculture: How Culture Moves Through the World*. Minneapolis: University of Minnesota Press, 2001. Print.

Yin-Poole, Wesley. "Capcom: Resident Evil 4 and 5 Didn't Ditch Horror." *Eurogamer*. N.p., 1 Nov. 2011. Web. 20 Nov. 2011.

The Strong, Silent Type:
Alice's Use of Rhetorical Silence
as Feminist Strategy

Suzan E. Aiken

She wakes, naked, disoriented, in a shower; the first person she "meets" asks for a "report," but the situation is entirely unfamiliar for her. When movie-goers first meet Alice, she seems powerless, a victim—but Alice is *not* power-less. The rhetorical situation of the movie *Resident Evil* (2002) is an envi-roment monitored and controlled by corporate computer, the Red Queen, and it is populated by groups of individuals attempting to survive: the mili-tary personnel dispatched to shut down the Red Queen, the security oper-atives Alice and Spence, and those persons who lived and worked in the Hive. Even those humans-turned-monster are attempting to survive, driven by what the Red Queen labels as their "most basic of needs" (*Resident Evil*). As an action-suspense thriller, the movie presents a situation in which the remaining humans fight for their lives as they attempt to escape the Hive and the reach of Umbrella Corporation. Among these humans is the security operative, Alice. Though she has no memory of events prior to waking up in the Mansion, Alice begins to develop her sense of self and her motivation to survive the experience throughout the sequences of the movie. Alice, like other action heroes, is able to physically grapple with the monsters as well as psychologically grapple with the antagonist, the Red Queen. Alice strategizes in many ways to survive. This study investigates Alice's use of rhetorical silence as a productive and positive feminist strategy to resist expectations that she is a victim who will not survive the events taking place in the Hive.

Contemporary and historic scholarship[1] in the field of rhetoric has demonstrated the value our society places on sound and speaking; and, film, too, relies on dialogue and visual action to advance plot, describe setting, and develop characters. Contemporary film values sound as a means for story-telling. In contrast to the concept that silence is connected to oppression or is a sign of victimhood, using rhetorical silence and rhetorical listening have been proven to be positive and productive strategies by some contemporary scholars (Glenn, Nakane, Ratcliffe). And, when movie audiences think of a typical action hero, they think of a strong, silent type of masculine hero such as Arnold Schwarzenegger or Bruce Willis—heroes who do not need much dialogue, who have catch-phrases. The strong, silent male action hero represents a masculine demonstration of strength: rather than gush dialogue, complain or worry, or explain his tactics to foil enemies, silence is a male hero's strategy; he *acts* on the world rather than speak. As a feminist strategy, the use of rhetorical silence may serve multiple functions such as resistance to dominant power structures or defiance of expectations and social-political constraints. While it is obvious that Alice is not a solely silent character, further close reading of the *Resident Evil* (2002) film shows that Alice does use rhetorical silence. Alice's use of rhetorical silence is a feminist strategy as the silences often present an opposition to expectations, an extension of masculine-feminine power dynamics, and a complication of scenes that might typically presume an action hero to use other tactics. For the purposes of this study, rhetorical silence is defined as an intentional use of silence with a determined function of making meaning in a given context with a specific audience. This study carefully examines the critical and intentional use of rhetorical silence as a positive and productive rhetorical strategy as a means of providing understanding of Alice's agency and power as a survivor.

Rhetorical Silence

Discerning the meaning of rhetorical silences draws on the work of scholars who have identified the various forms and functions of rhetorical silence, who have shown silence is a positive and productive strategy. Scholars have categorized the specific forms and various functions for silence, among them are Thomas Bruneau and Cheryl Glenn. Additionally, studies of silence have shown the importance of context, culture, social norms, and politics as necessary elements for meaning-making (Glenn, Ratcliffe, Saville-Troike). An effective silence is contextual; an effective silence can be an empowering example of agency against power structures rather than deference to those power structures. To better understand Alice's choices for and functions of rhetorical silence, the other aspects of the situation must be included—the context, the other characters, the cultures, the expectations. Saville-Troike asserts "a distinction be made between the absence of sound when no communication is going on, and silence which is a part of communication" and demonstrates that communicative acts of silence are part of a cultural framework in a speech community that serve to "organize and regulate its social relationships" (4). In Bruneau's socio-cultural category, he reveals that silence is "a strong rhetorical strategy to preserve socio-political ideology" (42). Communication, social, and cultural norms for silence and speech can advance and support political ideology—those norms guide the choices for characters like Alice to use silence, and the possible functions for silence. So, the scholarship supports a study of silence since the movie uses silence in several ways, and for multiple purposes. The rhetorical setting of the movie is a site for competing agendas, and the intersection of various social and political cultures. The uses of and meanings for rhetorical silence frequently draw on specific elements of context, audience, memory, culture, class, and gender for meaning-making and impact. The theorists and studies of silence allow for a closer and more complex understanding of Alice's use of rhetorical silence, and to show that Alice is *using* silence rather than *being* silenc*ed*. Alice uses rhetorical silence at several times during the film: during her first minutes of being awake, during times of memory recovery, during the hallway scene with Kaplan as he tries to shut down the Red Queen, and during a confrontation with the Red Queen.

Rhetorical silence is not just a break between words or a dramatic pause, it is the chosen absence of sounds and words by a rhetor-character (in this case, Alice) with a specific purpose and meaning. In *Unspoken*, Cheryl Glenn reminds us "like speech, the meaning of silence depends on a power differential that exists in every rhetorical situation: who can speak, who must remain silent, who listens, and what those listeners can do" (9). Differences in power can emphasize the roles permitted to individuals; using silence as a feminist strategy implies that silence may be used in unexpected or unanticipated ways. Glenn imagines placing "speech and silence in a reciprocal rather than oppositional relationship" (7). Rather than using only speech or silence, only masculine or feminine strategies, Alice may be using multiple strategies in reciprocity, in collaboration, or in opposition to power structures; rather than an *either-or* set of choices, Alice may apply *both-and* set of strategies. The rhetorical situation of the Hive and the Mansion provide a technological and scientific setting of manipulation, control, and power with The Umbrella Corporation and the military at the heart of a battle for control over the situation, and with Alice in a struggle against the Red Queen for survival. This chapter will provide an analysis of Alice's use of rhetorical silence as a means of survival, considering who can speak, who can listen, and the rhetorical strategies available. Alice employs silence as means of survival throughout the movie but this chapter focuses on one three minute exchange between Alice, the Red Queen, and the other survivors. This scene is critical to an analysis of rhetorical silence because Alice's silence stands in contrast to the conversation taking place between the Red Queen and the other survivors within the Hive.

Alice as Acting-Agent and Action Hero

Support for research methods is drawn from textual and discourse analysis (Johnstone, Eisenhart), from communication studies (Tannen, Saville-Troike, Nakane), and from other studies of rhetorical silence and rhetorical listening (Bokser, Glenn, Ratcliffe). Initial research for this chapter's study was observed, collected, and documented during the course of several independent screenings of the film *Resident Evil* (2002). By conducting multiple viewings, I was able to document the uses of rhetorical silence throughout the sequences of the movie—focusing primarily on the rhetorical silences deployed by the character Alice. The interactions between characters were tracked, and rhetorical silences were documented during each viewing of the film. This data was then reviewed, and attention was given to any emerging patterns. This study focuses only on the *Resident Evil* (2002) film, and centers on the rhetorical silences used by Alice—more specifically, the scene in which the group of survivors confronts the Red Queen.

While movie-goers are told that the Red Queen is made to look like the computer's creator's young daughter, it is implied that the Umbrella Corporation is the controlling construct, representing a masculine power structure. The Red Queen makes decisions which affect the lives (and which take the lives) of those living and working in the Hive and the Mansion. When the T-virus is released into the environment, the Red Queen initiates a lock-down of the Hive, begins procedures that would kill many humans still alive inside the Hive, and releases poison gas to knock out anyone left outside the Hive. The Red Queen uses her position of power as means for silencing those who are "beneath" her. She takes away the available rhetorical means at the disposal of those with less power by literally and physically silencing them through death. With the decision-making power, and the power as an acting-agent, the Red Queen (and, by connection, the Umbrella Corporation) represents a masculine and oppressive entity. As a central protagonist who uses silence to observe and manipulate the group of survivors, the Red Queen adds to the complexity of an analysis of rhetorical silence.

Among many divergent and significant concerns, the field of rhetoric is interested in the available means for communicating and creating meaning, and a feminist stance will question those possible strategies available to the character Alice as she represents a type of feminist resistance. A great deal of theoretical publication and numerous empirical studies provide glimpses of silence among the available rhetorical strategies, such as the work of Glenn's *Rhetoric Retold* or Sandoval's *Methodology of the Oppressed*. Glenn shows how women were able to strategize available tactics and wield those tactics effectively such as the women who adopted/adapted the use of silence-as-resistance.

Sandoval theorizes how oppressed groups develop modes of oppositional consciousness that allows a common community of understanding and decolonizes dominant power structures. These feminist theories provide a standpoint to understand how the use of rhetorical silence can be wielded as resistance, as protest, or as opposition to expectations for specific social and political roles, and as a means to survive. These theories provide a lens through which Alice's use of rhetorical silence can be considered as an intentional, productive, and feminist strategy. Rather than a sign of passivity, Alice's silence signifies a mind at work making rhetorical choices and decisions in order to undermine the power structure trying to destroy her.

With the advancement of technology, the broad spectrum of possible venues, the reduction of divide between global audiences, and so many other changes to our concept of the rhetorical situation, we are just beginning to reconsider the potential tools and decisions that make up the "available rhetorical means." Alice is an action hero who employs some of the same methods as male characters in other films; though, Alice does not subscribe to a feminine-only or masculine-only means of reacting and responding. One theoretical example of a separation of styles is Lindal Buchanan's careful research in *Regendering Delivery* which reveals much in the way of social convention, and rhetorical practices. She identifies and categorizes masculine and feminine delivery styles—concepts that would be helpful in considering the ways that Alice uses rhetorical silence with her fellow survivors and with the Red Queen. Buchanan, in her historic study, verifies "women selected the available (and gender-appropriate) means of indirect influence rather than direct persuasion and devised a manner of rhetorical presentation to match, one that simultaneously subverted social norms dictating women's silence and invisibility and cloaked the public and persuasive nature of their discourse" (79). A feminine delivery style meant "avowing a commitment to conventional gender roles while behaving contrary to them" (79). So, too, Alice's credibility and authority can be drawn from the delivery style of rhetorical silences. Roxanne Mountford observes that rhetorical delivery "is based in and on cultural norms and the breaking of those norms" (152). Turning back to Alice, the rhetorical silences are deployed in neither a solely masculine nor a feminine style. For example, in a move that might be considered feminine, Alice shows compassion in a silent gesture to Kaplan during a particularly tense scene in which Kaplan is about to attempt to shut down the Red Queen. This chapter claims that Alice is using rhetorical silence as a feminist strategy because the use of silence is often deployed in situations that require unique responses and reactions typical of scenes requiring significant dialogue which are often indicative of the differences in masculine and feminine silences.

The trope of the action hero has often been represented as the strong, silent type who often is gifted with short lines of dialogue and humorous quips. Alice is an action-hero; she survives the events of the Hive. Like many other action heroes, Alice is relatively silent. There are definite tropes in the movie such as opportunities to consider the Umbrella Corporation as patri-archical and to consider Alice as feminist opposition to the various power struggles played out in the film. This study assumes that, unless otherwise acknowledged in a scene, Alice has agency and makes choices based on her own perception and her own interpretation of events. By centering on the introduction of the character in the first film, I investigate Alice's first uses of rhetorical silence. Further, I explore the ways that Alice exists beyond the stan-dard "strong, silent type" of action hero by seeking the possible functions for her rhetorical silences.

Alice Is/Is Not *Silent*

After several viewings of the movie, it is easy to note that Alice is not a silent character; she responds to questions, she asks questions, she shouts and swears and cries, and she interacts with other characters. However, there are multiple ways that Alice uses rhetorical silence: at the sequence near the begin-ning when Alice wakes, during a scene in which the military team attempts to disarm the Red Queen, during a turning point of the film where the team tries to confront the Red Queen, and during moments of Alice's remembering (the times when Alice recovers memories). By using strategies of listening and obser-vation, Alice is a strong and silent hero who stands out from more traditional, masculine action heroes.

The first significant silence occurs at the Mansion. When the audience first meets Alice, she is waking, her body is on the floor of a bathroom shower. Similar to Schwarzenegger's Terminator, Alice arrives on screen naked, and thus begins her undertaking in the film. Alice proceeds to get up and explore the environment, clearly not remembering her own identity or "home." As she explores, she is quiet; Alice is on screen with both a film audience and the Red Queen observing her for three full minutes. During her third minute on screen, Alice says, "Hello" to an empty room. Alice is not forced to be quiet, though audiences find out later that the Red Queen had "gassed" the Mansion and caused Alice to pass out and lose her memory. Up until that moment of sound, Alice is silent by choice. Whether deductively or inductively, Alice has an awareness that she is in a communicative situation; in the style of a law enforce-ment officer Alice explores her environment, looking and listening. She only uses verbal communication when she believes there is another physical presence that she will draw out. She chooses to remain silent while she gathers information about her surroundings, herself, displaying an astute rhetorical awareness. This silence supports my point that silence is used by choice, intentionally.

Alice's loss of memory also provides frequent uses of silence. There are eight uses of flashback to reveal a memory during the *Resident Evil* film; seven of those memory-flashbacks belong to Alice, the eighth belongs to Spence. From the moment the film's audience meets Alice in the Mansion, Alice is actively seeking information: knowledge, or truth about herself, her surroundings, or her situation. Each of Alice's seven memories helps to reveal her identity and to advance the plot. The first six memories are internal and are meant for Alice-as-audience only (rather than shared with other characters). The first memory is Alice's own memory of losing consciousness in the shower inside the Mansion and falling down. The last memory places Alice as an observer in the hallway of the Hive looking in on a lab populated with scientists, and the memory reveals Alice's knowledge of the T-virus and the anti-virus, and this memory is accompanied by external visual and audio cues. Each of the memories, except the seventh memory, is internal and silent. While each memory represents a developing base of knowledge and meaning for Alice, the recovery of the knowledge and the interpretation of the knowledge is acquired primarily during Alice's silence. Here, rhetorical silence is a way of making meaning, and represents a kind of knowing—so, it follows that silence can serve multiple purposes. It also demonstrates a power over her own knowledge in that she chooses not to share these silent memories with her fellow survivors. By not sharing information regarding these memories, she retains control over those memories.

Another significant use of rhetorical silence occurs in the Hive. Alice uses a rhetorical silence during an operative scene in which Kaplan is approaching the Red Queen's central computer processing unit. The military team dispatched to the Hive has a mission: to shut down the Red Queen. In the process of moving down a hallway, four of the military team are killed in a surprise attack by the computer's defenses while Kaplan frantically tries to dismantle the computer's defenses. All characters verbally and physically expressing their own emotions during the crisis. Alice is the closest witness to the violent and visceral deaths of the four soldiers as she watches their deaths through a window. Once the computer's defense mechanism has been stopped, Kaplan takes up the military's mission, deciding to proceed through the dangerous hallway to the main computer room. The scene is especially tense, since four humans were brutally dismembered in the hallway. As Kaplan stoops to pick up the equipment bag from a dead soldier, a hand emerges from off-camera. Silently, Alice extends her arm, and touches the shoulder of the soldier; as he is startled and turns, Alice gently squeezes his shoulder and delivers a facial expression lending Kaplan support as both Alice and Kaplan proceed to the computer room to complete the mission to shut down the Red Queen. This silence represents a more feminine and collaborative style of communicating—Alice uses silence as a strategy to demonstrate support.

Alice's last use of rhetorical silence occurs during a pivotal scene between the remaining human survivors in The Hive and the Red Queen. Realizing that they are trapped, with little chance of escape or survival, Alice decides that the Red Queen must be turned back on and used as a source of information. In this case, she understands that the power of rhetorical silence rests with the dominant power structure. In contrast, if the Red Queen remains silent, then all the survivors will eventually succumb to death at the hands of the silent Red Queen. During the sequence just prior to the confrontation scene, Alice becomes a decision-maker and leads the group to the computer room to wake the Red Queen. No longer the amnesiac who waits for information or orders, Alice takes charge of the survival of the group. The scene takes place in the small room that stores the computer; Rain, Kaplan, Matt, and Spence deliver questions to interrogate the Red Queen. The dialogue of that scene is documented below in Table 1.

Table 1: Example of Dialogue, *Resident Evil* (2002)

Speaker	*Dialogue Spoken*
RED QUEEN	Ah, there you are. Things, I gather, have gone out of control.
RAIN	Give me that fucking switch right now. I'm gonna fry your ass!
RED QUEEN	I did warn you, didn't I?
RAIN	Tell us what the hell is going on down here.
RED QUEEN	Research and development.
MATT	What about the T-virus?
RED QUEEN	The T-virus was a major medical breakthrough. Although it clearly also possessed ... highly profitable military applications.
KAPLAN	How does it explain those things out there?
RED QUEEN	Even in death, the human body still remains active. Hair and fingernails continue to grow. New cells are produced. And the brain holds a small electrical charge that takes months to dissipate. The T-virus provides a massive jolt, both to cellular growth ... and to those trace electrical impulses. Put quite simply, it reanimates the body.
RAIN	It brings the dead back to life?
RED QUEEN	Not fully. The subjects have the simplest of motor functions. Perhaps a little memory. Virtually no intelligence. They are driven by the basest of impulses, the most basic of needs.
KAPLAN	Which is?

RED QUEEN	The need to feed.
RAIN	How do you kill them?
RED QUEEN	Severing the top of the spinal column ... or massive trauma to the brain are the most effective methods.
RAIN	You mean shoot them in the head.
MATT	Why did you kill everybody down here?
RED QUEEN	The T-virus escaped into the air conditioning system. And an uncontrolled pattern of infection began. The virus is protean, changing from liquid to airborne to blood transmission ... depending on its environment. It's almost impossible to kill. I couldn't allow it to escape from the Hive. So, I took steps.
MATT	Steps?
RED QUEEN	You must understand ... those who become infected, I can't allow you to leave.
SPENCE	Whoa. We're not infected.
RED QUEEN	Just one bite ... one scratch from these creatures is sufficient... and then you become one of them.... A check of my systems indicates my main drive circuit breaker has been disabled. May I ask why?
ALICE	Insurance. We need a way out of here. If you refuse to help, we flip the switch. Understand?

During the not-quite three minutes of dialogue, and the use of eight questions to interrogate the Red Queen, Alice is silent. Alice is on screen; during each question and answer, Alice is shown pacing, thinking, and she physically holds Rain back when Rain threatens the Red Queen. There is a significant rhetorical silence as Alice listens and waits during the confrontation with the Red Queen. Even though Alice initiates the "waking" of the Red Queen, and Kaplan serves as the computer expert, Alice listens silently. Eventually, Alice delivers an ultimatum: help the survivors or be shut down. The ultimatum shows that Alice now has the power to be silent as well as permanently silence. This key scene will frame the study of rhetorical silence as a productive, intentional, and feminist strategy. These silences help to prove that Alice is using rhetorical silence as a feminist strategy with the goal of survival.

Analysis and Observations: Alice as the Strong, Silent Type

This study began with my questions about silence—about the nature of silence, about the use of silence, about the meaning and interpretation of silence, and about Alice's use of silence. This inquiry began by asking how Alice might wield silence as any other rhetorical strategy or device; with asking whether silence might be used strategically to yield a specific effect or result with an audience—such as the use of rhetorical silence as a means for survival. The film's setting is a technological and scientific culture which values communication—both sounds and silences—but which often wields communication loaded with assumptions about context, audience, and the delivery of the messages. A more thorough understanding of the variables and of the "available rhetorical means" can be gained by using a careful analysis of Alice's use of and meaning for rhetorical silence in the confrontation scene with the Red Queen.

The dialogue in the confrontation scene begins with the Red Queen acknowledging the survivors. As the first to speak, the Red Queen assumes a level of authority and a position of power—the Red Queen points out the lack of control, indicating a weakness of the group. Rain is the first to respond, and first employs a threat and then asks a question: Rain demands to know what is going on. While Rain represents the raw fighting ability and aggression of a soldier, Rain's communication attack on the Red Queen is almost ignored. In her response to Rain, the Red Queen describes the situation as "Research and development"—a brief and cryptic answer typical of a corporate lackey. The communicative transaction initiated by Rain, first with a threat and then with a question, is completed by the Red Queen but is yet incomplete. The group does not have the means for surviving the events of the Hive.

Matt responds to the Red Queen's answer with a more specific question, "What about the T-virus?" It is at this point the Red Queen uses a corporate-like reply, cryptically incomplete information as a response to Matt's question. Further clarification is drawn out by Kaplan as he asks the Red Queen to "explain those things out there." The Red Queen does just that: her explanation seems almost excited as the Red Queen shares her scientific, observational data. It is through the back-and-forth of question-and-answer that the group is able to discover what happened in the Hive, what the Red Queen did to those persons in the Hive, what the Red Queen is capable of, and what information might help the group survive as they attempt to escape the Hive; ultimately, to draw out the Red Queen, and draw her in to dialogue.

When Rain first threatens the Red Queen, Alice physically holds Rain back but does not say a word. This was a moment during which Alice could have used the threat of shutting down the Red Queen, but did not. A strong, silent action hero might have cut to the chase and gone for a direct and concise resolution. Alice might have jumped in to ask for an escape route immediately since that was one goal for waking the Red Queen; instead, Alice is shown pacing, thinking, and quiet. Alice is motivated by survival, but is also insistent on the survival of the other humans in the group; the Red Queen is motivated to survive so that the Red Queen can retain power and control. For Alice, there is a connection between both Alice's and those other character's use of speaking and not-speaking; for the context of survival, interrogation, and combat presented Alice with the opportunity to utilize silence as one means among many to achieve a specific rhetorical goal—gathering information to help the group survive. The screen shows Alice is present physically, listening to the confrontation; the movie's audience knows Alice has chosen to be silent because of the dialogue that happens before the confrontation scene, and because Alice could have interjected during the questioning of the Red Queen. By her issue of a threat, the audience knows that in Alice's silence she has learned that the Red Queen fears what they all fear—being shut down.

With Alice, delivery of a silence comes in the form of the not-saying. Alice is physically present, has facial expressions to indicate her active listening, and moves about the small room which houses the Red Queen's computer. In the previous example of the Red Queen's constant observation, the silence is textual and on-screen—audiences know the silence exists because of the on-screen perspective that belongs to the Red Queen. During the confrontation, movie-watchers see Alice on screen but Alice does not speak until the end of the communication exchange. Alice weighs the ways a silence may be deployed to create an intended meaning or effect. Thus, the delivery of textual, gestural, bodily, and aural silences is complicated by the character's choices, the participation of the other human survivors as interrogators, and the context of the events in the Hive. She knows that the physical threats issued by the others are not going to intimidate the Red Queen, but rather inverting the power of silence will.

The Red Queen plays an important role when analyzing Alice's rhetorical silence. The Red Queen—when turned on—is always present. Viewers are aware of the Red Queen when the on-screen view switches to the Red Queen's perspective, an overlay of grids, graphs, infrared, and text. The movie's audience learns early in the film from One—the military commander—that the military is being sent in to shut the Red Queen down. In the confrontation scene, the audience learns that the Red Queen has taken charge of the Hive, decided that the T-virus cannot be allowed to escape, and then killed every person in the Hive in an attempt to contain the virus. (Interestingly, and to complicate the experiences of the survivors, there are still creatures in tanks that *are* alive.) The audience also learns from the Red Queen that the T-virus is nearly impossible to kill. The Red Queen objects during the first time the survivors try to shut her down, and when she is turned back on one of the Red Queen's roles is to educate the survivors. The Red Queen wields power, authority, and control over operations of the Hive and the Mansion, and, by extension, the survivors. It is reasonable for Alice to see the Red Queen as a resource for escape and survival. However, since the Red Queen has a mind of her own, Alice also needs to involve the Red Queen in a need for survival. The Red Queen wants to retain control, and the Red Queen must be the one to exert that control.

Throughout the film, the Red Queen is a silent observer-participant. Through the cameras (and on the film's screen) audiences see the Red Queen observe, document, and evaluate the events of the Hive. The Red Queen sees something, makes a decision, and takes action. She tells us this in the confrontation sequence after being turned on again by Kaplan: "The T-virus escaped into the air conditioning system. And an uncontrolled pattern of infection began. [...] I couldn't allow it to escape from the Hive. So, I took steps." The Red Queen is constantly an observer-participant, and—unless she is turned off—takes actions from a position of power. The Red Queen is in control of the Hive and the Mansion, and therefore represents a kind of masculine power and control over the beings who work and live in the Hive and in the Mansion. The Red Queen uses rhetorical silence as a means of exerting her power and control; and, from her position of power, the Red Queen can be juxtaposed with Alice.

Certain aspects of Alice's character should be considered when analyzing rhetorical silence. As a female hero in the movie, Alice contends with the often masculine situations such as the controlling environment, planning and decision-making, leadership, and combat. Based on the early conversation that Alice has with One about Alice's role with Umbrella, movie-watchers can assume that Alice has had extensive education, training, and is prepared for communications, tactical decision-making, and combat—indicating that Alice can bridge sets of expectations for masculine and feminine communication styles. Alice is identified as a high-level security operative by One after the group enters the Hive; prior to that, Alice discovers the storage drawer of guns in the dresser in the Mansion. Alice, with or without specific memory, utilizes that education and training to make rhetorical choices. Generally speaking, in the movie, Alice's use of responses, questions, memory, and silence indicate her agency and strategic choices. Preparedness and practice come from training and study, allowing Alice to possess multiple strategies and tactics and the ability to make decisions on how and when to deploy them. Alice appears to have little power in relationship to the Red Queen; although the use of rhetorical silence reveals that Alice does possess some agency and power.

As a societal and political acting-agent, in the unique and constrained setting of the Hive, within this set of socio-political expectations for women, Alice found ways to maintain her feminine role while engaging in other societal and political spheres that would be considered masculine—Alice is a security operative, a fighter, a strategic planner, but Alice is also compassionate in her insistence that everyone will escape (and she takes action to assure their escape). Alice rarely seems to be silenced; rather she makes the rhetorical choice to use silence. In the confrontation scene with the Red Queen, Alice listens. Other survivors—Matt, Kaplan, and Rain—ask a question of the Red Queen. The

Red Queen is in a position of power, revealing information and demonstrating her decision-making. Meanwhile, Alice listens and observes. It is not until the Red Queen asks a question about the computer's circuits that Alice wields the ultimatum: help us or be shut down.

The film's audience knows that the Red Queen knows Alice is present in the confrontation scene because the Red Queen can see every room of the Mansion and the Hive, and movie-goers know that the Red Queen has been observing the whole group. Agency and power exist in the ways that Alice chooses to interact with the Red Queen, with the rhetorical situation of the Hive and the Umbrella Corporation. Just prior to the confrontation scene, Alice acknowledges the gravity of the situation and makes a decision:

Table 2: Example of Dialogue, *Resident Evil* (2002)

Speaker	Dialogue Spoken
ALICE	I'm turning her back on.
KAPLAN	That is not a good idea.
ALICE	She'll know a way out of here.

Instead of being a passive victim of the Red Queen's poison gas and manipulation of the Hive's doors and "occupants," Alice decides to use the Red Queen's power to find a way to escape. With this plan to turn on the Red Queen, Alice also has a way to manipulate the Red Queen. Movie-watchers see in this sequence that Alice has support for her plan to succeed:

Table 3: Example of Dialogue, *Resident Evil* (2002)

Speaker	Dialogue Spoken
ALICE	That circuit breaker you were talking about—can you bypass it?
KAPLAN	Yeah.
ALICE	So do it.

Alice has something in mind for the Red Queen, she asks Kaplan to set up the potential for shutting down the Red Queen. Movie-watchers also know that Alice recalls the first visit to the Red Queen, and the Red Queen's insistence that she not be shut down. One reason to keep power on was the consequence that shutting down the power to the Hive also shut down the storage cells which contained the creatures—and, without power, a creature escaped. Knowledge of the creature is information that the Red Queen withheld from the group of human survivors. The Red Queen, throughout the movie, is most motivated by power and control, and by retaining that power and control. To undermine the masculinized power of the Red Queen, and the dominant discourse of the confrontation, Alice remains silent during the confrontation scene.

While it might seem possible that Alice is silent during the confrontation scene because she does not know what to do next, that is not true—Alice chooses to *use* silence. Alice has developed a way to involve the Red Queen in the need for survival—Alice waits for the Red Queen's question, the Red Queen's interest in her own circuits, to deliver the ultimatum. Alice communicates her understanding and knowing in the way that she carefully and intentionally shapes the form and content of speaking, listening, and rhetorical silence. Bruneau suggests that silence is "both a *concept* and an actual *process* of mind" when he discusses the ways that humans create, perceive, and interpret silence (author's emphasis, 17). Prior to the confrontation scene in the Hive, when faced with a situation that seems insoluble, Alice assumes control of decision-making, and Alice exerts assertiveness and confidence despite her loss of memory. Her decisiveness about waking the Red Queen, and her use of rhetorical silence and listening during the questioning of the Red Queen are examples of her agency and power.

Similarly, Alice's actions of defiance or resistance of expectations, and her argumentative rhetorical practices during masculine rhetorical processes such as interrogation are an example of Alice's agency. Even though the Red Queen looks and sounds female, the Red Queen represents the masculine power of the Umbrella Corporation, and the Red Queen serves the goals of that dominant power structure. Interrogation of the Red Queen is a masculine practice, and withholding her own voice is Alice's participation in that same kind of practice; Alice is calculating the right moment to speak with the right influence, and rhetorical silence helps to achieve that effect. For each interaction, for each intentional communicative and rhetorical practice, her agency or power exists within and between those positions allowed to women, between those spaces and actions monitored and controlled by masculine rhetorical practices, and between the expectations for women's abilities permitted in the given social and political context. For Alice, silence is used as one choice among many in specific instances, alongside the choices of words and rhetorical structures. Alice means to survive, and uses silence to help meet that basic need.

The rhetorical silence used by Alice in the confrontation scene is also dependent on Alice's role in the group as well as her relationship with the other survivors. Alice's credibility relies on the relationships with survivors and on relating to characters in the present—she has no previous memory or history with other characters or with herself on which to rely or construct that credibility. Often, Alice relies on a set of social and political expectations for her role, and her credibility. Considering her character in the whole of the film, Alice's many possible roles of security officer, captive, comrade-in-combat, or friend help to construct her credibility as compassionate and trustworthy—especially in the moments that her memory fails her and trustworthiness is a question. Alice uses the present moment to imbue her credibility and her authority, adding complexity to a delivered rhetorical silence. Each communicative instance—whether voiced or silent—provides understanding of the reliance upon a complex set of women's rhetorical practices and men's rhetorical practices in both the public and private sphere, and the utilization of this set of practices uniquely to achieve a specific rhetorical delivery of silence. In the confrontation scene with the Red Queen, Alice deploys a communication style that is more masculine than feminine, and Alice asserts a believable ultimatum. Her credibility and authority rests in the believable delivery of both silence and speaking.

To create the rhetorical silence, Alice called upon various rhetorical strategies and structures as well as her credibility, and her adherence to the roles assigned to women in a specific context. The rhetorical situation of the movie requires interaction and communication. The demand for interaction is heightened by the pressures and constraints of the Hive and the zombies, monsters; the demand to take action is also a pressure which heightens the decision-making of the characters as well as their sense of helplessness. To further complicate the use of speaking and not-speaking, there are the dissonant wills of the Red Queen, the military mission (to shut down the Red Queen), Alice, the survivors, and the zombies. These various pressures are often an instance which begs to be vocalized or explained. In one instance, Alice tells Matt "I don't remember the truth!" (*Resident Evil*) In different scenes, Alice calls upon or openly acknowledges the other character's expectations for her gender, for her role as amnesiac, and for the interactions with the Red Queen—making her credibility apparent to her fellow survivors and her audience. Alice's roles and credibility establish why the survivors would follow Alice's decision-making. Examining Alice's various roles and the multiple entities involved in the context adds to the complexity of Alice's use of and meanings for rhetorical silence.

In the example of the confrontation with the Red Queen, Alice is silent and listening. She withholds her voice and participation up until the end of the confrontation to deliver an ultimatum. Alice asserts to the Red Queen, "We need a way out of here. If you refuse to help at any time, we flip the switch. Understand?" The silence is delivered as listening, in the form of not-speaking, though Alice's facial expressions and bodily movement show her active presence. The impact of Alice's silent but strong presence relies on the questions and interactions of fellow characters with the Red Queen. Alice relies on fellow characters—including the Red Queen—to listen for meaning. Alice utilizes a kind of masculine authority and credibility through her many simultaneous roles as decision-maker, as peer of the survivors, and as woman-speaker to create a rhetorical silence. Rhetorical silence becomes apparent in the examination of the inter-relatedness of Alice, the context, and the other characters; yet, an effective silence is also reliant on the surrounding aspects of the rhetorical situation such as space, class, gender, and genre. The context and community shape the delivered message, including a delivered silence, through norms and expectations of that culture or community.

The competing cultures of control and authority from the Hive/Red Queen, the military's mission, with the need to survive each imbue a specific set of expectations and meaning for rhetorical silence. Similarly, the needs and motivations between the dissonant groups of humans and zombies/monsters also inherently inform the use of and meaning for a delivered silence. Throughout the film, Alice composes interrogatives and combative sequences typically delivered by male or dominant persons in power. Alice also draws on her credibility and authority anchored in her various social and political roles to create her own delivery denoting compassion or authority. The rhetorical silence delivered to Kaplan in the hallway in an early scene is a more feminine style of silence when contrasted with the rhetorical silence delivered during the confrontation with the Red Queen. The delivery of the various silences shapes the intended meaning by complementing or by conflicting with expectations and familiar rhetorical practices. Alice uses specific understanding and style when creating a delivery of rhetorical silence; an understanding of available means, and subsequent intentional use of rhetorical silence will best fit the context and the goals to survive.

Implications: The Strength and the Silence of Alice

In the book *Silence and Listening as Rhetorical Arts*, Cheryl Glenn and Krista Ratcliffe observe that rhetorical silence and listening "have been conceptualized and employed in different times and places by many people—some with power, some without—for purposes as diverse as showing reverence, gathering knowledge, planning action, buying time, and attempting to survive" (2). Though a fictional space, the Umbrella Corporation certainly represents a setting which contains a dynamic play of intellectual property, communication, and rhetorical silence: secret scientific experiments, data and products to be stolen, a mysterious computer-controlled environment, military and security operatives, and creatures and zombies. Alice, too, represents a site for the dynamic play of communication, agency, and decision-making; and, Alice uses both silence and sound strategically. When audiences first meet Alice, she uses the strategies of observer-participant that the Red Queen employs, and the audience discovers later that Alice is a trained security operative. Even though Alice's memory loss gives her a position of not-knowing, Alice utilizes silence as a means of surviving and, in doing so, gains some knowledge and power during the events of the movie. The four rhetorical silences noted at the beginning of this chapter help to document Alice's *concept* and *process* of using rhetorical silence throughout the movie. The confrontation scene is key because of the distribution of power, the use of masculine and feminine strategies, the expectations for heroes-in-action, and the use of rhetorical silence.

Throughout the movie, viewers see the potentially stratified ways that rhetorical silence can be applied in a specific context with an audience, similar to Lauer's suggestion that choosing a specific strategy can be used "to impact the audience and the faculty being addressed" (61). Rhetorical silence is used in various forms and performs various functions. Silence is employed by the military personnel, by the scientific and technological personnel, and by the Red Queen in different forms, performing different functions. The strategies of using rhetorical silence rely on those contexts, the cultures, and that specific set of characters to supply value and meaning for the silence. Alice's uses of rhetorical silence are also connected to Ratcliffe's discussion of interpretive invention and rhetorical listening because Alice is evidently thinking, observing, and evaluating (25). Generally speaking, Alice utilizes silence in specific and strategic ways; perhaps more importantly, Alice does not simply use silence because the context requires that she should be silent, or because she was silenced by either Umbrella Corporation or the Red Queen. So, the example of Alice represents a unique opportunity to consider rhetorical choices and strategies—and Alice's resistance to the situation. The Red Queen is a masculinized ideal of a woman who is programmed, a daughter, and is subservient to the status quo; Alice defies the status quo by resisting not only the Red Queen but also the world order that the Red Queen and the Umbrella Corporation represents. The juxtaposition of the silences used by the Red Queen and by Alice provides a more complex comparison of dominant rhetorical strategies versus resistant rhetorical strategies.

Under the constraints of the Hive and the Mansion, Alice retains and displays her humanity. Rhetorical silence is used as part of a productive set of rhetorical strategies to undermine expectations, to bridge both masculine and feminine communication styles, to express humanity; silence is a productive strategy used by Alice in a variety of ways. Alice's rhetorical silence relies on her relationships with others, her credibility and authority, and the dialogue before/during/after the silences for meaning. Even though Kaplan is the computer expert responsible for the computer shut-down, and even though Alice remains silent, Alice does retain rhetorical power and authority. She uses feminist rhetorical strategies such as silence to defy gender conventions. In the midst of life-or-death situations, Alice remains compassionate and she values the relationships with her fellow survivors. Alice acts as a representative feminine action hero using feminine rhetorical strategies in contrast to typical masculine means. Alice defies gender conventions as an action hero: devoid of memory (and, at times, devoid of a sense of self), Alice is able to wield strategies to fight monsters, to fight computers, and to fight the pressures to lose humanity.

Not only does silence shape the meaning of a given message but so, too, do bodily movement or stillness, environmental aspects or elements of setting, mental activities and memory—all that surrounds the rhetorical silence, as well as the memory of what came before and the memory for context, genre, gender, expectations and so on, shape meaning interactively. This study of rhetorical silence also highlights the importance of factors such as culture, gender, and class without relying on stereotypes for cultural or gendered silences. Different rhetorical contexts place value on speech and silence, and those values change as the context and participants change. A systematic study of rhetorical silence allows for a *both-and* approach to including and to considering the import of factors like culture or gender, but also for the ways that both speakers and audiences utilize and mediate delivery, style, and context. Similarly, including the contemporary perspectives that identity and agency are complex and often fluid is important, not limiting a character or a rhetorical silence to the potential rigid restrictions of a definitive factor such as a specific culture, gender, or class. Rather, there is a demonstrated dynamic play of roles and factors which contribute to a rhetorical context.

The analysis of Alice's rhetorical silences improves the understanding of her choice and intention to use a rhetorical silence as well as the import of the various possible elements connected to an effective silence. There are several uses of rhetorical silence during *Resident Evil*. Rhetorical silence is used as part of a productive set of rhetorical strategies to undermine expectations, to bridge both masculine and feminine communication styles, to express humanity; silence is a productive strategy used by Alice in a variety of ways. Rhetorical silence is used productively and positively to achieve a specific goal, and by centering on the confrontation scene with the Red Queen, we can better see the use of rhetorical silence as a means for survival—Alice strategically uses rhetorical silence as one among many means available to help herself, and to help the group (even if they did not make it), survive the events at the Hive.

Note

1. Scholarship juxtaposing sound and silence in communications, rhetoric, and linguistics includes but is not limited to Fernando Poyatos' *New Perspectives in Nonverbal*

Communication; Max Picard's *The World of Silence*; Ikuko Nakane's *Silence in Intercultural Communication: Perceptions and Performance*; Adam Jaworski's *The Power of Silence: Social and Pragmatic Perspectives*; Deborah Tannen and Muriel Saville-Troike's *Perspectives on Silence*; and Cheryl Glenn and Krista Ratcliffe's *Silence and Listening as Rhetorical Arts*.

Works Cited

Bokser, Julie. "Sor Juana's Rhetoric of Silence." *Rhetoric Review* Volume 25, Number 1 (2006): p. 5–21. Print.

Bruneau, Thomas J. "Communicative Silences: Forms and Functions." *The Journal of Communication*. Volume 23 (March 1973) p. 17–46. Print.

Buchanan, Lindal. *Regendering Delivery: The Fifth Canon and Antebellum Women Rhetors*. Carbondale: Southern Illinois University Press, 2005. Print.

Connors, Robert J. "Actio: A Rhetoric of Written Delivery (Iteration Two)." *Rhetorical Memory and Delivery: Classical Concepts for Contemporary Composition and Communication*. Edited by John Frederick Reynolds, Hillsdale, New Jersey: Lawrence Erlbaum Associates, 1993. p. 65–78. Print.

Glenn, Cheryl. *Unspoken: A Rhetoric of Silence*. Carbondale: Southern Illinois University Press; 1st edition 2004. Print.

_____. *Rhetoric Retold: Regendering the Tradition from Antiquity through the Renaissance*. Carbondale: Southern Illinois University Press, 1997. Print.

_____, and Krista Ratcliffe, eds. *Silence and Listening as Rhetorical Arts*. Carbondale: Southern Illinois University Press, 2011. Print.

Jaworski, Adam. *The Power of Silence: Social and Pragmatic Perspectives*. Newbury Park: Sage Publications, 1993. Print. Language and Behavior Series.

Johnstone, Barbara, and Christopher Eisenhart, eds. *Rhetoric in Detail: Discourse Analyses of Rhetorical Talk and Text*. Philadelphia: John Benjamins Publishing, 2008. Print.

Lauer, Janice M. *Invention in Rhetoric and Composition*. West Lafayette, Indiana: Parlor Press, 2004. Print.

Mountford, Roxanne. *The Gendered Pulpit: Preaching in American Protestant Spaces*. Carbondale: Southern Illinois University Press, 2003. Print.

Nakane, Ikuko. *Silence in Intercultural Communication: Perceptions and Performance*. Philadelphia: John Benjamins Publishing, 2007. Print. Pragmatics and Beyond New Series.

Poyatos, Fernando. *New Perspectives in Nonverbal Communication*. New York: Pergamon Press, 1983. Print.

Ratcliffe, Krista. *Rhetorical Listening: Identification, Gender, Whiteness*. Carbondale: Southern Illinois University Press, 2005.

Resident Evil. Dir. Paul W. S. Anderson. Perf. Mila Jovovich, Michelle Rodriguez, Eric Mabius, James Purefoy. Screen Gems/Sony Pictures, 2002. DVD.

Sandoval, Chela. *Methodology of the Oppressed*. Minneapolis: University of Minnesota Press, 2000. Print.

Saville-Troike, Muriel. "The Place of Silence in an Integrated Theory of Communication." *Perspectives on Silence*. Edited by Deborah Tannen and Muriel Saville-Troike. Norwood, NJ: Ablex, 1985. p. 3–20. Print.

Tannen, Deborah, and Muriel Saville-Troike, eds. *Perspectives on Silence*. Norwood, NJ: Ablex, 1985. Print.

"My name is Alice and I remember everything!" Surviving Sexual Abuse in the Resident Evil Films

James Stone

Introduction: Alice Wakes

Alice (Milla Jovavich) lays unconscious in a glaringly white operating theater. She is alone and almost naked, pierced and contorted by a tangled multitude of tubes, wires, clips, and electrodes. Regaining consciousness, she sits up, sees her reflection in a mirrored wall and screams in horror. Realizing she has been kidnapped and subjected to unnecessary medical procedures by the scientists of the Umbrella Corporation, she tears every intrusive device from her skin and makes her escape. Her persecutors track her relentlessly and Alice is eventually recaptured, confined to another medical facility, and rendered comatose. Encased in a womblike tank of green liquid and, once again, bereft of clothing, she is observed by Dr. Isaacs (Iain Glen), a megalomaniac geneticist intent upon using her body for his own nefarious ends. Alice wakes and begins to panic, grasping in terror at the network of tubing that encircles her. She has been reduced to an infantile state, a newborn emerging from a high-tech uterus. She demonstrates only the most rudimentary powers of speech and comprehension. "Do you know what that is?" asks Dr. Isaacs, holding up a pen. She stares at it blankly. He demonstrates its usage. "You try," he encourages. Holding the pen in her fist, Alice scratches simple lines onto the doctor's clipboard. "That's it," he tells her, as if praising a child. These are moments from *Resident Evil: Apocalypse* (2004), the second in an ongoing series of highly successful horror movies that also includes *Resident Evil* (2002), *Resident Evil: Extinction* (2007), *Resident Evil: Afterlife* (2010), and *Resident Evil: Retribution* (2012). The films frequently present Alice in an undressed and vulnerable state. In this, they are not dissimilar to countless horror pictures that trade in the spectacle of a scantily-clad woman in peril. But there is something different about Alice's predicament.

Her injuries are often sustained while unconscious. She is terrified, not by the prospect of an attack, or even by its execution, but by its aftermath. The horror she experiences comes from the knowledge that some terrible act has been visited upon her while she was unable to resist. Time and again, she wakes to discover that she has been overpowered, drugged, and injured. Though she may know who is responsible for her torment, the full details of her assault will become clear only later. She will piece together the past through a series of flashbacks. And as she struggles to take control of her mind and body, there is always something of the child about her. She will play the wayward daughter to the decidedly patriarchal Umbrella Corporation. By an obsessive focus on memory and childishness—coupled with an insistence on portraying Alice abducted, rendered unconscious, stripped, and surgically penetrated—the *Resident Evil* movies betray a fascination with sexual violence.

Millennial Horrors: Revelations of Abuse

The film series appeared in the wake of an outpouring of information—provided by all segments of the media during the 1990s and the early 2000s—regarding the prevalence and psychological consequences of sexual abuse. TV was the medium most responsible for bringing subjects like date rape and incest to unprecedented prominence in public discourse. As Luckhurst contends, "The inaugurating figure of contemporary trauma celebrity is undoubtedly Oprah Winfrey" (133) who "declared herself an abuse survivor in 1991" (75). From that moment on, the daytime talk show was refashioned into a confessional, an arena in which those with a tale of sexual trauma to tell might unburden themselves.

Media exposés were particularly focused on two topics: recovered memory and pedophilia. In the early nineties, certain therapists, by placing patients under hypnosis, offered access to what they deemed to be repressed memories of childhood sexual abuse. Myriad disturbing recollections were recovered in this fashion. Indeed, so numerous were the charges of father-daughter incest that resulted from these sessions, that therapists were frequently accused of planting false memories. An explosion of TV and press coverage resulted. As Walker claims:

> Popular media attention to the "problem" of "false memory" became intense in 1993, with newspapers and magazines reporting story after story of families sundered by a daughter's "false" accusations against her father, or of families struggling to come together again after a daughter's retraction of incest charges. The profes-

sional journal *Family Therapy Networker* reported that by 1994 over three hundred magazine and newspaper articles on "false memory" had appeared [12].

Despite widespread suspicion that recovered memories were often fabricated, many feminist commentators sprang to the defense of those women who found themselves branded as liars. For instance, Caputi claimed that to discount recovered memories was to mount "a misogynist backlash against perceived feminist threats to the patriarchal domination of women and girls" (296). This debate over memory, impossible to resolve since physical evidence of a decades-old assault was almost impossible to come by, revealed something both fascinating and disturbing: recollections of abuse—real or imagined—could be dredged up from the depths of many a subconscious. A vast number of individuals, given the requisite psychological goading, were able to pour forth a lurid set of stories and images. A familiarity with sexual violence, it seemed, had become an integral part of human identity.

The millennial period was also marked by a tidal wave of information regarding pedophilia. The discovery of institutionalized child abuse within the Catholic Church was, for many, particularly shocking. Isley, writing in 1997, informs us "over the last 10 years, the American public has been saturated with media reports regarding criminal and civil cases against religious ministers accused of sexually assaulting children" (277). In the 2000s there were many more disclosures regarding child abuse. The phenomenon of pedophile rings became widely acknowledged following a number of prominent police campaigns targeting child pornography. From 1999 to 2001 Operation Avalanche resulted in scores of well-publicized, if controversial, arrests in the United States; Operation Ore began in the UK in 2002; Operation Amethyst was implemented in the Republic of Ireland in 2002; Australia's Operation Auxin commenced in 2004. Several cases of child abduction, rape, and murder were kept firmly in the public consciousness over the course of these years. Fourteen-year-old Elizabeth Smart, abducted from her bedroom in 2002, was raped repeatedly over the course of nine months. She wrote a book about her experience and, in 2006, testified before Congress to support sexual predator legislation. She is now a commentator for ABC News, specializing in missing persons cases. In 2007, Madeleine McCann, a three-year-old, went missing in Portugal, sparking an international manhunt and a seemingly endless series of speculative articles regarding her fate. She has yet to be found. Although six-year-old beauty pageant contestant Jon Benet Ramsey was raped and killed in 1996, her rouge-imprinted face has stayed with us, becoming an iconic image of the 24-hour news cycle. Caputi noted in 2004, "Jon Benet Ramsey, a victim of sexual murder, haunts our culture" (105).

The media's obsessive focus on child abuse, and our apparent need to regularly revisit and memorialize its victims and survivors, enshrined the pedophile as the embodiment of ultimate evil. By the turn-of-the-century, largely as a result of the media's investment in stories of incest and child abuse, many were convinced the pedophile lurked around every corner. As Lee puts it: "During the early 1990s ... the pedophile was believed to be the freak across the road, always elsewhere" (10). But, he adds, "by the late 1990s everyone was a suspected pedophile. The monster was no longer the alien outside the clan, he was your dad, your teacher, your preacher, he was a you, whether you are male or female, innocent or guilty (but obviously guilty)—everyone was a suspect, particularly Catholic priests of course, so everyone was a 'monster'" (9).

The *Resident Evil* movies emerged from an age traumatized by new and disturbing knowledge. Their narratives are so replete with images of explicit and implicit sexual violence that they seem to embody a cultural anxiety brought on by the awful disclosures of the millennial period. They exhaustively confront a myriad of sex crimes. Abduction, rape, gang rape, date rape, and sex murder are an enormous influence on their imagery. And because Alice fights to remember the assaults perpetrated against her, is abused by domineering father figures, and often appears in scenes which render her childish, the series seems particularly intent upon tackling the phenomena of recovered memory and pedophilia.

Rape and Sex Murder: Explicit and Implicit

Alice is repeatedly threatened with the prospect of rape. For instance, she is nearly gang raped in *Resident Evil: Extinction*. Responding to a request for assistance, broadcast over the radio, she finds that she has been duped and lured into a trap. Instead of vulnerable survivors of the recent global apocalypse, she finds brigands who mean to do her harm. As they surround her, one pulls a large knife which he proceeds to press against the crotch of her shorts. The intentions of this band are all too apparent. In *Resident Evil: Afterlife* a shower scene, in which Alice disrobes, is fraught with the possibility that a peeping tom may attack her. One of the movie's chief villains makes it clear that he intends to sexually assault her after she is dead. "I'm looking forward to playing with your pretty face," he tells Alice.

Mostly, however, sexual violence against Alice is presented in figurative, though hardly subtle, terms. In *Resident Evil*, during our first encounter with Alice, it is strongly hinted that she has suffered a sexual assault. She awakens, groggy and shaken, lying naked on the floor of a shower stall. The shower curtain has fallen, draping itself decorously over her body. Water cascades from the faucet. Gingerly getting to her feet and looking into a nearby mirror, she discovers bruising and scarring on her shoulders. A brief flashback occurs, showing her falling in the shower, but not revealing the reason for her collapse. Exiting the bathroom slowly and apprehensively, Alice finds herself in an exquisitely furnished mansion which she begins to explore, decidedly ill at ease. We are offered a series of hints that her collapse may have been connected to an amorous encounter. She approaches a double bed, upon which a red cocktail dress is laid out, and discovers a handwritten note that reads, "Today all your dreams come true." A kiss is appended to the message, suggesting a communication from a lover. Opening a chest of drawers, she discovers men's undershirts, women's silk blouses, some table linens, and then, to her surprise, a cache of guns. Tellingly, the accoutrements of domestic life are nestled alongside instruments of violence. Alice discovers a photograph that depicts her in a wedding dress standing alongside a bridegroom. Since she stares wistfully at this image, we are primed to ask whether this man has caused her injuries. Suddenly, there is a fleeting movement behind her and a startlingly loud noise erupts from off screen, linking the image of romantic union with terror. Alice whips around to meet the apparent threat but finds nothing. Instead, her attention is drawn to a winged, figurative statue covered in polythene sheeting that is reminiscent of a shrouded corpse. A domestic space adorned with tokens of romance has been well and truly imbued with a sense of dread. After a few more tense moments, Alice is grabbed from behind by a man. As she shouts, "Stop! Get away from me!" he throws her to the floor and climbs on top of her. Suddenly, the windows of the room explode inward as a team of gas-masked commandos invade the mansion. Pulling the man from atop Alice's body, a member of this group saves her from an attacker whose potential as a rapist has already been elaborately hinted at. This scene establishes Alice, and the *Resident Evil* movies themselves, as riven through with anxiety about sexual abuse.

Within these moments can be found the series' inaugural references to drug-facilitated date rape. In the decade leading up to the millennium, new attention was brought to date rape (often referred to as acquaintance rape) and, in particular, sexual assaults against individuals made unconscious due to the ingestion of alcohol or drugs. An article in *The National Institute of Justice Journal* notes:

> in the mid- and late 1990s, ethnographers and rape crisis centers began hearing reports of drugs, often referred to as "roofies" and "liquid ecstasy," being administered clandestinely to immobilize victims to impair their memory and thus facilitate rape.... These drugs can produce loss of consciousness and the inability to recall recent events. Victims may not be aware that they have ingested drugs or that they have been raped while under the influence of drugs. Reports of such assaults and increases in the recreational consumption of the drugs used in these assaults have brought drug-facilitated rape into sharp focus in recent years [Fitzgerald and Riley 9].

That the phenomenon of drug-facilitated date rape had reached epidemic proportions was made clear in 1996 when President Clinton signed the Drug-Induced Rape Prevention and Punishment Act. This legislation increased penalties for those persons utilizing "date rape drugs," such as Rohypnol. Greater awareness of date rape made sexual assault seem a terrifyingly ubiquitous crime and suggested that individuals were ever more powerless to protect themselves.

Alice is rendered unconscious by narcotics (a puff of soporific gas delivered from the shower faucet), discovers bruising, and cannot remember the recent past. Other details—the picture, the love note—each suggesting that she has been assaulted by a loved one, point yet more strongly toward a date rape scenario. One of the most disturbing revelations connected to the new cultural prominence of date rape was that women were statistically most likely to be raped by a boyfriend, fiancé, or spouse. In the mansion scene, the rapist becomes a disconcertingly domestic figure.

The *Resident Evil* series imbues the mansion with great significance. It will be returned to via flashback in *Resident Evil* and *Resident Evil: Apocalypse*. Every time we return to this scene of an apparent sex crime, its details are transformed and further tinged with the aura of sexual violence. In *Resident Evil: Extinction*, Dr. Isaacs creates numerous clones of Alice that he tests and trains in an underground replica of the mansion. At the climax of the film Alice, preparing for a showdown with the doctor, explores this space. Instead of the mere suggestion that something monstrous stalks its corridors—as was the case in *Resident Evil*—we are now certain that this domestic realm, still possessed of its marriage bed and wedding photograph, will be visited by a truly malignant presence.

Through overzealous self-medication, Isaacs has turned himself into a hulking, grotesque monster. As Alice waits for him to appear, she is momentarily distracted by the sight of the wedding photograph. She stares at it, as if looking for answers. At this precise moment, Isaacs attacks her. Just as in *Resident Evil*, the contemplation of the photograph results in an attack by a man. Once again, it is suggested that domestic relationships between men and women are colored by abuse. While the "abusive husband" of *Resident Evil* merely grabbed Alice, this more monstrous version will try to suffocate her with his newly acquired tentacles. He then attempts an act of penetration that is an extreme manifestation of sexual violence. Thrusting his mutated limbs toward Alice's face, he tries to enter her mouth and eye sockets simultaneously.

Apparently a survivor of rape and domestic violence, Alice will also be portrayed as the victim of a sex murder. After the death of Alice's clone in *Resident Evil: Extinction*, Dr. Isaacs regards the corpse impassively and coldly tells an assistant "get rid of that." In referring to a woman as "that" rather than "her," Isaacs aligns himself with the philosophy of fellow Umbrella patriarch Albert Wesker who, in *Resident Evil: Afterlife*, informs Alice that she will be killed because "the Umbrella Corporation is taking back its property. You just didn't work out." The films make clear that when a human is regarded as an object, any form of sexual violence becomes possible. As the corpse of the Alice clone, clad in the red cocktail dress from the mansion, is thrown into a ditch, the camera tracks back to reveal about a hundred dead and mutilated "Alices." The moment is rife with suggestions of sexual murder. Every bloody corpse, each a victim of Isaacs' experiments, is wearing the same alluring dress and boots. Several have their legs splayed open, others are arranged in different quasi-pornographic poses. It is a scene redolent of necrophilia, the sexually desirable corpse laid out for our gaze. The image of scores of bodies dumped into a ditch with no regard for their humanity evokes the Holocaust but also, since each corpse is female, the mass graves filled with victims of the Juarez, Mexico, "femicide."

Alice is not the only character in the series threatened with rape and sexualized murder. In *Resident Evil: Apocalypse*, as a terrified woman flees a pack of ravenous zombies, the scene plays out like the prelude to a gang rape. The woman is young, attractive, and alone, running up the stairwell of an inner-city tower block and pursued by a gang of rapacious assailants. It is a moment iconographic of urban decay films such as *Death Wish* or *The Exterminator*. If we are not sufficiently convinced of the perverse undertones to the attack, we are offered a zombie's-eye-view of the fleeing woman, complete with a shot that allows us to glimpse her underwear. The pack succeeds in running down its quarry and the woman is bitten. In this heavily sexualized scenario, the bite signifies the rape toward which the scene has been building. Because she realizes that the zombie's bite will soon make her a member of the living dead, the woman chooses to throw herself from the roof of the building. In doing so, she acts in sisterhood with all those heroines of Victorian literature and early cinema who would rather die than live with rape and its aftermath. Indeed, the most famous attempted rape in cinema history, the attack on Elsie Stoneman (Lillian Gish) in *The Birth of Nation*, ends with the woman flinging herself to her death from a great height.

Another zombie attack heavy with suggestions of gang rape occurs in *Resident Evil: Extinction*. Dr. Isaacs has decided to test a new breed of somewhat controllable zombie by unleashing a group of them upon a convoy of survivors and their newest compatriot, Alice. Placing about thirty into a shipping container, he drops them into a desert location where they lay in wait for the convoy. When the zombies burst forth, they are virtually identical to one another. Dressed in gray, one-piece jumpsuits they are almost all male and bald-headed. Though the convoy is made up of men and women, much of the scene involves male zombies attacking screaming, running women. When they manage to overpower their victims, the zombies fall upon them *en masse*, exacerbating connotations of gang rape. Since their jumpsuits make them look like prison inmates, and they are consumed by a ravenous desire for mostly female flesh, the zombies embody one of our most cherished, and stereotypical, images of the incarcerated male: the convict who, given half a chance, will unleash his libidinal frustrations on the nearest woman. Even the zombies' baldness evokes the shaven heads of jail-house gang members.

The act of rape is alluded to in the many scenes of violence that revolve around aggressive biting or licking. Contamination by the T-virus frequently results in the acquisition of a fearsomely voracious mouth. *Resident Evil: Afterlife* introduces a type of zombie whose entire face splits open, like an unfurling flower, to form a facial cavity all the better to rend flesh. In each of the movies, contaminated attack dogs menace Alice with their snapping, drooling jaws. In *Resident Evil: Apocalypse*, the mountainous physique of Nemesis (Matthew G. Taylor) is topped by a mouth constantly agape, angrily red, and filled with razor sharp teeth. And then there are the Lickers, huge, muscular quadrupeds that seem to have leapt out of the most perversely erotic nightmare. It is entirely fitting that a film series so filled with anxiety regarding sexual abuse should present as its most feared monster an abomination with a fifteen-foot tongue. The Lickers will be punished for putting their tongues where they are not wanted. In scenes underpinned by a medieval sense of retribution, the creatures will be dragged around by their signature appendage and suffer its removal. Every one of these remarkable mouths suggests an appetite for sexually abusive behavior.

Of course, the zombies that stumble through the series are eager to bite their victims. The sexual connotations of biting have been noted before in discussions of zombie cinema. Simon Clark argues that "the zombie's mouth—the very thing that consumes living flesh and turns it into decaying matter—becomes nothing less than the manifestation of the vagina dentata. The bloodied mouth of the undead corpse can be interpreted as a horrific depiction of the consuming female genitals" (203). While this may be true of other zombie films, in the *Resident Evil* series the zombie mouth is notably male. In these movies, the act of devouring is associated with gang rape—usually a male activity—and inextricably linked with that remorseless coterie of sex attackers, the men of the Umbrella Corporation. In *Resident Evil: Afterlife*, Umbrella boss Albert Wesker attacks Alice by opening his mouth and allowing a spidery growth to emerge. At the climax of *Resident Evil: Extinction*, Dr. Isaacs informs Alice, "I ingest you, I gain control." Rejecting his violent orality, she replies, "I'm not on the menu."

Flashbacks, Repetitions and Transformations: Resident Evil and the Traumatized Psyche

The aftermath of sexual assault is often marked by amnesia. Walker comments: "studies have shown that amnesia for childhood sexual abuse is not only possible but a characteristic feature of such abuse" (65). While many trauma survivors display an inability to remember, others demonstrate an inability to forget. They mentally revisit a terrible event, experiencing flashbacks or nightmares. This repetition compulsion is theorized in the work of physician Mardi Horowitz who, during the 1970s, discovered, "Stress events contained information difficult to terminate. The images got stuck in cycles of repetition rather than fading into conventional memories" (Luckhurst 148). Alice experiences so many flashbacks in the *Resident Evil* series that they become a defining element of her character. Indeed, because the films return so obsessively to times and places that have particularly troubling associations for the protagonist, their very narratives suggest the workings of a traumatized psyche.

Alice will experience numerous flashbacks that enable her to fully comprehend the extent of her abuse. In *Resident Evil: Apocalypse*, after she awakens in Dr. Isaac's uterine tank, a series of flashbacks informs her that she has undergone abduction and experimentation. In the same movie, as her body is wracked by convulsions, she flashes back to scenes of her maltreatment. Remembering the ominous words, "prepare her for exposure," she winces, recalling penetration by needles. Such moments bolster an argument made by Luckhurst that the flashback is "the central device of cinema's representation of trauma" and highly suggestive of "the protagonist's enslavement to a buried traumatic past" (179).

It is not only flashbacks that suggest Alice's psyche is plagued by repetition. On several occasions, the films revisit sections of an important scene, not as a flashback but as a reprise. For example, the moment in which Alice awakens in an operating theater, first seen in *Resident Evil*, is shown to us again at the beginning of *Resident Evil: Apocalypse*.

In *Resident Evil: Extinction* there will be a reprise of much of the mansion scene from *Resident Evil*. The scene plays out exactly as it had in the first movie: waking in the shower, looking into the mirror, discovering the bruising, looking at the wedding photo, encountering the statue. But then we are offered images absent from the earlier film, moments that seem to challenge the accuracy of the original scenario. Repetition gives way to nightmarish transformation.

The scene will play out like a bad dream but, in terms of the trauma paradigm, like an embellished memory. Trauma survivors are prone, not only to revisit their suffering through flashback and nightmare, but also to transform it. As Walker notes:

> [a] "radically remolded" but not absolutely untrue memory may be one of the most characteristic responses to traumatic experience. This is especially true for childhood sexual trauma, where traumatic experiences tend to be repeated and often occur prior to the child's development of integrated identity patterns.... A trauma from an external source, is very likely to trigger a memory pattern marked by gaps and misperceptions ... [74].

After Alice sees the eerie statue, her experience starts to resemble an embellished memory, the original trauma remolded and misperceived. She opens a door but, instead of walking down a leaf-strewn hallway, as she had in the initial version of the scene, she finds herself in a glass walled, fluorescent-lit corridor. If we recall *Resident Evil*, we may recognize the corridor as part of the Hive, a massive underground complex that sits beneath the mansion. It was the site of a massacre in which several members of a commando team were sliced to ribbons by lasers. But since the Hive corridor is a considerable distance from the mansion, we are presented with a disorienting, dreamlike melding of spaces. Alice touches the walls of the corridor and memories flood back in quick succession. A flashback presents the commando's bodies, dismembered and decapitated. Alice will not suffer the same fate. As the lasers advance upon her, she acrobatically avoids them, narrowly avoiding injury and climbing into the ductwork of an air-conditioning system. After crawling forward a few feet, she drops into yet another new space, a hospital corridor. Our memories of *Resident Evil* may cue us to the confusing fact that this hospital is not in close proximity to the Hive. Traffic noise becomes apparent, suggesting that an urban space lies just outside. Alice begins to run toward an exit, pushing a gurney before her in order to smash her way to the street. Suddenly, a huge blade plummets from the ceiling, chopping the gurney in half and stopping Alice in her tracks. She only has a moment to recover from this surreal and incongruous event when from the floor a spinning, bullet-spewing disk appears. Alice's torso is horribly wounded and she drops to the ground, dying.

In the next few moments of the film we realize that the character we have been following is not Alice, but her clone. The events we witnessed took place in a research facility where scientists experiment on a multitude of manufactured "Alices," putting them through their paces in convincing recreations of rooms in the mansion, the Hive, and the hospital. We therefore have an explanation for the oddly disjunctive quality of the previous scenes and yet, though we now know the truth, this does not diminish the sense that what we have experienced feels very much like the retreading of a traumatic incident via embellished memory.

Pedophilia: The Resident Evil

The *Resident Evil* films present Alice, not only as a survivor of sexual abuse, but as a child who must endure pedophilic, incestuous attentions. Alice is, in many respects, a strong woman yet, at every turn, she demonstrates characteristics associated with children. The very fact that she is played by Milla Jovovich ensures that she will appear, in Rabin's words, "a gamine with a gun." Jovovich's waiflike frame connotes that she is still the teenage model who came to prominence on the covers of international fashion magazines. Her diminutive qualities are fully exploited in *Resident Evil*. Exploring the mansion, she turns door handles placed at shoulder level. This element of mise-en-scène, as Alfred Hitchcock demonstrated in *Rebecca*, is bound to make an adult heroine appear girlish. As she rounds each corner, a look of curiosity and wonderment upon her face, Alice is the quintessential child of fairy tale exploring the forbidden castle.

Of course, the fairy tale protagonist that Alice resembles most is her namesake in the well-known books by Lewis Carroll. The *Resident Evil* movies persistently ask us to draw a comparison between their Alice and Carroll's Alice, perhaps the most famous child in all of literature. For instance, when the filmic Alice enters a dreamlike, labyrinthine space and does battle with the Red Queen, a homicidal computer intent upon beheading her enemies, we are left in no doubt of whom she is meant to remind us. Though these parallels to *Alice's Adventures in Wonderland* constitute, in Harper's words, "a bid for cultural capital," another result of such allusions is to infantilize the protagonist.

Alice's childish qualities are further developed when she interacts with the men of the Umbrella Corporation. In *Resident Evil: Apocalypse*, she is born from a womb devised by Dr. Isaacs. Like Dr. Frankenstein, he has fathered a figurative child without the aid of a woman. As the newborn Alice lies naked, shivering, and wet, her "father" approaches and kneels down. Adopting a calmly paternal tone, as if comforting a waif, he gently pulls her to her feet. "You're safe," he says. "Come on. That's it. There we are," he continues as Alice gradually stands up. As the relationship between the doctor and Alice develops, their father-daughter dynamic becomes more pronounced. "Good girl," he says, as an Alice clone advances successfully through one of his initiative tests. As Alice breaks into his laboratory to exact her revenge, he wryly intones "welcome home."

It soon becomes clear that Alice will demonstrate the characteristics, not just of a child, but an abused child. Isaacs' tone changes abruptly and he becomes a figure of menacing control and intrusion. "I want her under twenty-four hour observation. I want a complete set of blood work. Chemical and electrolyte analysis by the end of the day," he barks to his underlings. Alice remains uncharacteristically weak, her body bereft of strength, her mouth only able to form partial words. She has been robbed of her identity and is apparently in awe of the scientist's overwhelming presence. A study on the psychological effects of child abuse observes that abused children "feel physically and morally helpless, their personalities are not sufficiently consolidated in order to be able to protest, even if only in thought, for the overpowering force and authority of the adult makes them dumb and can rob them of their senses" (Rashkin 163). Such is Alice's affect at this juncture: a child whose body and mind are in thrall to her abuser.

When the doctor asks Alice if she remembers her name, the question is a catalyst for a rapid series of flashbacks that suggest an incestuous component to their relationship. Alice's subconscious begins to pour forth images of her recent past and her fight against Umbrella. Prominent amongst these are shots of Alice lying, naked and vulnerable, on a surgical gurney, juxtaposed with images of Angela Ashford (Sophie Vavasseur), a child whose life Alice has recently saved. The flashback sequence climaxes with Isaacs leaning over the supine Alice in a threatening and proprietary fashion, his face moving ever closer to hers. As he looms over her helpless body, a half-smile on his face, he appears the villain of melodrama, about to take from the heroine what, he might say, is rightfully his. By presenting Isaacs' treatment of Alice as a figurative rape, and by visually linking Alice with a threatened girl, the scene is steeped in connotations of incestuous assault perpetrated against a child.

Like many an abused child, Alice moves from a psychological position in which she has no conscious memory of abuse to one in which she is fully cognizant of these memories. When Dr. Isaacs wakes her, he tries to ascertain whether she remembers anything of their relationship. He touches her gently on the neck, stares meaningfully into her eyes, and intones seductively, "Look at me. Can you remember anything? You remember your name?" Isaacs asks these questions in the hope that she does not remember. He wants a malleable subject, not a rebel who resents his litany of surgical atrocities. The subsequent flashback sequence, in which Alice remembers her abuse at the doctor's hands, allows her to quickly leave behind her helpless, infantile state. Adopting an assertive and wry expression, she states, "My name is Alice, and I remember everything." This is no small statement in an era of recovered memory. Like a woman who has become suddenly aware of abuse suffered as a child, the heroine takes control of the past and declares that her recollections are factual.

Alice will tangle with other abusive father figures. Major Cain (Thomas Kretschmann), like Isaacs, is associated with penetrative imagery, needles and tubing thrust into the bodies of his unfortunate test subjects. He injects the T-virus into Alice and another survivor of the events of *Resident Evil*, Matt

Addison (Eric Mabius). Matt is a particularly youthful-looking adult. He is defined by the notably boyish motivation of rescuing his sister from inside an Umbrella facility. Matt is chosen by Cain to become the main guinea pig in the so-called Nemesis Program. Thereafter, he is transformed into Nemesis, a grotesque, lumbering, growling beast with no will of his own. Matt is robbed of language, left with only a glimmer of his former self, and dominated by his creator, Major Cain. Like Alice, he demonstrates the personality of an abused child.

"You're like brother and sister," Cain tells Alice and Matt. "Don't you understand how important you are to me?" he asks in paternal fashion. Like many an abusive patriarch he will employ language which is, by turns, uplifting and damning. "You are magnificent," he tells Alice, but later concludes "you're such a disappointment to me." He will even force his creations to fight one another. While he does so ostensibly to discover which of the pair might be utilized as a prototypical weapon marketed by the Umbrella Corporation, he has engineered a nightmarish scenario of domestic abuse in which two children are goaded to fight for their father's affection.

The series includes only one literal father, Dr. Ashford (Jared Harris), a wheelchair-bound Umbrella scientist who spends much of *Resident Evil: Apocalypse* searching for his missing child, Angela. At first glance, Ashford would seem to be quite a sympathetic character. His relentless quest to recover his daughter seems to stem from genuine feeling. He may have invented the T-virus which will, over the course of the series, lay waste to the planet, but he did not intend that his creation get out of hand. "He's not a bad man. He didn't mean for any of this," Angela tells us. The virus was originally a serum intended as a cure to a debilitating disease that Ashford passed on to his daughter. And yet, we are never quite sure whether to trust him. He is, after all, an important figure in a malevolent corporation. And most damningly, like the other fathers we have met, Ashford has been reckless with his daughter's body. When Alice and her compatriots discover Angela, the girl pulls up her sleeve to reveal a multitude of puncture marks. At this point in the narrative, it is unclear what the source of these wounds may be and the movie allows us time to develop our suspicions. We soon discover that the holes in the girl's arm were caused by her father's experiments. Because we have witnessed Alice and Matt undergo procedures comparable to this, Angela seems another in a long line of children abused by Umbrella's patriarchs. Ultimately, we discover that Ashford penetrated his daughter's body, and risked great injury to her, because he loved her. Many sexually abusive fathers have made a similar claim.

Although Alice may recover, to some extent, from her fathers' unwelcome attentions, the *Resident Evil* movies remain haunted by the specter of incest and pedophilia. The Red Queen and the White Queen are Umbrella computer systems represented visually by holograms of prepubescent girls wearing night-dresses. Interaction with the computers is achieved by talking to these ghostly images. Each is able to reply in a natural, conversational manner so that to communicate with them is, essentially, to talk to a child. The children who have lent their image to the Red and White Queens are the daughters of Umbrella scientists. The Red Queen, we hear, is "modeled after the head programmer's daughter." In scenes that feature these computers we are offered the spectacle of little girls created and programmed by their fathers. These "children" are disturbing manifestations of complete paternal control.

While the Queens are immensely powerful devices, they frequently represent vulnerability. Their strangely inappropriate attire and placement in sterile, underground laboratories suggest utter defenselessness. The Red Queen will undergo an assault by a team of commandos attempting to gain access to the underground facility over which she presides. For most of *Resident Evil*'s running time, the paramilitary team will attempt to "access" the Red Queen, get through her "defense mechanisms," and "shut her down." As the group makes its way further and further into the Red Queen's inner sanctum, by attempting to hack into her programming, we witness a disturbing invasion of a little girl's private space. The insurgents struggle for superiority. "Red Queen's defenses are in place, she's making it difficult," complains one of their number, continuing, "She'll say anything to stop us shutting her down." At one point, a commando calls the Red Queen a "homicidal bitch." It is quite disconcerting, but entirely appropriate in a sequence that plays out like a protracted sexual assault, to hear this abusive term applied to the child. The process of invasion reaches an end with the child pleading, "Get out, get out. You can't be in here" and, "I implore you please, please."

Conclusion: "My Name is Alice"

During the last two decades, explicit references to sexual abuse have been incorporated, as never before, into virtually every arena of culture. Cinema has embraced the subject. *Natural Born Killers*, *Happiness*, *Magnolia*, *The Pledge*, and *Mystic River* all focus on the sexual abuse of children. The most hard-hitting films on sexual violation—such as *Baise-moi*, *Irréversible*, and *The War Zone*—emerged from European art-house cinema. TV shows, such as *Law and Order: Special Victims Unit* and *To Catch a Predator* build narratives around the bringing of a pedophile to justice. Online videogame players routinely "rape" each other. For instance, many in the *Gears of War* gaming community make sure to perform a ritualistic sexual assault on the bodies of their slain enemies. Their avatar can be made to perform pelvic thrusts over a virtual corpse, the action known among aficionados as "raping." Jokes about sexual abuse have become a staple of the comedy landscape. The satirical British comedy show *Brass Eye* presented its pioneering and highly controversial "Paedogeddon!" episode in 2001. The animated comedy series *Family Guy* introduced a neighborhood pedophile as a regular character in 2005. In the U.S., jokes about prison rape have become so common that the Justice Department recently released a statement acknowledging that, "In popular culture, prison rape is often the subject of jokes," and adding "sexual abuse is never a laughing matter" (Cushman 17). In 2011, Zinoman suggested that jokes about rape were becoming a motif in the work of female comedians. Pornography has, of late, become more invested in the iconography of assault. Hedges comments that "the most successful porn films keep pushing the physical and emotional boundaries of the women on screen and incorporate an expanding array of physically and verbally abusive acts" (68). Whether our cultural products encourage us to laugh at, celebrate, or be horrified by abuse, they betray a deeply felt anxiety surrounding the subject.

Even though the *Resident Evil* movies seem highly influenced by our culture of sexual trauma, they rarely make explicit mention of rape and never openly discuss incest or pedophilia. They take a far more veiled approach. Scholars have repeatedly contended that an artwork's profound interest in sexual trauma may not be immediately apparent. Rashkin makes a convincing argument that *The Picture of Dorian Gray*, a novel popularly regarded as having a homosexual subtext, also incorporates "a complex saga of child abuse ... inscribed cryptically within the narrative" (158). In an influential essay on *Last Year at Marienbad*, Higgins claims that rape may be discernible, not so much in the film's narrative, as in its imagery: "If rape as event has been suppressed from the story, it is present as discourse, dispersed in multiple thematic codes. It is represented symbolically by a series of broken things: a glass, ... [a] shoe, later a balustrade.... It is present in the theme of penetration (into rooms, into thoughts)" (19). As Rashkin notes, we must sometimes look "deeply into ... [a] text's overdetermined language (including visual, filmic language) to locate dramas too distressing or disruptive to be put into words" (17).

While there is a cultural need for explicit exploration of sexual abuse, there often exists a desire to tackle this fraught subject in a more indirect manner. The *Resident Evil* movies allow us this indirect approach by offering a modern myth: a vast, cataclysmic, otherworldy universe within which the terrible subject of sexual violence is confronted but never named. The story of Alice comes complete with journeys to the Underworld (in each movie she breaches the portals of an underground Umbrella facility), an apocalyptic backdrop (the end of the world is nigh as almost every human is transformed into a zombie), and the slaying of fearsome father figures (the abusive corporate patriarchs). Along the way, she must defeat a parade of towering monsters. And, as the series goes on, Alice will become godlike. In *Resident Evil: Extinction* she harnesses the elements, creating a vast, fiery vortex to destroy a flock of homicidal birds. In *Resident Evil: Afterlife* she is able to rupture the ground with a thought. Indeed, she will become a Fury, revenging herself upon the hubristic Umbrella Corporation.

By mythologizing our collective trauma, the *Resident Evil* movies offer hope that the evil of abuse might be defeated. The more explicit portrayals of sexual abuse rarely offer such optimism. Indeed, they usually admit defeat, stressing only blighted lives and endless contagion. As Lee notes, "the film industry, the fantasy industry" frequently maintains "that pedophilia and child sexual abuse is unstoppable" (12). He demonstrates how, "*Mystic River's* unsubtle use of ... [the trope of vampirism] maintains the myth that the abused are forever tainted, for once bitten there is no release" (223). Rejecting such a philosophy, Alice will struggle with her abusers and often succeed in besting them. "They thought they were safe in their hi-tech fortress, but they were wrong," she tells us in *Resident Evil: Afterlife*, before leading a devastating assault against an Umbrella citadel. In becoming a figure of vengeance, Alice forcefully states that sexual abuse can be eradicated, its legacy terminated. In the real world, this outcome is, of course, an impossibility. But, in the realm of myth, we may accept it and achieve a catharsis, a temporary relief from despair that more naturalistic portrayals of sexual abuse do not provide.

Another optimistic pleasure offered by the *Resident Evil* movies is their focus on survival. Alice will endure her ordeals, reliably returning to the fray, bloodied but unbowed. In every *Resident Evil* movie the heroine will place great emphasis on uttering the words, "My name is Alice." By doing so she asserts that, despite the Umbrella Corporation's abuses, she retains a coherent identity. In naming herself, Alice also suggests that she is engaged in a form of therapy. The preamble, "My name is..." is widely recognized as a motif of the survivors group, the first words of a confessional statement delivered by someone recovering from the ravages of alcohol, incest, or any other debilitating experience. Alice declares that she is a survivor, engaged in a series of psychological triumphs and setbacks, that one day, maybe, will lead to freedom from the past.

The emphasis on retribution and survival might explain why the *Resident Evil* films have built such a loyal following. The critical community often expresses exasperation that these popcorn blockbusters have achieved enormous popularity. The late Roger Ebert, America's most renowned movie commentator, angrily argued of *Resident Evil: Apocalypse*, "The movie is an utterly meaningless waste of time. There was no reason to produce it, except to make money, and there is no reason to see it, except to spend money.... Parents: If you encounter teenagers who say they liked this movie, do not let them date your children." While such critical admonitions are amusing, they may be missing the point. The *Resident Evil* films fulfill a need to see the vast, disturbing panorama of sexual abuse played out on an epic scale. Certainly, their success is partly due Milla Jovavich's nubile charms. However, there are many other movies, in the horror genre and elsewhere, that place greater emphasis on their heroine's sex appeal. It is notable that, over the course of five *Resident Evil* films, there exists not one conventional sex scene. It might also be claimed that the moments of spectacular violence keep audiences coming back. Of course this is true, but if violence is what viewers want, there are a plethora of far more gory works to choose from, for example the "torture porn" movies that appeared concurrently with the *Resident Evil* franchise. What the *Resident Evil* movies offer, the factor that makes them unique and enormously popular, is an ability to transport us to a place where the monster of sexual violence can be confronted and, at least temporarily, slain.

Works Cited

Baise-moi. Dir. Virginie Despentes and Coralie Trinh-Thi. FilmFixx, 2000. DVD.

The Birth of a Nation. Dir. D.W. Griffith. Epoch Producing, 1915. DVD.

Caputi, Jane. *Goddesses and Monsters: Women, Myth, Power, and Popular Culture.* Madison: University of Wisconsin/Popular Press, 2004. Print.

Carroll, Lewis. *Alice's Adventures in Wonderland; And, Through the Looking-glass and What Alice Found There.* New York: Penguin Classics, 2009. Print.

Clark, Simon. "The Undead Martyr: Sex, Death, and Revolution in George Romero's Zombie Films." *The Undead and Philosophy: Chicken Soup for the Soulless.* Chicago: Open Court, 2006. 197–210. Print.

Cushman, John H. "U.S. Issues Far-Reaching Rules to Stem Prison Rape." *New York Times.* 17 May 2012. Web. 23 May 2012.

Death Wish. Dir. Michael Winner. Paramount Pictures, 1974. DVD.

Ebert, Roger. "Resident Evil: Apocalypse." Rev. of *Resident Evil: Apocalypse. Chicago Sun Times.* 10 Sept. 2004. Web. 15 June 2012.

The Exterminator. Dir. James Glickenhaus. Avco Embassy Pictures, 1980. DVD.

Fitzgerald, Nora, and Jack Riley. "Drug Facilitated Rape: Looking for the Missing Pieces." *National Institute of Justice Journal* 243 (2000): 9–15. *National Institute of Justice.* Web. 10 June 2012.

Happiness. Dir. Todd Solondz. October Films, 1998. DVD.

Harper, Stephen. "I Could Kiss You, You Bitch": Race, Gender, and Sexuality in the *Resident Evil* Movies." *Jump Cut* 49. Spring (2007). Web. 27 Apr. 2012.

Hedges, Chris. *Empire of Illusion: The End of Literacy and the Triumph of Spectacle.* New York: Nation, 2009. Print.

Higgins, Lynn A. "Screen/Memory: Rape and Its Alibis in Last Year at Marienbad." *Rape in Art Cinema.* New York: Continuum, 2010. 15–26. Print.

Irréversible. Dir. Gaspar Noe. Mars Distribution, 2002. DVD.

Isely, Paul J. "Child Sexual Abuse and the Catholic Church: An Historical and Contemporary Review." *Pastoral Psychology* 45.4 (1997): 277–99. Print.

Jarzombek, Mark. "The Post-traumatic Turn and the Art of Walid Ra'ad and Krzysztof Wodiczko: From Theory to Trope to Beyond." *Trauma and Visuality in Modernity.* Hanover, NH: Dartmouth College, 2006. 249–71. Print.

Kaplan, E. Ann. *Trauma Culture: The Politics of Terror and Loss in Media and Literature.* New Brunswick, NJ: Rutgers University Press, 2005. Print.

Lee, Jason. *Pervasive Perversions: Paedophilia and Child Sexual Abuse in Media/Culture.* London: Free Association, 2005. Print.

Lowenstein, Adam. *Shocking Representation: Historical Trauma, National Cinema, and the Modern Horror Film.* New York: Columbia University Press, 2005. Print.

Luckhurst, Roger. *The Trauma Question.* London: Routledge, 2008. Print.

MacFarlane, Seth, prod. *Family Guy.* Fox. Television.

Magnolia. Dir. Paul Thomas Anderson. New Line Cinema, 1999. DVD.

Morris, Chris, prod. "Paedogeddon!" *Brass Eye.* BBC. London, 26 July 2001. Television.

Mystic River. Dir. Clint Eastwood. Village Roadshow Pictures, 2003. DVD.

Natural Born Killers. Dir. Oliver Stone. Warner Bros., 1994. DVD.

The Pledge. Dir. Sean Penn. Warner Bros., 2001. DVD.

Rabin, Nathan. "Resident Evil: Apocalypse." *The A.V. Club.* 14 Sept. 2004. Web. 4 June 2012.

Rashkin, Esther. *Unspeakable Secrets and the Psychoanalysis of Culture.* Albany, NY: SUNY, 2008. Print.

Rebecca. Dir. Alfred Hitchcock. Selznick International Pictures, 1940. DVD.

Resident Evil. Dir. Paul Thomas Anderson. Screen Gems, 2002. DVD.

Resident Evil: Afterlife. Dir. Paul Thomas Anderson. Screen Gems, 2010. DVD.

Resident Evil: Apocalypse. Dir. Alexander Witt. Screen Gems, 2004. DVD.

Resident Evil: Extinction. Dir. Russell Mulcahy. Screen Gems, 2007. DVD.

Resident Evil: Retribution. Dir. Paul Thomas Anderson. Screen Gems, 2012. DVD.

To Catch a Predator. MSNBC. Television.

Walker, Janet. *Trauma Cinema: Documenting Incest and the Holocaust.* Berkeley: University of California, 2005. Print.

The War Zone. Dir. Tim Roth. Lot 47 Films, 1999. DVD.

Wolf, Dick, prod. *Law and Order: Special Victims Unit.* NBC. Television.

Zinoman, Jason. "Female Comedians, Breaking the Taste-Taboo Ceiling." *New York Times.* 15 Nov. 2011. Web. 09 June 2012.

The Woman in the Red Dress: Sexuality, Femmes Fatales, the Gaze and Ada Wong

Jenny Platz

The world of *Resident Evil* is eerily similar to the worlds of film noir, reflecting noir plots and themes of betrayal, paranoia, the unknown, destruction, and the constant interaction with death. At the center of the mysteries of the *Resident Evil* games 2, 4, and 6 is the beautiful Ada Wong. Ada is constantly covered in shadows, hiding behind her many facades, and she never allows Leon or the player to fully understand her motives. Through her connection to the Umbrella Corporation, Ada is part of the darkness that surrounds Raccoon City and is a threat, a figure that uses her charms to further her own agenda. Ada is a femme fatale, a force out of film noir whose power lies in her sexuality. Through this power, the femmes fatales are given access to traits typically associated with male agency, money, and the pursuit of knowledge. Like the other femmes fatales from the 1940s, Ada's sexuality grants her power over men, causing her to alter the status quo of gender norms, and become a threat to male heterosexuality.

Ada closely follows theorist Yvonne Tasker's definition of the femme fatale in her book *Girls: Gender and Sexuality in Popular Cinema*, where Tasker qualifies the aspects that create a femme fatale (120). According to Tasker, femmes fatales are defined by four aspects. First, the women are always seductive with heightened sexuality. Second, this sexuality is what grants the women power over men. The third point states that the femme fatale is surrounded by confusion and deception. Her role in the story is ambiguous. And finally, the women are an enigma themselves, placed in the center of a story where the main character is seeking the truth (120).

All these traits result in male anxiety due to the woman's refusal to fit into patriarchal values. These women are often juxtaposed to the "good" women of film noirs. These "good" women follow the rules of the patriarchy and are depicted as lacking sexuality, and therefore become symbols of purity (121).

Ada's sexuality is tied to her identity in the games, where she is often introduced in the game through her body parts, revealing her sexual charms to both Leon and the players. Ada fulfills Tasker's second trait through her interactions with Leon, manipulating him in *Resident Evil 2* into aiding her on her quest, and in later games, repeatedly saving her life. Because Leon never reveals his reasoning for loving and trusting Ada, the player can only rely on cinematic clues that suggest that Leon is fascinated with her because of her alluring body. Tasker's third and fourth aspects of a femme fatale are revealed through Ada's mysterious role as a double agent, a role that is never fully explained in any of the games, as well as her central linkage to the plot in each game. In *Resident Evil 2* and *4* her role as a double agent moves the plot forward, providing crucial information to Leon and the player, as well as establishing transitions to the 5th and 6th games. Finally, the plot of *Resident Evil 6* literally revolves around Ada and the mystery that surrounds her.

But Ada differs from her femme fatale counter parts of the 1940s and 50s, and proves to be the ultimate incarnation of Tasker's femme fatale. As Tasker reveals, femmes fatales are mysterious creatures that can never be fully understood (120). But femmes fatales usually lose their aura of mystery during the climax of the films, where their double motives are revealed and the hero of the noir figures out her agenda. He knows that she is a non-trustworthy vixen who will stop at nothing for money, power, and revenge. *Scarlet Street* illustrates the reveal of the femme fatale's mystery when Edward G. Robinson's character Chris learns that his kept woman is cheating on him, and only pretending to be interested in him for money. Through this reveal, the femmes fatales become monsters and corrupted women capable of murder. In contrast, Leon and the player never understand Ada, and it remains unclear whether or not her motives are tied to money, power, or revenge. Ada is the real puzzle of the *Resident Evil* series that will never be solved. Because the puzzle of Ada is never solved, she is also never viewed as a monster.

In opposition to classic femmes fatales who are never granted the power to alter the gaze or use their bodies as physical weapons, Ada proves to have bodily and narrative powers outside of her sexuality. Ada uses her body to fight zombies and infected villagers throughout the games and is not forced to use unreliable guns that run out of bullets, proving to be useless. Through this trait Ada is astute where other characters of the games can be clumsy, and can transform her sexuality into a physical manifestation where femmes fatales can only have sexual powers. Although femmes fatales Phyllis from *Double Indemnity* and Kathie from *Out of the Past*, played by Barbara Stanwyck and Jane Greer, are master seductresses, they are both useless in a physical fight, and would meet their ends quickly in the zombie filled hallways and corridors of the *Resident Evil* series.

In the mini game in *Resident Evil 4* and her section in *Resident Evil 6*, Ada possesses the power of the gaze. She is the only femme fatale to have a continuous point of view that the player must experience the games through. Although femmes fatales are at times granted momentary point of view shots in films, the femmes fatales are never allowed to be the main character of the story, and must rely on the hero's gaze to be brought into the world of the noir. Ada is the main character of her stories, and at times forces the male heroes to rely on her point of view to exist in the games. Most importantly is Ada's power of the gaze and her ability to grant the player valuable information in *Resident Evil 2*. In the game, Ada learns through Annette of Dr. Birkin's death and the spread of the T-virus to Raccoon City. Through the flashbacks Annette sets up, Ada's disrupts the traditional male power of the gaze by infiltrating point of view shots of the male characters in the flashback sequence. Although the male characters Dr. Birkin and HUNK have point of view shots in the sequence, the player only sees these sequences through Ada's vision of the events Annette is describing. The shots therefore become point of view shots of a woman. Therefore, the way noir heroes grant life to femmes fatales through their gazes, Ada's grants life to the mysterious origins of the Raccoon City Incident.

Perhaps most noteworthy is Ada's ability to be reborn. Because femmes fatales disrupt the gender restrictions society places onto women, they are always eliminated in the films. The women are punished for their power through prison or death. Kathie from *Out of the Past* dies in a car crash/shoot out, and Brigid goes to jail at the end of *The Maltese Falcon*. Despite dying several times in all games, Ada rises from the ashes, and gives a much-needed helping hand to Leon during his final confrontations with his foes, and therefore continues her necromantic adventures in other games. Ada thusly becomes a femme fatale worthy of celebration. She holds all the strong characteristics of a femme fatale of the 1940s and 50s, but does not have to come to a tragic end in exchange for her power. Ada has a future, where the other femmes fatales only have an end.

Film Noir's Origins and Modern Concerns in Society

The film noir style emerged in the 1940s during World War II. The original style lasted until the mid–1950s, and was reborn again as neo noir in the 1960s and 70s (Krutnik 15). In the mid 1940s, French critics labeled the films noirs, or black films, addressing the dark nature of the Hollywood films (Doane

102). Films such as the 1940 film *Stranger on the Third Floor*, 1941's *The Maltese Falcon,* and *Double Indemnity* from 1944 are classic examples of noir.

The style of film noir was a response to the horrors of the war, which were reflected through the dark mise-en-scène of the films, low-key lighting, the loose morals of the film's characters, and the crime centric plots (Cowie 126–127). Because of the trauma of the Holocaust and the Nazis, the world was no longer a sunny beautiful place, but a dark world where no one could be trusted and death lurked around every corner. Noirs physically represent this cinematic transformation in Hollywood where brightly lit and joyous musicals such as *The Wizard of Oz* and *Top Hat* were replaced by dark and dreary films of noir. The reality of death is seen in every film noir where the body count is always high, and in some cases such as *Sunset Boulevard* and *Double Indemnity*, the hero of the film even dies, revealing that no one is safe anymore, even in films. The main character dying in a film in an unromantic and pointless way was practically non-existent in Hollywood before noirs.

The world of noirs is uncannily similar to the world of survival horror in the *Resident Evil* game series. Although noir motifs often appear in action and detective style video games, most notably in Rockstar's *L.A. Noire*, the *Resident Evil* series is one of the few survivor horror games to rely on the film style for visual and thematic effects. The striking feature of film noir is low-key lighting and dark atmosphere. In all *Resident Evil* games the setting is usually at night, and in dark and shadowy places such as an abandoned police station, gothic mansion, sewers, a castle, or a laboratory. The sequences that take place during the day in *Resident Evil 4* and *5* never allow the mise-en-scène of the games to become bright and cheery. Instead the sky is overcast such as in *4*, or the players have to go into dark caves or buildings with no light. The general atmosphere of noirs and *Resident Evil* is also filled with death. In noir films, characters often die midway through the film and detectives are routinely coming across dead bodies. In the world of *Resident Evil*, dead bodies are literally walking around, and usually bloodstains and grime make up the art direction.

Underneath the blood, grime, and shadows that make up the world of noirs and *Resident Evil* is the belief that no one is safe anymore and no one can be trusted. Pearl Harbor and the Japanese Internment suggested that there were spies in America, implanting paranoia in the nation. In noirs, paranoia proves to be founded in truth in that characters constantly betray each other, wives cheat on and kill their husbands, partners steal from each other, and childhood friends are revealed as killers of children. Noirs such as *Double Indemnity*, *The Maltese Falcon*, and *Kiss Me Deadly* reflect the concern with the ability to trust others, where all the leading women of each film initially present themselves as victims, and then betray and even kill their male counter parts. The inability to trust partners is apparent through Wesker and Barry in the game *Resident Evil I*, and Nicolas in the game *Resident Evil 3: Nemesis*. Moreover, these games address noirs' concerns with women and their inability to be trustworthy.

Much of the mistrust associated with film noir is located through the femme fatale. The femme fatale character emerged in the film style as a response to males' fears and anxieties associated with women's new place in society. During World War II women infiltrated the male workplace, working in factories, offices, and other places their husbands, fathers, and brothers once worked (Martin 203). This female invasion resulted in male anxiety of losing their place in society to women, who were increasingly gaining power in the world. This fear is addressed in film noirs through the femme fatale. In *Double Indemnity* Phyllis' powers to infiltrate the male patriarchy is seen through her hand in the murder of her husband, as well as her ability to control Walter and bring him into the world of crime. Through her power Phyllis invades the space of the male patriarchy, resulting in the death of two men.

The Resident Evil video games can also be connected to the social climate of the times each game was released in. The games depict contemporary fears of global terrorism, bio warfare and pharmaceutical control, as well as government conspiracies. This is seen in the games through the spread and modification of Las Plagas parasite and the various incarnations of the G, C, and T-virus. These diseases infect villages and cities, eliminating the resident population. *Resident Evil 4* and *6* complicate the use of the infection by allowing the player's character to become infected with the virus. This happens in *Resident Evil 4* when Leon is implanted with the Las Plagas parasite, and in *Resident Evil 6* where the characters Leon and Helena can be turned into zombies by a poisonous fog. Fears of the global spread of terrorism have become valid after 9/11, and the potential spread of uncontrollable diseases can be seen through the media's portrayal of SARS, swine flu, and the avian flu. Mirroring real life concerns, in the *Resident Evil* series no one is safe anymore, and bio warfare and other uncontrollable diseases can strike at anytime.

Through the *Resident Evil* series' reflection of society's new concerns and fears, the games resemble the way film noirs reflect society's fears during and after World War II. The incorporation of film noir aesthetics and tones into the survival horror game genre also indicates the cultural need to return to the film style. The games do not reflect the same fears as the noirs however, suggesting that the femme fatale may not have to suffer the same consequences as the classic femme fatale. Ada's refusal to die or simply go away indicates the transformation of society's fears and its ability to deal with strong, and therefore threatening women. Interestingly, Hollywood does not seem as ready as the video game genre to reward the femme fatale, where neo noirs such as *L.A.*

Confidential and *Brick* either purify the fatale into marriage, or punish the fatale through assumed imprisonment. As the paper will explore, unlike the other fatales Ada does not have to die, or stay dead after she is "killed" because of her power.

Tasker's First Trait: Women with Heightened Sexualities

Tasker reveals the first aspect that defines the femme fatale is her sexuality, therefore revealing the women are always identified through their bodies. Author Janey Place writes in her article "Women in Film Noir" that women are defined by their physical appearances in film noirs (54). Place also explains the role the camera plays in the objectification of the women. In film noirs the femmes fatales are linked to the composition of the film and use their sexuality to attract the camera's and viewers' gaze. This is exhibited in such films as *Gilda*, where the camera constantly lingers on Rita Hayworth's title character. In the film, Gilda is usually placed in the center of the screen, visually attracting the viewer. In other films such as *Double Indemnity*, low angles are used to both accent Phyllis' legs, as well as reveal her seductive powers. She is attracting the direction of the camera's gaze.

Although the women possess power through their sexuality, the gaze consequently exploits the women. The gaze in the films not only objectifies the women by placing her identity onto her appearance, but it also fragments the women (54–55). Again, this is seen in *Double Indemnity* where the camera slowly tilts up Phyllis' legs during her introduction, and also in *Gilda* where the gaze is focused on Gilda's hair and face, also during her on screen introduction. Through the camera angles, the women's body parts are fragmented from the rest of their bodies. The scenes introducing Phyllis and Gilda only allow the women's legs or head to appear on the screen, detached from the rest of their bodies. They are only identified as their legs or hair. Place suggests that this fragmentation of the femmes fatales' bodies is in order to punish her. The women's fragmented parts, legs and hair, are sexually threatening. For this threat, the women must be punished through objectification and fragmentation. Visual control is not allowed. Otherwise this power will remain unchecked, and will destroy the male patriarchy (57). In most cases this punishment is very severe and the women are killed during the film's climax.

The role of the camera and its negative effect on women is also apparent through Ada in *Resident Evil 2* and *4*. The introductions of Ada closely follow the conventions of the male gaze, which Laura Mulvey addresses in "Visual Pleasures of Narrative Cinema." According to Mulvey's theory, the woman is the object of the male gaze, and acts a threatening reminder of castration (14–

19). Because of this the woman is punished through the film's narrative or cinematography, fragmenting her body (22). Ada allows herself to be the object of the male player's and characters' gaze, and any threat of castration she may possess is removed through her punishment. When Ada is first visually introduced in the world of *Resident Evil*, her feminine assets are made clear through Leon's and the player's gaze. After an unknown person narrowly misses shooting Leon, the camera cuts to Ada. The gaze starts at the bottom of her feet, and then slowly tilts up her legs. Ada is wearing a dress with black leggings, garments that reveal and accentuate her shapely form. Through this introduction, Ada is linked to her appearance (Mulvey 19).

In *Resident Evil 4*, Ada is introduced similarly. The first glimpse Leon and the player have of Ada is after she saves Leon from Bitores Mendez. During this scene, a mysterious stranger shoots Mendez's arm, freeing Leon from his grasp. When Leon looks up to his savior, all he can see is a woman in a red dress and her bare legs. The mysterious woman/Ada is later seen again when she puts a gun to Leon's head. After Leon gets the best of her by knocking the gun out of her hand, the two engage in a slow motion fight, where the camera once again remains on Ada's legs as she does cartwheels in her high slit dress. Her *Resident Evil 4* introduction continues the display of Ada's bodily identification. Ada is linked to her appearance; she is known and even recognizable by her feminine charms, specifically her legs and her trademark red clothes. She cinematically fulfills Tasker's first trait of what a femme fatale is, a woman with heightened sexuality (120). But like the femmes fatales of classic noir, Ada's role as seductress is at the price of her visual fragmentation. The close-ups of her legs cinematically chops off her limbs from the rest of her body, fragmenting her and allowing her legs to become fetishized.

Tasker's Second Trait: Femme Fatale's Power and Strength as Located in Their Sexualities

The femmes fatales' heightened sexualities are what grants them power over men. Through the women's allure, they are able to manipulate men into doing their bidding and trusting and following the fatales into crime. The power femmes fatales have over men often results in plots where the fatale and her new lover kill her husband, the hero "saves" her from her gangster boyfriend, and he aides her in the betrayal and theft of the wealth of the fatales' past lovers. Most of the actions the heroes commit are in regards to the femmes fatales' desires, or in the least connected to her in the overall trajectory of the story. The doings of the heroes are often actions they would not take if they were not under the thrall of the fatale. The power of the fatale to influence men to go against their character is notably seen in *Out of the Past* and *Double Indemnity*, films where both heroes betray their friends and morals because they are in love with a femme fatale.

Ada's fighting style and role of seductress also grant her power. Ada's greatest power over Leon is her sexuality and aura of mystery. In *Resident Evil 2*, because Ada is intriguing and alluring, Leon is drawn to her and feels he must protect her. Leon's attraction towards Ada is visually displayed through his point of view shot when he scans Ada's body in *Resident Evil 2* and *4*, and his constant flirtation with her throughout all the other games. Leon's interactions with Ada are also markedly different than his interactions with Claire, who represents the "good" woman of noirs that Tasker juxtaposes with the femme fatale (121). After the game's opening, Leon does not insist on escorting Claire throughout the police station in order to protect her. In contrast, Leon always insists on protecting Ada, and is annoyed when she runs off. The only difference between Leon's relationship with Claire and Ada, is Leon's fascination towards Ada and the gaze he casts onto her. Leon never objectifies Claire, despite her revealing biker shorts. He cannot understand Ada's mysterious ways and her refusal to submit to his patriarchy power, whereas Claire submits to his power by agreeing to go and temporarily stay in the police station. Claire listens to a man, the way the patriarchy informs women to do. Notably, Rebecca Chambers and Jill Valentine of *Resident Evil 1* are other incarnations of Tasker's "good" women (121), where both are desexualized, and in Jill's case, masculinized through army fatigues.

Because of his fascination with Ada, Leon takes a bullet for her and struggles to save her, despite the realization that she is a double agent for an Umbrella-like company. In *Resident Evil 4*, now knowing Ada's to be a double agent, Leon still actively tries to save her, and even trusts her enough to lower his weapons when face to face with her. Ada's power over Leon is once more made apparent through his verbal and physical proclamation of his feelings toward her in *Resident Evil 2*, his mourning for her during the ending sequence in *2*, his constant flirting with her in *Resident Evil 4,* and his shielding of her from bullets in *Resident Evil 6*. Leon is attracted to and cares for Ada, despite her constant rejection of him and her dubious behavior.

Ada's power of sexuality in manipulating men is also apparent in her power of body. In all of Ada's game appearances she proves capable of surviving in a world of monsters. She is able to easily defeat zombies and lickers, and can match strengths with Leon and the super monsters of the games. But Ada's strength is different than Leon's strength, or even Claire's and Jill's, and is located in her body and not in guns, bombs, or other weapons that all other characters must rely on in *Resident Evil 1–5*. The power of body Ada possesses is seen during her fight sequence with Leon in *Resident Evil 4*. During the scene where the two pull weapons on each other, Ada uses an oriental fighting style of cartwheels and other gymnastics. Everything about Ada, especially her fighting and escaping skills, are graceful. Her movements are not only functional, killing or disabling her attackers, but also are beautiful. Ada uses the same artistic methods of fighting against the villagers and Krauser during the *Separate Ways* mini-game. These movements are unique in the game, where other women and men do not engage in the delicate and dance like fighting styles, but instead just stab, or shoot each other and rarely use physical attacks. Ada's power is her body, and although she proves herself to be a weapons expert as well, her body remains her main strength; although interestingly, it is not until *Resident Evil 6* where characters and players are able to freely rely on physical attacks to fight zombies and other creatures. This is a contrast to *Resident Evil 4 and 5,* the only other games to allow physical combat where players are only able to use physical attacks during specific quick time scenes or as combo plays. However, Ada's exotic fighting style still remains unique in the series, where the new combat feature lacks the grace and poise of Ada's skills.

In addition, Ada also uses accessories to aide in her fights and escape methods. During the scene where Ada first reveals herself to Leon, she depends on her feminine powers of accessories by using her pink glasses to blind Leon with a flash. Because Leon disarmed her, without the glasses Ada would not have been able to distract him, retrieve her gun, and cleanly escape. Ada's merging of her sexuality and weapons is also located in her grappling gun. Although not a feminized weapon, Ada's use of the grappling gun when she is with Leon becomes sexualized. During the scene where Ada and Leon are on the boat traveling to the island, Ada uses the gun to escape from Leon and continue on her secret mission. Through the use of the gun, Ada allows Leon and the player to see up her dress and her bare legs. The use of the gun seduces Leon and calls attention to her femininity. Although not a weapon, in *Resident Evil 6* Ada uses a makeup compact to hide a data chip regarding Derek C. Simmons and his worldwide crimes. Through the makeup compact Ada's power of intellect and espionage become physically and literally placed in the feminine, a linkage to her body.

As Tasker's second trait of femmes fatales describes, fatales' powers are located in their bodies and seductive powers over men (120). Ada proves this definition through her manipulation of Leon's aide, and later the ability to hold his favor after he learns of her double motives. She also uses her body as a weapon when she fights Leon and villagers in *Resident Evil 4*, and her skills in her feminized and sexualized weapons and accessories such as the grappling gun and sunglasses. Although Ada's sexuality allows for the diminishing gaze of the camera, a fate classic femmes fatales share, her sexuality and body is what empowers her to attack and defend herself against foes and creatures, a trait that classic femmes fatales do not carry. Through her power of body, Ada transforms the negative effects of the objectifying gaze into another tool she can use to provide safety and security for herself.

Tasker's Third and Fourth Traits: Women as Deceptive Figures and Women as Enigmas

The two other traits Tasker assigns to femmes fatales, her role as an ambiguous and deceptive figure, and her role as a puzzle in a story built around investigation, can also be easily linked to Ada (120). Mary Ann Doane describes the femme fatale and her mystique in her book *Femme Fatales: Feminism, Film Theory, and Psychoanalysis.*

> The femme fatale is the figure of a certain discursive unease, a potential epistemological trauma. For her most striking characteristic, perhaps, is the fact that she never really is what she seems to be. She harbors a threat which is not entirely legible, predictable or manageable. In thus transforming the threat of the woman into a secret, something which must be aggressively revealed, unmasked, discovered, the figure is fully compatible with the epistemological drive of the narrative, the hermeneutic structuration of the classical text [1].

According to Mary Ann Doane and Tasker's third qualification of a fatale, all femmes fatales are located in mystery (120). The characters and the viewers are ignorant of the fatale's agendas and only know what they are allowed to see by the film. Moreover, while solving the central narrative mystery of the film, the male characters must also solve the femme fatale. Is she to be trusted or will she turn on him during the end of the film? These concerns are usually addressed during the climax of the film, where the femme fatale removes her façade of innocent victim and betrays the main character. The femme fatale's apparent goals are then revealed, such as their desires for money, power, or freedom. The mystery of the femme fatale is then solved, and the plot is nicely wrapped up through her death or imprisonment. But through understanding the femme fatale's motives the women lose their mystery. Therefore, they not only lose part of their identity, their aura of mystery, but lose their place as a femme fatale. The woman no longer carries the "discursive unease" (1) Mary Ann Doane writes about because the male hero has solved her mystery, which most likely resulted in her death. With the removal of her mystery, her threat is released and therefore she has no place in a film noir anymore, she ceases to exist.

Ada is a mystery that is never solved. When Ada is introduced in *Resident Evil 2,* she is in an aura of mystery. In the game Ada is constantly running off unannounced, and Leon and the player do not know aspects of her agenda until the end of the game. The characters in actuality only learn of her agenda as a double agent and not whatever personal or other agenda she may possess. The same can be said for *Resident Evil 4*, where again Leon and the player do not know what organization Ada is working for, or what Ada's relationship with Wesker is. The audience only knows she is a double agent with unknown motives. During the *Resident Evil 4* mini game, *Separate Ways*, and Ada's playthrough in *Resident Evil 6*, little information about her is given despite the game being told from Ada's point of view. Leon and the player are never granted access into Ada's mind beyond her point of view as a playable character, and what the game allows us to see and hear is all we know of her.

Ada cannot be placed onto one moral side and her agenda is never known. Although she works for Wesker, she often helps Leon by going against her orders. She is neither good nor bad, and is placed in a vexing middle ground. Because of this lack of information and unclear loyalties, Leon and the player are determined to figure her out, and define who she is. Although Leon is able to solve the mystery of why Ashley was kidnapped and who were responsible for the G virus, Ada and the secrets she carries are never revealed. Her conflicting actions allow her to float between the realms of good and bad, seductive and menacing, and become frustratingly unpredictable. Where Phyllis' of *Double Indemnity*'s bloody past is brought to light, and Brigid's greed and murders are revealed during the end of *The Maltese Falcon*, Leon and the players are only left with questions regarding Ada at the end of each game. Ada is never nicely wrapped up during the end of the games. Ada cannot be defined. Ada is not just a collection of society's fears and concerns of the time the way the classic femmes fatales function. Through her refusal to be solved, Ada moves away from the finite powers of classic femmes fatales, possessing all the power and sexuality of classic femmes fatales without any of the limitations. Without the limitations and the solving of Ada's mystery, unlike the other fatales, Ada is allowed to remain a femme fatale. She does not lose her function in the plot by being solved, and therefore can continue to exist. Because her agenda is never revealed, whatever it may be, Ada is saved the fate of most femmes fatales; she does not become a monster.

The Monstrous Femme Fatale

With the acquisition of power, her sexuality, and control of men the femmes fatales must pay a price. Of course the femme fatale is brutally punished, as will be explored later, but she also becomes a monster. Once the agenda's of femmes fatales are revealed, the femmes fatales are depicted as immoral vixens who care for nothing but themselves and power. As stated earlier, Brigid proves to be the murderer of Sam Spade's partner, and Phyllis' past murders are revealed shortly before she kills Walter. They are fixated as being evil with no morals. The femmes fatales who are revealed to have pure motives or prove themselves by saving the hero are stripped of their femme fatale powers through the formation of the couple. By becoming the hero's girlfriend, or more likely wife, the femmes fatales are no longer threats to the patriarchy because they have been safely brought into the patriarchy. They thusly become the "good" women Tasker describes (121). In *Resident Evil 5*, Jill represents the femme fatale's reincorporation into the patriarchy when she is removed of the powers Wesker implanted her with, and is no longer a threat to Sheva and Chris.

Because the mystery of Ada is never solved and due to her selfless aid of Leon, Claire, and other characters Ada never becomes a monster. Instead she remains in a neutral state of being neither bad nor good. In *Resident Evil 2* she helps Leon and Claire escape Raccoon City, but she steals the G-virus sample. In *Resident Evil 6* she often saves Leon's and Helena's life, but much of the reason she does so is to continue her quest for revenge against Simmons. Similar to the inability to solve the mystery surrounding Ada, her moral compass is also never truly defined. In contrast, the only other female character with questionable morals and heightened sexuality in the *Resident Evil* series does become a monster. Excella Gionne, who wears similar high-cut dresses to Ada's, physically transforms into a disgusting monster with tentacles and black sludge, visually representing her descent, as well as the descent of classic femmes fatales, into evil.

Ada's ability to blur the lines of morality is a commentary on the patriarchy's notions of gender, a rare attribute for video games which usually follow the stereotypical structures of gender in western society (Fox and Bailenson 148). Usually the women are given two options in video games, the role of the sexual object such as Excella, or the role of the sexless object such as a virgin or tomboy, Rebecca and Claire. There is no gender fluidity for the women (Watts 252–53). Video games outside the series that feature strong female leads such as *Tomb Raider*, the *Final Fantasy* series, or *Silent Hill 3* still follow the traditional tropes of the overtly sexualized action star, Lara Croft, or the sexless child, Heather Mason. Ada fulfills this gender fluidity. She has attributes typically associated with males, such as physical strength and intelligence, and traits typically associated with females, such as beauty and poise. Unlike Lara Croft or women in *Final Fantasy* games, Ada's sexuality is not so exaggerated that it becomes an unrealistic display of the female body. Ada has a normal, although very beautiful body, and breasts that are not disproportionate to her frame, unlike the voluptuous Lara or Tifa Lockhart.

The incidents of Ada's use of feminine weaponry additionally reveal her ability to enjoy gender fluidity. Although Ada's choice of weapons is located in the gender realm of the feminine, the act of fighting, especially with the phallic gun, is located in the realm of the masculine. In film noirs the women who are granted this dualism of gender are punished and depicted as immoral and reprehensible. Although Ada is punished, she is never the villain. *Resident Evil 6* complicates this by having a sub villain of the game as an Ada doppelganger. Ada instead is celebrated. She moves beyond poststructuralist conventions of gender and the problems of essentialism in second-wave feminism, and defines what being a powerful, feminine, and perhaps even moral woman is for herself.

Femme Fatale's Agency, Narrative Control and the Gaze

As stated earlier, femmes fatales are implanted with power because of their sexuality, but this power also carries over into a power of agency, where the femmes fatales are able to pursue their desires of money and knowledge. These desires are unique for women in films of the 1940s and 50s because usually their only goals are to get married and have children. The desire to gain money and knowledge is usually reserved for men (Place 54). *Casablanca* exhibits the male agencies of revolution and honor through the character Rick, where Ilsa's agency is only connected to her love for Rick and her husband Victor. Her agency only exists to be a lover and wife in the film. Femmes fatales such as Christina from *Kiss Me Deadly*, notably played by Cloris Leachman, who desires knowledge, and Kathie from *Out of the Past* who fights for freedom and money, display the fatale's agency. The femmes fatales' agencies are often identical to agency of the sinister male characters in the films. In addition, femmes fatales often have narrative powers in films, again a unique trait in that the narratives do not center around marriage, dating, or raising children. The femme fatale's narrative powers are also seen through Christina and Kathie. It is because of Christina that Mike becomes engrossed in the mystery of the film, and Kathie's betrayal of Whit and then Jeff propels the film's narrative forward.

Ada clearly possesses narrative power in all of her appearances, although the agenda behind her agency remains unknown. In the two games, Ada's actions are crucial parts to the player and Leon finishing the game. In *Resident Evil 2*, Ada gives Leon the last key to the police station, provides him first aid after he is shot, and throws him the rocket launcher that saves his life while fighting Mr. X. In *Resident Evil 4* Ada's action have an even greater affect on the player's and Leon's goals. During the beginning of the game, Ada alters the puzzles Leon encounters and rings the church bell saving him from the villagers. Ada also turns on the gondola lift Leon will later use, and prevents Krauser from stabbing Leon. Similar to *Resident Evil 2*, Ada also provides Leon with the rocket launcher he uses to kill Saddler. Through these actions, Ada directly influences Leon's and the player's gameplay.

Ada has more than just narrative powers, but can also control the gaze of the games, although only momentarily. Ada's narrative powers of the games is most evident during the sequence where she confronts Annette Birkin. In *Resident Evil 2*, shortly after Leon is shot, Ada chases down Annette. During this sequence the player is granted access to Ada and plays as her character. Once Ada corners Annette, the two engage in a very informative conversation, where Annette comments on Ada's role as a double agent. The scene then cuts to a flashback, where the player and Ada learn of the source of the Raccoon City outbreak. This information is revealed nowhere else, and without Ada, the player would never know how the virus spread. The information Ada learns is not granted to Leon, but only to her. More importantly however, through these scenes Ada controls the gaze.

Through the reveal of these flashbacks, Ada undermines the male gaze that controls mainstream Hollywood cinema. According to Mulvey's "Visual Pleasure of Narrative Cinema" women are not only the object of the gaze, but lack the ability to control the gaze (19–20). Women are only granted the control of the gaze through their placement in women's pictures that adhere to the male patriarchy, where their actions are associated with getting married, raising babies, and staying beautiful. Although Claire controls the gaze in her gameplay of *Resident Evil 2*, it is located in the world of the patriarchy in that Claire plays the pseudo mother to the child Sherry. She is fulfilling her gender role. Men are the only characters that are able to shape and control the gaze (21). According to Mulvey, male control of the gaze and their objectification of women is part of the language of society and is embedded in cinematic language. This language is so ingrained that it cannot be changed (14–15).

But in *Resident Evil 2,* Ada has point of view shots during scenes that are not associated with the typical gender roles usually enforced by films. Furthermore, the player sees through Ada's eyes, forcing the player to align with a woman. Because *Resident Evil 2* places importance on Ada's gaze, the scenes reveal crucial information to understanding the reasons behind the Raccoon City incident; the game elevates the female gaze to the same level as the male gaze. Ada's gaze brings the player, and later Leon, into the central plot of the game, allowing them to participate and thus exist in the world of *Resident Evil*. Without Ada's gaze and aid of Leon, the player would still be stuck in Raccoon City's sewers, and would know nothing of the events leading to the outbreak. This transformation of the gaze results in the transformation of the male patriarchy, reflecting the changing language of society and its view of women and power. Although Ada is punished through torture and fake deaths, she does not have to lose her life for this power. She may still be threatening to the male order, but the femme fatale no longer has to pay for male insecurities with their lives. But this is a power classic femmes fatales never have access to. Seldom are femmes fatales given point of view shots, and never are femmes fatales allowed to be the main character. Although femmes fatales can have narrative powers, unlike Ada, the only power of the gaze they have results in the sexualization of their bodies and attraction, not control of the gaze.

The Punishment of the Femme Fatale

But women are not allowed to drive the narratives forward over the male characters. In film noirs these femmes fatales with narrative control are killed or imprisoned. In the 1940s and '50s femmes fatales reflected the male fears of women taking over male space, in particular the workplace (Martin 203). This fear translated to film through the femmes fatales, where these women were powerful and controlled aspects of the narratives. Therefore they are killed in order to protect male patriarchy. Jans B. Wager describes the femmes fatales' fate in her book *Dames in the Driver's Seat*.

> The femme fatale, meanwhile, fights against male economic and social domination, usually at the cost of her life or her freedom. She is murdered, tortured, jailed, or at the very least contained by marriage in the final reel of the film. The femme fatale's resistance is fatal, sometimes to the men who fall for her, almost always to herself [4].

Femmes fatales are allowed to be powerful, but it is at the price of their lives. The punishment of femmes fatales such as Cora in *The Postman Always Rings Twice*, and Christina in *Kiss Me Deadly*, result in the fatales' death, where fatale Candy of *Pickup on South Street* is bound in a relationship at the end of the film, thus losing all of her powers.

In *Resident Evil 2* Ada's threat to the male order is revealed during her introduction. When the player first sees Ada she tries to shoot Leon in the head. She is a danger to the good Leon, and later a constant frustration. Almost instantly after the two meet Ada runs from Leon, refusing his role of protector during the zombie apocalypse. Ada continues to refuse Leon's aid throughout the game, by always running off when he tries to take control of her. Leon expresses his frustration over his lack of controlling her during the middle of the game, where he lectures that running off is reckless and stupid. Ada obediently replies, "alright, we'll do it your way" (*Resident Evil 2*). Because Ada is a woman, she must do what Leon tells her, otherwise she will be killed by one of the monsters. But at this point in the game what has Ada done to prove she needs Leon's constant protection? She has survived alone like Leon, and has presumably killed just as many zombies and lickers as he has. In contrast, Leon does not feel the need to escort Claire throughout the game. Regardless, Ada is being reckless and stupid.

Leon is the one who is apparently in charge. Ada cannot constantly run away from him, because he believes he is the one who decides the course of action. Ada must do it his way. The male character's belief that he has authority over the female character is also apparent in film noirs where the femmes fatales play along with the male's authority, when in actuality she is undermining his alleged power at every move. Leon's refusal to follow a woman is also expressed in *Resident Evil 4*. Before the two engage in a battle of arms, Ada holds a gun to Leon's back and tells him to put up his hands. Leon smugly replies "sorry, but following a lady's lead just isn't my style" (*Resident Evil 4*). Leon will not take orders from a woman unless she is under the patriarchy's order, like Ingrid Hunnigan, and even then he shows his resistance by flirting with her. Leon upholds the ideals of the male patriarchy and puts Ada into two categories, the beautiful woman he desires, and the woman who must be reprimanded for her refusal to follow male authority.

Ada is punished for her rebellion against gender norms and male control, but unlike the femmes fatales of the classic noir period, she lives and profits from her social misdeeds. The classic femmes fatales are usually killed because of their agency; therefore preventing them from pursuing their thirsts for power and money into other adventures or films (Wager 42). Ada is able to live through several games, continuing her adventures and pursuits. But, before she can continue her adventures she must be punished. In both games, Ada is physically punished for her crimes against society and even "dies" several times. In *Resident Evil 2* Ada is wounded by Dr. Birkin, and in *4* Saddler knocks her unconscious and captures her. During the climax of *Resident Evil 2* Ada's punishment results in her apparent death, when depending on the player's scenario, she dies in Leon's arms or falls to her death. But Ada does not die, and instead rises from the grave just in time to save Leon from Mr. X. Through this rebirth, Ada becomes more powerful than the femmes fatales she is based on. She is never jailed and she cannot be killed. She is already the equal of her male counterparts and even surpasses them in terms of intelligence and often survival skills, thusly challenging the male patriarchy and winning. Through her rebirth she does what other femmes fatales are not able to do. Unlike Kathie who cannot enjoy her fortune because she is killed, or Phyllis who dies shortly before finally being granted her freedom, Ada enjoys the benefits of her crimes and lives to accept many more secret missions. Furthermore, the ability for a femme fatale to survive is notably in the genre of video games, and not film. This suggests that video games may be ready for the strong, and maybe immoral, woman to be rewarded, where film still mostly relies on punishment for the threatening and morally complex woman. *Sin City*, directed by Robert Rodriguez, closely follows film noir styles, and interestingly does not punish the femmes fatales, but idolizes them. This is greatly different than neo noirs such as *Brick*, *The Grifters*, and *Inception* where the femmes fatales are punished and turned into monsters. Perhaps part of the reason why a video game allows for unpunished femmes fatales, where film does not, is because video games allow for the physical control of the fatales through granting playable characters, something film cannot do. By allowing the player to have physical control of Ada, or any other female character, her powers become less threatening and more manageable. It is only when she has full control of her own during cut scenes that the male player is totally at the mercy of the femme fatale.

Conclusion

Ada Wong of *Resident Evil 2, 4,* and *6* is a femme fatale like the cunning women of film noir. She is a seductress of the men she encounters, and gains power through her ability to persuade the men to protect her with their lives. In *Resident Evil 2, 4,* and *6* Leon constantly risks his life for Ada, often getting shot in the process. True to the standard definition of the femme fatale, the mystery surrounding Ada links her to the mystery of the game's narrative, allowing her to ignite the game's plot forward. Through this agency Ada is given access to the control of the gaze, forcing any male players to view the events of her gameplay through the eyes of a woman, an unimaginable point of view for the male patriarchy. It is only through the eyes of a woman that the player exists and is able to continue his or hers in game journey.

Ada additionally gives power to the role of the femme fatale by refusing to die for her powers. Unlike the classic femmes fatales, Ada is only mildly punished, and gets away with her crimes. Julie Grossman states in her book, *Rethinking the Femme Fatale in Film Noir: Ready for Her Close-Up*, that the femme fatale is the celebration of unchecked power (1). But Ada is the true celebration of unchecked power. She is granted immortality by surviving her three game appearances, living forever through the players' gameplay, and just like a zombie, she always comes back from the dead.

Works Cited

Bailenson, Jeremy N., and Jesse Fox. "Virtual Virgins and Vamps: The Effects of Exposure to Female Characters' Sexualized Appearance and Gaze in an Immersive Virtual Environment." *Springer Science + Business Media* (2009): 147–157. Project Muse. Web. 26 Oct. 2012.

Cowie, Elizabeth. "Film Noir and Women." *Shades of Noir: A Reader*. Ed. Joan Copjec. London: Verso, 1993, 121–165. Print.

Doane, Mary Ann. *Femme Fatales: Feminism, Film Theory, Psychoanalysis*. New York: Routledge, 1991. Print.

Grossman, Julie. *Rethinking the Femme Fatale in Film Noir: Ready for Her Close-Up*. New York: Palgrave Macmillan, 2009. Print.

Kruntnik, Frank. *In a Lonely Street: Film Noir, Genre, Masculinity*. London: Routledge, 1991. Print.

Martin, Angela. "'Gilda Didn't Do Any of Those Things You Have Been Losing Sleep Over!': The Central Women of 40s Films Noirs." *Women in Film Noir*. Ed. Ann E. Kaplan. London: BFI, 1998. 202–228. Print.

McAlister, Elizabeth. "Slaves, Cannibals, and Infected Hyper-Whites: The Race and Religion of Zombies." *Anthropological Quarterly* 85. 2 (2012): 457–486. Project Muse. Web. 24 Oct 2012.

Mulvey, Laura. "Visual Pleasures and Narrative Cinema." *Visual and Other Pleasures*. New York: Palgrave Macmillan: 1989. Print.

Place, Janey. "Women in Film Noir." *Women in Film Noir*. Ed. Ann E. Kaplan. London: BFI, 1998. 47–68. Print.

Resident Evil 2. 1.04. Capcom. 1998. Video Game.

Resident Evil 4. 1.10. Capcom. 2005. Video Game.

Resident Evil 6. 1. Capcom. 2012. Video Game.

Tasker, Yvonne. *Working Girls: Gender and Sexuality in Popular Cinema*. London: Routledge, 1998. Print.

Wager, Jans B. *Dames in the Driver's Seat: Reading Film Noir*. Austin: University of Texas Press, 2005. Print.

Watts, Evan. "Ruin, Gender, and Digital Games." *WSQ: Women's Studies Quarterly* 39.3.4. (2011): 247–265. Project Muse. Web. 26 Oct 2012.

Chris Redfield and the Curious Case of Wesker's Sunglasses

Nicolas J. Lalone

"To see the true nature of things, we need the glasses: it is not that we have to take off ideological glasses in order to see reality directly as it is—we are 'naturally' in ideology, our natural sight is ideological."—Slavoj Žižek, *The Plague of Fantasies* (11)

In *Resident Evil 5* (*RE5*), a pharmaceutical consortium designs a virus that will target specific strands of DNA. To do this, the consortium has displaced millions of African citizens living where a key ingredient of their virus—a flower called "stairway of the sun"—is located. Simultaneously, the consortium is testing the virus (and others) on the same Africans. Because this plant grows only in this area and because it plays an integral part in the tribal history of those Africans, the consortium can only test this product on the residents who live near a tiny cave in Kijuju—a nation located somewhere in or near Nigeria. This virus will release the "potential" of its victim's DNA and "re-establish" humanity's connection with nature (in that only the strong survive). The purpose of this essay is to explore the dialectic proposed by the tension between the protagonist and antagonist of *RE5*'s narrative.

There are two white men standing at opposite ends of a dialectic that could be referred to as American ignorance in *RE5*. On one side of the dialectic is the white male who wants to release the virus—Albert Wesker. On his side of the dialectic exists a conscious application of ignorance employed as a means through which corporate entities can pursue an agenda without ethical consideration. The consortium's agenda, personified by Wesker, shows how culturally insensitive profit-seeking enterprise can be when the residents or culture of an area stand in the way of profit or power disguised as "scientific progress." On the other side of the dialectic is another white male—Chris Redfield— who represents the cultural ignorance that comes from being a member of a core component of the capitalist world economy (Wallerstein 382–83). The mixture of these two brands of ignorance makes *Resident Evil 5* a unique, though inadvertent, critique of American society.

It is inadvertent because it would be an error to presuppose that the designers of *RE5* had a purposefully constructed, consistent philosophical dialogue in mind when constructing this game. Instead, we presuppose that *RE5* is an example of Žižek's evaluation of the Matrix trilogy during which he says, "a work whose very inconsistencies point towards the antagonisms of our ideological and social predicament" ("Reloaded" 198). And there are many inconsistencies in the setting of *RE5*. For example, like the Congo, where so many insurgencies are focused on the monetary gain from coltan mines, Kijuju was only called into question because of a rumor of biological weaponry being smuggled into the country. The people of Kijuju inadvertently but literally become the mindless masses who trusted that foreign investors had their best interests in mind. Because the people had been ignored in the events leading up to the terrorist threat that got the core's attention, the central component of *RE5* is Wesker and his virus. It is more important to secure the rare plant and resulting virus that was about to be released, at whatever the cost, because it was going to impact the core. So, while insignificant, Africa often remains the central focus of corporate greed because of the rare materials found there—not the people who live there. The representation of Africa within the game mimics this lack of detail past "Africa." These inconsistencies actually point to a very real reality—what do we mean when we say "Africa?"

Africa is represented in interpretations of *RE5*—reviews of the game itself. The ignorance manifests itself wherein reviewers consistently state that *RE5* is merely an expression of colonialism—an exercise in what Wallerstein calls a "core process" whereby the core (or First World) has designated an entire periphery (or 3rd World) nation's DNA as the labor they need to achieve their goal ("The Construction" 385). Again, the interesting thing about *RE5* is that the game is not about the Third World. It is more about the perils of science mixed with ambition that completely ignores what it must do to meet that ambition. While colonialism is represented on the surface, the details of the game say more about the horrors the corporate world has visited upon Kijuju rather than how Kijuju had fared before it began to be interfered with or labeled as some form of terrorist-related area.

According to in-game lore, Kijuju has received many gifts and investments from the richer nations of the world in appreciation of its building techniques. The consequences of what they have received are manifest by comparing it with a nation that has had similar consequences to face: Nigeria. So, what *RE5* asks is similar to what Slavoj Žižek posited when he asked would happen if terrorists targeted DNA for ideological reasons instead of structures that represent ideology they do not agree with ("Welcome" 36). Ideology, or, the way we understand how the world is and should be, is the object at the center of the disagreement that has driven the world since 2001. Unlike most social theorists, Žižek believes that ideology is not something that masks reality; reality is something that pierces ideology. This was the case with 9/11. The fantasy that everything America did was just and universally loved had built a shelter for Americans from the consequences their actions had outside their borders ("Plague" 16). An indication that reality had pierced fantasy was through popular response to the World Trade Center and Pentagon attacks, "this is just like a movie or a video game."

Starting in 2001, the faceless terrorist took over a majority of antagonist slots in nearly every entertainment medium. Shows like *24* (Season 3) capitalized on terrorism by trying to inform audiences that terrorism is complicated by money from the military-industrial complex. By funding terrorists, the military-industrial complex can continue its endless expansion. In our fantasies, our entertainment, it is rare to see true critiques of the reality. Instead, our fantasies often mimic the tensions between ideology (the world we live in) and reality (the consequences that world creates) (Boucher and Sharp 3). Most fantasy simply expands an ideology's reach or attempts to justify action taken in other countries by highlighting a danger to the homeland that exists far away in a foreign land ("Welcome to the Desert" 14).

This is how terrorism is routinely shown in our entertainment. However, given that the immediate and actual threat of terrorist attacks is now over ten years old, terrorism has begun to breed with a variety of old science-based fears that were never made real ("Welcome to the Desert"). At least the old science-based fears never came true for the nations of the core; the periphery has had to live within those fears. Medical testing has detached itself from moral obligation in the periphery. Further, terrorism has become a business, a new fantasy that is sheltering us from the horrors our medical enterprises are bringing to other parts of the world. These actions will also have consequences. In video games, this is a unique and intercultural exchange of information that began because of a technology developed in tandem with missiles after World War II. Because of the intercultural nature of video games, there exist quite a few critiques of American culture. However, citizens of the United States rarely produce within the United States or these games. Each of these games was met with resistance before their release (e.g., *Metal Gear Solid 2* [2001], *Grand Theft Auto 3* [2001], *Metal Wolf Chaos* [2004], *Resident Evil 5* [2009]). The *Resident Evil* series was one such critique.

In 2007, a Japanese video game maker named Capcom released a trailer for the fifth chapter of their *Resident Evil* franchise. *RE5* follows a Bioterrorism Security Assessment Alliance (B.S.A.A.) agent named Chris Redfield as he investigates a report of biological terrorism in a small autonomous region of

West Africa named Kijuju. This trailer featured Redfield entering a small African town rife with violence as a man with a megaphone agitates the crowds. The ominous scene takes a violent turn and Redfield suddenly has to fight for his life. Every person in the town wants to murder Redfield and throughout the rest of the trailer, he tries to fight his way out of town. The dark skinned residents of this African town are seemingly bereft of free will, as there seems to be no one in the town who resists the will to kill this newly arrived white man.

Critics reacted with discomfort. Stephen Totillo of MTV noted that "[*RE5*] presents a fantasy I don't desire. It looks like it's an advertisement to virtually shoot poor people" (Totillo, "Notorious"). N'Gai Croal (then of *Newsweek*) said that, "It's like they're all dangerous; they all need to be killed" (John, "N'Gai Croal"). Evan Narcisse went so far as to say; "this game will make plenty of people uncomfortable in racially specific ways" (Narcisse, "Uncomfortable Echoes"). It is important to note that all of these reviewers were responding to a trailer for a video game that was not released yet and ended up telling their readers an interpretation of a story they could not fully access. Through Žižek's frame, we understand that the ideology of race relations in the United States was pierced by the fantasy of *RE5* though it seems like *RE5*'s designers are actually trying to persuade the reader to notice more than American racism. The key to understanding what *RE5*'s creators meant to portray is seen in the development of the *Resident Evil* franchise as an "accident[s] that could actually happen" (TheBatMan, "The History and Making") into an accident made purposefully to advance an ideology.

An "Accident" That Could Actually Happen

When *RE5* was released, the narrative had a little more depth to it than the initial reviews assumed—though analysis of *RE5* rarely went past that acknowledgment. In this game, Redfield arrives in Kijuju and begins to hear about a weapon called Uroboros. As he walks around town with a local, the hyper-sexualized light-skinned African female soldier named Sheva Alomar (Brock 437–38), they observe scenes of unrestricted violence and eventually come upon a man agitating a crowd of angry villagers in Swahili. Sheva, it was said, was placed in the game to help balance the equation between the Caucasian male and the killing of Kijuju citizens (Narcisse, "Uncomfortable Echoes"). Her appearance on camera through a long take of her butt before we see her face, serves to distract the target audience from the horrors that they are about to experience. After a brief acclimatization of how to move and shoot as Redfield, we are introduced to the first point whereupon Kijuju's hostility boils over to aggressive rage.

The agitator yells, "Uroboros is a gift! A way to paradise!" Then, pointing toward Redfield and Sheva, "There! In the house! Get them! No one must know what has happened this day." The agitator is a character that links the in-game back story (told through various diaries, scenes, and dialogue) to out-of-game advertisements. Capcom placed viral advertising for the game through the Google-run Blogger. In this blog, Adam, a character living in Kijuju, reveals that the agitator had been placed in the town as a sickness began to spread throughout Kijuju (Adam, "World Crashing"). Town residents were sent to a clinic for treatment and came back "different." The reason for this difference was a virus from a previous chapter of *Resident Evil*—a parasite named Las Plagas. Previous *Resident Evil* games featured mindless zombies. However, the Las Plagas Type 2 virus does not turn the person undead but destroys the moral center of the infected. Further, Las Plagas allows the infected to maintain some semblance of regular day-to-day activities. This infection is not what Redfield was there to investigate (as it is not an arms deal) but it quickly escalates to the very reason Redfield has to fight for his life. The entire country of Kijuju is assigned to kill Redfield in order to mask the completion and attempted dissemination of Uroboros—a virus derived from a native plant called "Stairway of the Sun."

"Stairway of the Sun" has been part of the local Ndipaya tribal mythology since it began passing oral history. The legend was told that if the plant were ingested and did not prove to be fatal, it would grant the person great power. The person who ingested this plant and lived would become the village leader. In the 1960s, the founder of the Umbrella Corporation discovered that "Stairway of the Sun" contained a virus that altered DNA. Given the right type of host, this virus would grant the infected person increased physical attributes. After several modifications and failed trials, the virus from this plant came to be known as the Progenitor Virus. This virus has played a central role in each chapter of *Resident Evil*. Redfield, throughout the course of *RE5*, discovers that Albert Wesker, a biologically modified white male being who has been a villain in nearly every *Resident Evil* chapter, has re-established Umbrella's secret facility beneath Kijuju. Combining the virus from the flower with the mind-control of Las Plagas, Wesker attempts to free the world from the confines of capitalism and return it to a state of nature (Bibliomaniac15, "Cut Scene 48").

Running parallel to this narrative is a growing sense of despair generated from medical tests performed on unwilling subjects by corporate entities so large and complex they cannot be litigated (Washington, "Why Africa Fears"). Early in *Resident Evil*'s development, Shinji Mikami—the original designer of the franchise—said that, "The game [*Resident Evil*] unfolds itself in the near future of the USA and shows an accident that could actually happen" (The-

BatMan, "The History and Making"). *Resident Evil* has not lost this original design principle. Despite gaining a terrorism-derived motivation, *RE5* still could "actually happen." In fact, the likelihood of an accident like *RE5* occurring is more likely than the rest of the games. Just two years before this game was published, pharmaceutical giant Pfizer was forced to settle with the country of Nigeria after injecting children with meningitis with a drug that had not been fully tested or approved (Kovac, "Nigerians to sue"). Cases like this have happened repeatedly around the world as competition and secrecy between drug companies result in a continuous loosening of ethical guidelines (Rebecca Project 4). Many times, these events seem far beyond the scope of our standard fantasies. For example, this essay focuses on a single event that resulted in six individual cases: *Abdulahi v Pfizer I, II, III, Ajudu Ismalia Adamu v Pfizer*, and two court cases in Nigeria. These cases were spread out over nearly twenty years involving in two different countries, dozens of families, medical doctors, and lost children, ultimately resulting in an international conspiracy between the United States, Pfizer, and Nigeria because of cables released by Wikileaks (Bosely, "Wikileaks Cables").

Court cases and incidents like this are rarely discussed in the United States and so reality is often missing during discourse about international content in popular culture in the United States. The reality set forth by the Japanese creators of this game has not fully pierced the shield of fantasy around American action outside of America. The proof for this is in the way reviewers responded to *RE5*. We only notice that there are African people dying (in another country). Or, to put it another way, this game's content was controversial enough to impact avoidance of race discussion but not enough to unsettle American ideology. Reviewers did not attempt to discuss how our way of life impacts others or that the Africans in *RE5* are a near perfect representation of American ideological renderings of Africa (Wainaina, "How to Write"). If this were not the case, the initial discussion about *RE5* may have centered on the impact of American pharmaceutical research on the rest of the world instead of assuming a colonialist representation of Africa.

In some cases, the news from tests like these in various African nations is anesthetized and placed into movies that do represent colonialist representations of Africa. Fantasies about corporate presences in Africa like *Blood Diamond* (2006), *The Constant Gardener* (2005), or *Babel* (2006) offer surreal moments in which white Americans take action due to the sacrifice of a significant other. These movies often propel ethical mishaps of large international organizations into the spotlight. Unfortunately, these movies rarely pursue the consequences of these cases inside the nations they occurred. Instead, they offer a moment when the world notices something bad has happened and correct it by reprimanding entities that exist outside the nation they occurred in.

RE5 is a game that is made to explore how we learn about world issues—and ultimately how we figure out how to ignore them. Ultimately, this game represents a moment in popular culture whereupon the consequences of ignoring these drug trials actually result in the genocide of those being tested on. However, as we have seen, this moment is fleeting and mostly ignored.

This essay will pursue this clash of fantasy and reality through the thin veil of a court case. In reality, the only option for Kijuju's government would be to pursue litigation against the Global Pharmaceutical Consortium, G.S.A.A., Tricell, and Umbrella for their unethical and illegal treatment of Kijuju's citizens. While there are no true plaintiffs in this case as there is most likely no one left alive in Kijuju, realistic precedent is on the side of the corporate entities, not the governments of those nations; unless, of course, those citizens can prove that any of the entities involved broke the Nuremburg Code or the Declaration of Helsinki. At most, Kijuju may be able to convince a court that they are due reparations for damages done to its citizens at the time of the outbreak; again, if there are any members of those families left to pursue legal action. In the opening comments of this court case, we will outline the characters of these two defendants. Once defined, we will use these qualities to elucidate how the clash between these two metaphorical entities obscures public discourse and evaluate if the game designers managed to resolve this clash.

Wesker v. Redfield: *Opening Statement—Chris Redfield*

If we are to judge Redfield's journey through Kijuju, we must first come to understand his character as an agent of American ideology and strategic ignorance. Strategic ignorance is best defined as a socially constructed blind spot. In these spots lay the foundation for ignoring the plight of those "in the margins" (Bailey 77). The very beginning of *RE5* introduces us to the fact that Redfield has these spots. He tells us that he should have seen "it" coming. His actions, directly responsible for the downfall of the Umbrella Corporation, have thus allowed terrorists to begin to amass biological weapons (Bibliomaniac15, "Cut Scene 01"). Possession of these weapons has destabilized the regions already associated with terrorism. These "unstable regions" constantly shift the power balance. As a member of the newly formed BSAA, Redfield is sent to Kijuju to investigate how the locals are getting access to biological— or DNA—targeting weapons. Note that where these weapons were simply viruses in the previous game, they have become terrorist weapons now that they have left "stable regions" (United States, Spain, France).

At the beginning of the game, Redfield seems poised to simply go to

Kijuju, investigate, and get out. He ignores the problems in Kijuju, but is told to pay attention to the possible problems Kijuju could cause the "stable areas," or the Global North. Like most of America, he believes that this area is a "haven for terrorists" but little else. There is not much showing of local culture as there is in "Adam's Blog" (Adam, "Experience Kijuju"). Instead, we are treated to the world as Redfield sees it with all eyes uncomfortably on him. Sheva Alomar, a local soldier who is meant to be his guide during the investigation mentions how the locals seem hostile to Americans. Within minutes, Sheva and Redfield are on a course that ends with them murdering what seems to be an entire African nation. Motivationally, Redfield initially fights for his life and to find Irving, the Caucasian arms dealer who was reported to be dealing in the area; however, he soon learns that his former partner, who he believed dead, is alive and associated with whatever is happening in Kijuju. Redfield never mentions saving the people of Kijuju because, as the introductory scene indicates, the nation is a haven for terrorists. Kijuju has been written off as "un-savable." Redfield does not fight to free or correct Kijuju's wrongs; he simply wants to get his job done (Bibliomaniac15, "Cut Scene 01"). While later this focus shifts slightly to rescue his former partner, Jill Valentine, he does not consider the people of Kijuju at any time during the game.

Once Redfield manages to track down the figures behind the disaster in Kijuju, his focus shifts from getting his job done to desperately struggling to stop the end of the world. This struggle climaxes at a volcanic eruption with Wesker growing uncontrollably unstable. After a dramatic gesture (knocking Wesker's head off with a rocket shot from a helicopter as he escapes a volcanic eruption), Redfield accomplishes his goal. The world is saved. However, once this goal is accomplished, Redfield wonders if it is all worth fighting for. He glances at Jill and Sheva, ideology once again descending around him, the fantasy of safety. It reassures him. Yes, the safety of everyone through capitalism is worth fighting for. Redfield has a shallow goal throughout the entire game. He simply sets a point B and walks toward it: investigate arms deal, save Jill, kill Wesker. Redfield is manifested American ideology. He only thinks of finishing his job and fulfilling his own desires. Standing in contradiction to Redfield is Wesker. Wesker is only capable of seeing the big picture and in doing so, often misses many little things happening around him.

Wesker v. Redfield: *Opening Statement—Albert Wesker*

Albert Wesker is not a villain. He is more of a representation of the demeanor needed to consciously pursue the things corporate entities need to retain power. Wesker, unlike Redfield, was not raised as a human being. He was developed by the Umbrella Corporation as part of the "Wesker Children" program. Umbrella's founder, Oswell E. Spencer, felt that humanity had grown weak and that genetic engineering was the only means through which humanity could be corrected. Through the "Wesker Children" program, hundreds of children were kidnapped and brainwashed to believe that they needed to seek out and work for Spencer. With genetically superior children brainwashed to serve him before he augmented them, Spencer dreamed of establishing a utopia on earth with him at the center (Wiki, "Oswell E. Spencer"). Of all the Wesker children, Albert was the first to show real promise in the program. Soon, thirteen children were chosen to be injected with a virus that eventually became the Progenitor virus. Almost all of these children died due to their exposure to the virus. Albert was the only confirmed survivor.

All of these events occurred throughout the 1970s, a time of fear, government mistrust, and corporate interference (PBS, "Discontent with Government") in Kijuju at the behest of the Umbrella Corporation. Because of his purposeful breeding and genetic manipulation, Wesker represents the aggressive and cold reality of a purely capitalist world. Wesker's sunglasses are a symbolic device that allows him to see outside ideology. In this way, Wesker maintains the psychology to do as he needs throughout the *Resident Evil* series. It is not until Wesker literally loses his head due to an RPG hitting it in an erupting volcano that his ability to maintain his form and his sight is ruined. The hideous mass that expands and melts in the fires of the volcano is symbolic of reality itself, melting away as Redfield, Sheva, and Jill fly somewhere else disillusioned with everything that has transpired. With Wesker gone and reality no longer infecting their world, they can once again settle back into the fantasy they came from—and re-enter America.

Breaking Down Wesker v. Redfield

Video games offer a means through which a player can explore ideas about the world (Bogost 2–3). Because video games are made by people, this exploration takes place in an approximation based on subjective ideas limited by the resources game makers have to express those ideas. Žižek's *Plague of Fantasies* reminds us that at all times we are inside ideology ("Plague" xiii). Our ideology at current is that of globalization or neo-liberalism. Ideology, technology, and the drive for better products will thus allow us to realize the vastness of human potential and a unified humanity (Bauman 16). This "improvement" of humanity in the Global North has been the driving force throughout the 20th and 21st centuries. Under neo-liberalism, corporate entities have pursued less and less ethical means to produce products and the citizenry that benefits from it remains strategically ignorant but dependent upon these products. Theoretically, neo-liberalism is an extension of the modernist agenda—technology will save us, we just need to follow the path to get there. In practice, this modernist fantasy has been commoditized. As a commodity, the future has been made into the constant want for "more" of everything from the First World (Bauman 16–17).

Returning to *Resident Evil,* we do see countries in the Global North fighting to contain the infection that has been loosed upon them. The disasters in the North, sometimes referred to as accidents, usually result in an entire city (usually remote) being decimated and ultimately destroyed. But there is something unique that occurs when referencing First World countries and disasters—they are often portrayed differently than disasters that happen in the Global South or the Third World ("Welcome to the Desert" 13). If a disaster happens in the global south we see scenes of destruction and chaos, dead bodies, blood, and violence. During September 11, we saw very little of this ("Welcome to the Desert" 13). These games are more about the horrors of what happens in the night. When *RE5* was released, there was a shift to a nation outside the global north. Suddenly, all of the violence that took place in the dark now exists in the light; a nearly oppressive amount of light is present at all times in *RE5* (Capcom-Unity, "Famitsu Interview") It tells the player that the things going on in Africa over the last few years of *Resident Evil* games are coming to light. This is because while all of the previous games were going on, the African nation of Kijuju was being manipulated, tested, and eventually fell under the power of the type two Las Plagas. At the beginning of the game we are reminded of this. Redfield should have known "they" would get their hands on the weapons he had stopped previously. The Global South was ignored and this ignorance was not acknowledged until Redfield was sent to Kijuju at the beginning of *RE5*.

Wesker and Redfield's confrontation displays many of the conflicts that occur between the realities corporate entities pursue outside the ideology they install in the Global North. The only difference is that instead of zombies, there is bureaucracy and bureaucrats, and this makes it more difficult to comprehend. For example, medical drug trials are conducted using the same rules for U.S. drug trials in nations like Nigeria, Cameroon, Uganda, or even more recently, rural India (Krosin, et al., 306). The corporations doing the testing present test subjects with complex English documents meant to provide informed consent. These documents are often too complex for these subjects to understand. To get around this problem, pharmaceutical companies routinely use local doctors who are promised money and prestige through publications in North American journals of medicine (Rebecca Project, "Outsourcing Tuskegee").

These native doctors then administer and test medications in their home countries that would not be legal to test in the United States. If this testing is discovered, there are sticky legal precedents to consider. Cases that involve Alien Tort statutes have been aggressively rejected in many courts in the United States (where these pharmaceutical companies often have their headquarters). The Supreme Court case *Sosa v Alvarez-Machain* created a dizzying array of complicated decisions to be made before possible legal action can be taken (*Harvard Law Review*, "Federal Statutes"). The *Sosa* decision stated that the courts of the United States should not, in any way, interfere with the sovereignty of another nation. This precedent suggests that U.S. courts cannot intervene if private actors participate in an illegal act perpetuated by a U.S. corporation while working with local government officials or in an official government capacity. Acts considered illegal in the United States performed elsewhere may be considered legal in those places.

In 1996, Pfizer tested a medication named Trovan on one hundred children, causing five deaths and a variety of detrimental side-effects. By 2001, several families in Nigeria began a court case that would remain in the system, undecided and rejected three times over a ten year period. This court case, *Abdullahi v Pfizer, Inc.*, was ultimately dismissed by the Court of Appeals because none of the defendants could prove that Pfizer had violated the Nuremburg Code or the Declaration of Helsinki (Bosely, "Pfizer used dirty tricks"). If Pfizer had violated either of these binding international documents, the doctors and corporations involved could be brought forth before a judge and punished for crimes against humanity. However, from 1997 to 2010, none of the defendants in this case could convince a jury that Pfizer had violated these laws (*Harvard Law Review*, "Federal Statutes").

Pfizer finally settled with the families of the children who died during the Trovan tests after the court case moved to the courts of Nigeria (*Guardian*, "Pfizer Nears $75m Settlement"). Unfortunately, shortly after the settlement had been agreed upon, Pfizer hired an investigator to blackmail the Nigerian Attorney General (Bosely, "WikiLeaks Cables"). The resulting controversy, spurred forth by WikiLeaks, revealed that the United States Ambassador in Nigeria had collaborated with the Pfizer representatives to see it through. Unsurprisingly, the files that had been used in the court case disappeared which makes it impossible to pursue appeals (Umar, "Pfizer—Victims'"). Pfizer ultimately paid ten million dollars of the agreed upon seventy-five million before the blackmail scheme. They have not paid further reparations. Pfizer, like Umbrella, Tricell, or the Global Pharmaceutical Consortium, seems to have an uncanny ability to keep existing past their own failures due to people like Albert Wesker, though it is rare that we actually know their names.

Wesker v. Redfield—*Summary Judgment* | *The Makers*

Game makers often do not spend the time researching topics like this down to their legal precedent roots. Game maker intent is to create a system that is "fun" and "entertaining" (Juul 18–20). Jun Takeuchi, design head for *RE5*, argued this point constantly when American game critics challenged his discussion of Africa during interviews about the game (Narcisse "Uncomfortable Echoes"). This discussion also takes the form of Wesker and Redfield. If we take the initial reaction to *RE5* as its impact on players, we would see this game as a racist, colonialist piece of trash entertainment meant to further indoctrinate young white males into believing how people from Africa "really are" (Totilo, "That Notorious").

In reality, *RE5* is a critique of American ideology and American corporate practice whereupon a fantasy Africa is placed in the same ideological position it is in reality—powerless against a hope for economic stability and growth. No doubt, the reason Oswell E. Spencer managed to originally open the research facility in Kijuju was due to growth, job creation, and economic stability. The Ndipiya tribe, displaced by Spencer's work, was most likely a sacrifice made by the other peoples in Kijuju even if they were not entirely sure why Umbrella wanted the land or wanted to open a research facility. Like in so many parts of Africa (e.g., the Congo and coltan; AIDS vaccines in Uganda; diamonds in Kenya), it is unfortunate that such a rare resource exists before the people there had the means to defend it for themselves. Wesker, in his bid to try and bring the rest of the world back to nature through the Uroboros virus developed from the original plant found in Kijuju, uses the DNA of the rest of Kijuju to try and stop white America from hindering his plan. Powerless to stop Wesker, powerless to stop the sickness that lead to most citizens of Kijuju being infected with Las Plagas, and powerless to stop themselves from trying to kill Redfield and Sheva Alomar, the nation of Kijuju is a massive exaggeration of realistic political events that players should be persuaded to think about. However, anyone playing this game, as Žižek notes of existence, is not in reality and that is the thing that makes players feel uncomfortable when they play *RE5*.

Wesker v. Redfield: *Closing Remarks*

We live in ideology ("Plague xii"). It is the stuff all ideas about the world are built with. Players, like game makers, are limited by their own experiences. Our education, family income, peer groups, and popular culture all impact our ability to perceive the world. When we engage with something like *RE5*, we use that experience to make sense of what we see. Video games, it is said, are made primarily by male Caucasian groups for male Caucasian players. This too is an ideology for the primary makers of this game come from an ethnic group that sued the United States in an effort to be recognized as white. The Japanese were officially denied access to being considered anglo or white. We come full circle to Žižek's *Plague of Fantasies*. In America, particularly white America, we use an epistemological tactic referred to as selective ignorance to avoid discussing or reflecting too long on the horrors of what has to be done to get products to American shelves. Even though *RE5* is "just a product made to entertain us," it shows us just how far selective ignorance could go.

Africa is often forgotten when the discussion is about "world-affairs" (Matinyi, "Why Africa Is Ignored"). Dark-skinned people seem to be transported out of where they live when seen with American eyes. They are transported into a sort of oubliette they cannot escape—the ideology of America. Inside, they are told that they are underprivileged, and that their ethnicity has a myriad of identity problems when faced with living in a world in which they do not live—that of whites. This often blinds whites to the actual problems people who live in Africa face. These actions typically are caused because of things performed by corporate entities run by European or American interests that directly impact goods those people purchase. *RE5* as critiqued by professional game industry press was judged using these criteria. The people of Africa, infected by a disease developed in a quest for first-world immortality, are not victims of white action by reviewers, but are assigned race-based ideological components because they could not see outside of their everyday ideology.

This ignorance, personified by Redfield is literally destructive in this game. Kijuju itself is the victim because it is a poor country. Even the Japanese, a group outside of America and Europe, cannot resolve the problems the ignorance personified by Wesker and Redfield contain inside their dialectic. The fiscal, environmental, and biological ruin caused by Wesker is never stopped, hindered, or resolved. Their immediate cause was eliminated and Redfield, American ideology, simply flies away on a helicopter while pondering the impact of everything he has done to protect those around him. He looks at Jill Valentine, his partner from the previous game, who he rescued from mind control, and Sheva Alomar, his new partner, who had helped him through his current tribulations.

"Was it worth it?" Redfield asks at the end of *RE5*. Redfield looks at Sheva and Jill in the helicopter as they fly away from a nation that many would claim to have just suffered massive genocide at the hands of American corporate interests and shakes his head, smiling about how his companions make it all worth it. The final lesson of *RE5* is that all the people in the stable countries of the world are worth the mass murder of a victimized people. By the end of this game, Redfield has avoided putting on Wesker's sunglasses that would allow him to see how horrible the world is outside of the Global North. With the game over and no one left to kill, the player most likely has as well.

Works Cited

Adam. "Experience Kijuju" Blogspot. Web.

Altheide, David. *Qualitative Media Analysis.* Thousand Oaks: Sage Publications, 1996. Print.

Archivebot, Nowgamer. "The Making of *Resident Evil.*" *Now Gamer: 2010.* 11 November 2011.

Bailey, Alison. "Strategic Ignorance." *Race and Epistemologies of Ignorance.* Eds. Shannon Sullivan and Nancy Tuana. Albany: State University of New York Press, 2007, 77–94. Print.

Bauman, Zygmunt. *Liquid Modernity.* Malden: Polity Press, 2000. Print.

Bibliomaniac15. "Resident Evil 5 Game Script." *GameFAQs.* 2009. 10 October 2011. Web.

Bogost, Ian. *Persuasive Games: The Expressive Power of Video Games.* Cambridge: MIT Press, 2007. Print.

Boseley, Sarah. 2010. "WikiLeaks Cables: Pfizer Used Dirty Tricks to Avoid Clinical Trial Payout." *The Guardian—The U.S. Embassy Cables.* December 2010. 14 November 2011. Web.

Boucher, Geoff, and Matthew Sharpe. "Introduction: "Žižek's Communism' and *In Defence of Lost Causes.*" *International Journal of Žižek Studies*: 4 : 2: 1. Web.

Brock, André. 2011. "'When Keeping It Real Goes Wrong': *Resident Evil 5,* Racial Representation and Gamers. *Games and Culture 2011.* 5: 429. Web.

Capcom-Unity. "Resident Evil 5 Famitsu Interview with Takeuchi-san." April 2008. 12 May 2012.

"Federal Statutes—Alien Tort Statute—Second Circuit Looks Beyond Complaint to Find State Action Requirement Satisfied—*Abdullahi v Pfizer, Inc., 562 F.3d 163* (2d Cir. 2009). *Harvard Law Review* 768 (2010). Web.

Guardian U.K. "U.S. Embassy Cables: Pfizer Nears $75m Nigeria Settlement." *The Guardian: U.S. Embassy Cables: The Documents.* Dec 2009. 5 May 2012. Web.

John, Tracey. "Newsweek's N'Gai Croal on the 'Resident Evil 5' Trailer: 'This Imagery Has a History.'" *MTV Multiplayer: MTV Geek.* Apr. 2008. 6 April, 2012. Web.

Juul, Jesper. *Half Real: Video Games Between Real Rules and Fictional Worlds.* Cambridge: MIT Press, 2005. Print.

Kovac, Carl. 2001. "Nigerians to sue U.S. drug company over meningitis treatment." *BMJ Group* 15: 323 (7313): 592. Web.

Krosin, Michael T., Robert Klitzman, Bruce Levin, Jianfeng Cheng, and Megan L Ranney. 2006. "Comprehension of Informed Consent in Rural and Peri-Urban Mali, West Africa." *Clinical Trials* 3: 306–313. Web.

Lenzer, Jeanne. 2007. "Nigeria files criminal charges against Pfizer." *BMJ Group* 334:1181–1187. Web.

London, Jacqui Wise. 2001. "Pfizer accused of testing new drug without ethical approval." *BMJ Group* 322: 194. Web.

Mastrapa, Gus. "Into Africa with Resident Evil 5." *Crispy Gamer: Gaming Culture Unlocked.* June 2008. 12 November 2011. Web.

Matinyi, Ng'osi. "Why Africa is ignored in global affairs." *The Citizen: "It's the Content That Counts."* March 2011. 20 July 2012. Web.

McWhertor, Michael. "Resident Evil 5 Not Redesigned After Race Criticism, Says Producer." *Kotaku* Accessed: June 2008. 15 April, 2012. Web.

Murray, Senan. 2007. "Anger at deadly Nigerian drug trials." *BBC News* June 2007. 15 April, 2012. Web.

Narcisse, Evan. "Thought/Process: More on Resident Evil 5 and Uncomfortable Echoes." *Crispy Gamer: Gaming Culture Unlocked.* March 2009. 15 April 2012. Web.

_____. 2009. "Uncomfortable Echoes: A Conversation with Resident Evil 5 Director Jun Takeuchi." *Crispy Gamer: Gaming Culture Unlocked.* March 2009. 15 April 2012. Web.

Nundy, Samiran, and Chandra M. Gulhati. 2005. "A New Colonialism?—Conducting Clinical Trials in India." *The New England Journal of Medicine* 352:16:1633–1636. Web.

Presidential Commission for the Study of Bioethical Issues. *"Ethically Impossible": STD Research in Guatemala from 1946 to 1948.* Washington, D.C. September 2011. Web.

Rebecca Project for Human Rights; United Africans for Women and Children Rights; National Council of Negro Women. *Non-Consensual Research in Africa: The Outsourcing of Tuskegee Policy Brief.* Web.

Stephens, Joe. "Panel Faults Pfizer in '96 Clinical Trial in Nigeria." *The Washington Post.* May 2006. 15 April 2012. Web.

TheBatMan. "The History and Making of Biohazard '96." *Biohaze.* 2009. 22 June 2012. Web.

Totilo, Stephen. "That Notorious '*Resident Evil 5*' Trailer and the People I Met in Africa." *MTV Multiplayer.* August 2007. 15 April 2012. Web.

Umar, Auwalu. "Nigeria: Pfizer—Victims' Medical Records Missing." *All Africa.* October 2009. 24 May 2012. Web.

Wainaina, Binyavanga. 2005. "How to Write About Africa." *Granta: The Magazine of New Writing* 2013: 92: 97. Web.

Wallerstein, Immanuel. 1987. "The Construction of Peoplehood: Racism, Nationality, Ethnicity." *Sociological Forum* 2011: 2:2:373–388. Web.

Washington, Harriet A. 2007. "Why Africa Fears Western Medicine." *The New York Times.* July 2007. 10 March 2012. Web.

World Health Organization. *Observations on Vaccine Production Technologies and Factors Potentially Influencing Pandemic Influenza Vaccine Choices in Developing Countries: A Discussion Paper.* World Health Organization: Regional Office for South-East Asia. 2009. Web.

Žižek, Slavoj. *The Plague of Fantasies.* Brooklyn: Verso. 2008. Print.

_____. "Reloaded Revolutions." *More Matrix and Philosophy: Revolutions and Reloaded Decoded.* Edited by William Irwin. Chicago: Open Court, 2005. 198–208. Print.

_____. *Welcome to the Desert of the Real: Five Essays on September 11 and Related Dates.* London: Verso, 2002. Print.

Zyl, Mikki van, Jeanelle de Gruchy, Sheila Lapinsky, Simon Lewin, and Graeme Reid. *The Aversion Project: Human Rights Abuses of Gays and Lesbians in the South African Defence Force by Health Workers During the Apartheid Era.* Cape Town, South Africa: Simply Said and Done, 1999. Web.

Through the Looking-Glass: Interrogating the "Alice-ness" of Alice

Hannah Priest

Paul Anderson's 2002 film *Resident Evil* contains a number of verbal and visual references to Lewis Carroll's nineteenth-century novels *Alice's Adventures in Wonderland* and *Through the Looking-Glass*. These range from character names—the protagonist Alice and the Red Queen computer—to settings that vaguely echo the *Alice* books—entry to another "world" via a mirrored room—and visual details that remind the audience of the earlier novels—a white rabbit in a laboratory, a paperweight with an Alice in Wonderland design. The frequency with which these references appear suggest a conscious intertextual relationship between the *Alice* novels and Anderson's film, and suggests that some parallels might be drawn between Carroll's texts and the *Resident Evil* (filmic) universe.

However, this intertextuality is notable for its superficiality and tenuousness. The paperweight with the Alice design is almost impossible to discern on first viewing the film; a white rabbit in a laboratory need not necessarily be a reference to Carroll's novels. More significantly, were these references removed there would be little effect on the film's overall plot and characterization, which is underlined by the fact that the subsequent films in the series make far fewer explicit *Alice* references. It is possible, therefore, to view these references as a sort of "Wonderland window dressing," similar to that employed in the first *Matrix* film (dir. Andy and Lana Wachowski, 1999), intended to indicate the move from the "real" world to somewhere "other" and to signpost the strangeness of the otherworld.

The journey "down the rabbit hole" from Carroll's original children's novels to a filmic shorthand for otherworldly strangeness, via surrealist art, modernist literature and psychedelic pop culture, deserves a study in its own right; it is not, however, the focus here. Rather, this essay will explore what remains of *Alice* in the *Resident Evil* films when one looks beyond the "Wonderland window dressing." With or without leporine visual cues, the *Resident*

Evil films undoubtedly feature a protagonist who shares her name with Carroll's heroine—to what extent, then, can we read Alice alongside Alice?

It would be odd (to say the least) to claim *Resident Evil* as even the loosest retelling or revision of Lewis Carroll's *Alice* novels. A former head of security at a secret corporate laboratory battling against increasingly monstrous opponents unleashed by her former employer in the wake of an apocalyptic viral outbreak has little in common with a prim and bossy English schoolgirl's playful adventures in a nursery rhyme-inspired fantasyland. Nevertheless, there are striking similarities between the construction of *Resident Evil*'s Alice and the protagonists of texts that are more explicitly interpretations or sequels to Carroll's: examples include Simon Fellows's *Malice in Wonderland* (2009), American McGee's Alice games for PC and Xbox and, to a lesser degree, Jeff Noon's novel *The Automated Alice* and the *Warehouse 13* series one episode "Duped" (2009). Additionally, parallels can also be drawn with another group of texts which, like *Resident Evil*, resist being read as versions of *Alice's Adventures in Wonderland*, but contain a repertoire of "Wonderland window dressing" and construct their protagonist along similar lines to *Resident Evil*'s Alice: this second group of texts includes Zack Snyder's *Sucker Punch* (2011), John Carpenter's *The Ward* (2010) and Jay Lee's *Alyce* (2011). This chapter explores the models of femininity presented in the *Resident Evil* film series, and its connection to these other twenty-first-century "Alice" texts, arguing that, while the films cannot be read as interpretations of Carroll's novels, they belong to an "Alice tradition" of presenting feminine identity through madness, fragmentation, agency, violence, and disengagement.

As Mad as a Hatter

In recent years a number of scholars have recognized the peculiar malleability of Carroll's *Alice* novels. Michael Hancher notes the "dreamlike, episodic structure of both books, the heavily charged psychological subtext, and the explicit privileging of pictorial illustration," which "have from the start led her audiences to register her story in terms of character, scene, myth, and image, rather than of plot, narrative voice, or (save for some memorable phrases) diction." He describes *Alice* as "a happily overdetermined and polymorphous text" that "thrives in an infinite number of forms" (202). Considering the novels' child-protagonist specifically, Helen Pilinovsky writes: "In the hundred years since her copyright expired, she has passed from being a specific character to being a near archetype: images of Alice appear in every medium" (182). The plurality of Wonderland, and the rejection of authorial control or master narrative in its many incarnations, proliferates across "an infinite number of forms" and "every medium"; nevertheless, in order for this to make sense, there must also be some uniformity through which an audience can recognize a text as participating in this tradition. For Hancher and Pilinovsky, as for other scholars of post–Carroll Wonderlands, the common ground is to be found in "character," in "a near archetype," in "her story." Not only is this sense of "character" as much concerned with post–Carroll traditions as it is with the *Alice* novels, it is manifested clearly in the *Resident Evil* series of films. While the plot, narrative voice, medium and diction of these films owe little (if anything) to Carroll's *Alice* novels, the female protagonist is an Alice character.

One of the primary markers of Alice's identity in the first *Resident Evil* film is her loss of memory; indeed, this both facilitates and drives the film's plot. In the opening sequence of the film, Alice regains consciousness on the floor of a shower. She experiences brief flashbacks, but these are incomplete and reveal nothing about her loss of consciousness. She leaves the bathroom and enters a bedroom, finding objects that appear significant but about which she knows nothing. Alice's amnesia continues on her abduction and transportation into the Hive. While other characters reveal information about her past—specifically about the falseness of her life with her "husband" Spence—Alice's only access to any of this is through further fragmented flashbacks. Even as her role in the events leading to the Hive's lock-down is revealed, Alice's mind struggles to connect with anything prior to the events of the film. Questioned by Matt about her role in his sister's death, Alice is forced to admit, "I don't remember the truth."

This amnesia, and its relationship to the "truth" about Umbrella's purpose and intentions, continues throughout the series. Despite Alice's defiant claim in the second film (*Resident Evil: Apocalypse*, dir. Alexander Witt, 2004) that "I remember everything," this is undermined by a lack of revelation to the audience about Alice's life before the events of the first film. Her voiceover at the beginning of *Apocalypse* announces that she was the "Head of Security" at the Hive, but there are no flashbacks or other evidence of Alice's memories of this role. Alice, as the viewer comes to know her, begins at the moment she awakens in the shower. Furthermore, Alice's peculiar susceptibility to unconsciousness and (potential) amnesia is underscored by the frequency with which she is rendered insensible during the course of the series: Alice reawakens twice in *Resident Evil* (in the shower and, towards the end of the film, on a hospital bed in quarantine), once in *Apocalypse* (in a water tank in an Umbrella laboratory); numerous times in *Resident Evil: Extinction* (dir. Russell Mulcahy, 2007), including an opening scene which recreates the shower awakening from the first film; and *Resident Evil: Retribution* (dir. Paul Anderson, 2012) recreates the laboratory awakening from the end of the first film/beginning of the second. In the third and subsequent films, these depictions of unconsciousness and amnesia are heightened by the fact that not all the "Alices" who wake up are the same. The introduction of the clone–Alices troubles a sense of coherent and complete memory in the protagonist, implying that Alice's consciousness has literally become fragmented.

While Alice is not described or portrayed as "mad" in the *Resident Evil* films, the presentation of her mind and her mental connection to the events around her is unsettled. The audience rarely see or learn anything that Alice herself is not aware of—notable exceptions include the multiple clone–Alices in *Extinction* and the survival of Jill Valentine which is first signaled in an in-credit sequence at the end of *Resident Evil: Afterlife* (dir. Paul Anderson, 2010)—and the viewer learns about Umbrella at the same pace as the protagonist. More significant, however, is the way in which the viewer experiences Alice's engagement with the world around her and the recovery of her memories. The frequent use of brief, disjointed flashbacks throughout the series, including one in which the Alice of the present walks amongst embodied hallucinations of the past (*Resident Evil*), allows the audience to view the events of the film via a psyche that is ruptured, damaged and, possibly, unreliable.

The association of Alice-inspired characters with madness is a long one. Inspired, perhaps, by Carroll's Cheshire Cat's assertion that "we're all mad here" (35), twentieth- and twenty-first-century Alices are frequently figured in terms of mental illness, amnesia and psychosis. Carroll's *Alice* novels were first associated with neurosis and mental infirmity in the 1930s. In an essay now widely thought to be tongue-in-cheek, A.M.E. Goldschmidt proposed a Freudian reading of Carroll's novels as heavily symbolic and suggestive of the subconscious; this reading was followed by further psychoanalytic readings of the novels, which lacked the (probable) irony of Goldschmidt's original. Such readings of Carroll's novels are not universally accepted, and frequently rely on an imagined projection of the author's own subconscious desires and neuroses—to which I will return in the final section of this chapter. Nonetheless, these interpretations mark the beginning of a longstanding association of Wonderland with a *mental* landscape, and Alice's participation therein with subconscious and unconscious development (and decline).

In the 1970s, an alternative psychoanalytic reading of Alice was proposed by feminist writers of the "French" school of theory. Specifically, Luce Irigaray and Hélène Cixous read in Alice a powerful exemplar of the fragmentation and impossibility of feminine subjectivity. The metaphor of the looking-glass is key here, and Rachel Falconer has traced this mode of understanding the "fragmentary" female "nonsubject" through Alice and Wonderland from Irigaray and Cixous to later autopathographies of female mental illness, such as the semi-fictionalized memoirs of Marya Hornbacher and Susanna Kaysen, which contain numerous references to the Carrollian Wonderland (6).

And yet, while *Resident Evil* shares some ground with the psychoanalytic appropriations of Alice, and with the madness memoirs that reflect similar readings of female subjectivity, the film series also resists a reading based unproblematically in Irigaray and Cixous's looking-glass metaphor. While the narrators of the autopathographies examined by Falconer learn to recognize their own fragmented selves and return, to some extent, to "the normal spaces of social interchange," (9) *Resident Evil*'s protagonist embraces fragmentation and focuses it outwards. Indeed it could be argued that Alice's "madness" is a necessary weapon that will ensure her survival in a hostile world. The memoirs examined by Falconer present the Wonderland/underworld as a territory of the unconscious. The narrator-authors of Hornbacher and Kaysen's texts are both institutionalized, but in order to "escape" Wonderland they must embrace their respective institutions as a site of treatment rather than incarceration. However, if we look to an earlier semi-fictionalized memoir of female madness—Antonia White's 1954 novel *Beyond the Glass*—we can discern the beginnings of another tradition of figuring the relationship between female madness and Wonderland, which has relevance to the portrayal of Alice in the *Resident Evil* films.

In White's novel, the protagonist Clara experiences a manic episode which leaves her hospitalized. Unaware of where she is or what has led to her incarceration, she views her surroundings as a nightmarish distortion of Wonderland—the title of the novel itself comes from her looking at a beautiful garden through a window but being unable to actually get to it, a reference to an episode in *Alice's Adventures in Wonderland*. In the early parts of the novel, Clara hints at an understanding of her own identity and subjectivity based in *Alice*-related imagery. She employs the looking-glass image frequently, with her reflection representing not only a sense of fragmentation, but the outright threat of "a twin sister" who "became mocking, even menacing" (White 31). However, it is not until she is institutionalized that Clara explicitly understands herself as being "Alice Through the Looking-Glass" (233). Unlike the narrators of Hornbacher and Kaysen's books, who find in their respective hospitals "a sorority" of fellow patients (Falconer 11), Clara is surrounded by "strange-looking people," like "an old lady who wore very elaborate white draperies and a strange headdress like the Duchess in Alice in Wonderland" (White 237). In a telling scene, Clara makes a futile attempt to interact with other patients by teaching them how to play croquet. Her attempt fails and she realizes, like Carroll's Alice, that "[s]he was imprisoned in a place full of mad people" (243). This externalization of "madness" is presented alongside images of Clara's brutalization at the hands of doctors and nurses. Although much of what she describes appears to be the product of her psychosis—for example, she believes she is the subject of medical experimentation by the military—it is also, in fact, her "treatment": she is drugged, force-fed, restrained, put on display for other doctors, mocked and only avoids having her hair sewn into a plait by dint of it being too short. Clara only escapes "Wonderland" in the end by admitting that she is *not* like the other patients, that "what *they* say doesn't always make sense" (257, my emphasis).

It is possible to read Clara's "Wonderland" as, at least in part, a product of her own mind: she imagines patients, doctors and nurses through the lens of the *Alice* books to which she has referred prior to her committal. Nevertheless, the references to the dehumanization she undergoes, as well as the fact that none of this "treatment" appears to have any effect on her recovery, externalizes the threat of Wonderland. It is important, at this point, to consider *where* Clara has been taken. She is in the "Nazareth Royal Hospital," a barely fictionalized version of the Royal Bethlehem Hospital (commonly known as Bedlam), the institution to which the author was committed in the 1920s. A byword for brutality, cruelty and dehumanization, "Bedlam" (at least in fiction) is only superficially related to the wards and treatment facilities in which the narrators of contemporary autopathographies begin their road to "normal spaces of social interchange." White's Clara is not sent to a hospital; she is sent to an asylum, with all the threat that word conveys.

Resident Evil's Alice is neither committed to a hospital nor an asylum, but her experience of a threatening Wonderland, partly a creation of her own fragmented psyche and partly of an external and threatening institution, has more resonance with White's memoir than with those of Hornbacher or Kaysen. Like Clara, Alice *must* accept her Wonderland as external in order to survive it; neither Alice nor Clara can accept any "sorority" with fellow inhabitants. In *Apocalypse*, for example, Jill Valentine is exhorted to stay and fight for Raccoon City by Peyton: "These are our people, Jill!" This is contrasted sharply with Alice's later nonchalance at the nuclear attack on the city; she displays no sadness or pity because, though they might be Jill's, they are not her people.

The relationship between White's memoir and *Resident Evil* is further heightened by comparison with two other texts in which "Alices" are incarcerated in asylums. In John Carpenter's *The Ward*, a young woman called Kristen is sent to an institution following an act of arson. The asylum—and I choose this word over "hospital" given the institution's labyrinthine corridors, instruments of medicalized brutality, supernatural manifestations, and disappearing inmates—is populated by one small group of patients, also all young women. One by one, these patients are killed by a malevolent ghost named Alice (depicted in life as wearing an Alice band and carrying a stuffed white rabbit). When Kristen is the only patient left alive, her doctor reveals to her that in truth she is Alice, and that she, like her fellow patients, is one of Alice's multiple personalities, a fragmentation of self resulting from her abduction and rape at the age of eleven. In order to allow Alice to recover, Kristen must submit to being killed by her.

The ending of Carpenter's film allows for some ambiguity, particularly as the final "scare" comes from the supposedly dead Kristen bursting from a cupboard as Alice leaves with her parents, undermining the efficacy of any treatment. Dr. Stringer's final explanation clearly suggests that the asylum–Wonderland was entirely a product of Alice's imagination, with the whole scenario occurring internally during hypnosis. However, the methods employed to "kill" her personalities evoke the external threat of the Bedlam-like institution, with one personality having an orbitoclast forced through her eye and into her brain and another being electrocuted with an ECT machine. Even the revelation of the "truth" is told as Dr. Stringer forces "Kristen" into a hypnotic state to the ticking of a Gothic metronome. *The Ward*'s undermining of a completely internalized Wonderland through the tropes of the threatening asylum finds echoes in the presentation of female madness in Zack Snyder's *Sucker Punch*. Like *The Ward*, this film has no explicit association with *Alice*, aside from a heroine who wears an Alice band and the use of a cover version of Jefferson Airplane's *White Rabbit* in the soundtrack. Nevertheless, the parallels with Carpenter's film, White's *Beyond the Glass* and the *Resident Evil* films are striking. Sent to the Gothic Lennox House following the accidental murder of her younger sister, the protagonist Babydoll is the victim of her abusive stepfather and a corrupt orderly who quickly ensure she is scheduled for a lobotomy. As the orbitoclast (again being used as a symbol of the brutality of the asylum) is raised, Babydoll enters a double fantasy world. First, Babydoll is a dancer in a sinister burlesque club, and then from there she fantasizes a series of set pieces in which she and several other young women must fight dragons, Samurai warriors and steampunk Nazis in order to escape. Eventually, one woman (Sweet Pea) does escape, and Babydoll undergoes the neurosurgery. Again, the internalization of Wonderland is made clear—the events of the film happen in Babydoll's head as she awaits a lobotomy. But this is undermined by the threat of the asylum. It is revealed at the end of the film that the violent and abusive acts that took place in the "fantasy" world were versions of events that took place in the "real" world and that each player in the "fantasy" has its double in the "real." Sweet Pea's escape from Lennox House really does happen, suggesting that the menacing Wonderland really was something she had to evade.

These asylum–Alice films stand in clear relationship to the *Resident Evil* series. Like Kristen/Alice and Babydoll (and Clara before them), Alice is continuously threatened by the external world. She is not fighting inner demons, but rather the monsters created by an institution exterior to her. While Alice does not find herself incarcerated in an asylum, she frequently wakes up in a laboratory and is the subject of literally dehumanizing experimentation as she becomes "Project Alice." The constant threat of medicalized brutality, symbolized by the lobotomy in *Sucker Punch* and *The Ward*, is emphasized by the continued creation and disposal of clone–Alices (*Extinction* and *Retribution*), the attempt to "shut down" Alice at a distance (*Extinction*), and the specter of Jill Valentine and (temporarily) Claire Redfield's "reprogramming" with Umbrella's biomechanical devices (*Afterlife* and *Retribution*). Far from accepting the need to treat her fragmented self and internalize her ruptured psyche, Alice utilizes this as a means of survival. Like Babydoll and Kristen/Alice, she externalizes her anger through increasingly violent actions, embracing and weaponizing her confusion and fragmentation. Instead of experiencing anxiety at the sight of her cloned self, Alice builds herself (into) an army and confronts Umbrella: "I'm gonna be bringing a few of my friends" (*Extinction*).

Nothing but a Pack of Cards!

Resident Evil's Alice is characterized throughout the film series by her capacity to enact physical violence upon others, and to endure physical violence enacted upon her by others. Despite the insistence that Alice's status changes from human, to genetically enhanced superwoman, to human again, her ability to sustain and cause injury remains constant. From the first time she runs up the walls of the Hive and kills a zombie dog with a well-aimed kick (*Resident Evil*), the audience is left in no doubt that Alice possesses the ability and inclination to carry out stylized acts of hyperviolence. At first glance, this appears to differentiate her from her Carrollian namesake; however, *Resident Evil*'s Alice belongs to a tradition of violent Alices that can be traced back to her Victorian ancestor. Moreover, the capacity for violence revealed in these Alices is directly related to the threat of Wonderland and the presentation of agency-through-madness discussed above.

At the end of *Alice's Adventures in Wonderland*, the seven-year-old protagonist becomes frustrated at the absurdity of her surroundings. The final straw, it seems, is the farcical trial of the Knave of Hearts. By the time Alice is called to give evidence, she has begun to grow tall again, causing her to scatter members of the jury "on to the heads of the crowd below" (73). Eventually Alice goes further and dismisses the business of the court (and, by implication, the business of Wonderland) as "[s]tuff and nonsense!" and the persons within it as "nothing but a pack of cards!" (78). At this, the court fly into the air and fall on her as playing cards, Alice gives a scream "half of fright and half of anger," and she leaves/escapes Wonderland (78). This method of returning to the "real" world is echoed at the end of *Through the Looking-Glass*, which climaxes in Alice exclaiming "I can't stand this any longer!" (167) and shaking the Red Queen "backwards and forwards with all her might" until she turns into a kitten (168).

Alice's violence is not wanton, though it can be read as childish petulance or impatience. Rather, it is a final act of frustration against an increasingly bizarre and menacing world. Moreover, as Will Brooker notes, early editions of *Through the Looking-Glass* highlighted this further by presenting a possible avatar for Alice that is more explicitly associated with violent acts. In considering the poem "Jabberwocky," which appears in Alice's second adventure, Brooker writes: "[W]e might remember that the Beamish Boy who defeats the Jabberwock looks, in Tenniel's illustration, rather like Alice herself; he wears her striped stockings under a tunic, and has her flowing long hair. In the original *Looking-Glass*, then, we already have seen a kind of substitute Alice, another alternate mirror version, perhaps, wielding a vorpal sword against monsters" (245).

Brooker uses this Alice who is "already" "wielding a vorpal sword against monsters" to offer a heritage for the presentation of a violent Alice in the PC game American McGee's *Alice* (Rogue/EA Games, 2000); I suggest that the characteristics outlined by Brooker as being shared by McGee and Carroll's Alices are also found in the presentation of Alice in *Resident Evil*. Furthermore, the *Resident Evil* series and American McGee's *Alice* games are not the only texts in which we find an Alice who responds to the cruel and brutal menace of Wonderland with extreme violence. As discussed above, both *Sucker Punch* and *The Ward* present Alices who are menaced by an asylum–Wonderland that threatens both physical and psychological assault. Additionally, the eponymous heroine of the straight-to-DVD slasher film *Alice in Murderland* (dir. Dennis Devine, 2010) enacts the familiar role of "final girl," learning to respond to the attacks of an unknown assailant with her own acts of violence. In this case, Alice is also "mad," but does not realize this until the final sequence: the murderers were her sisters, therefore she assumes homicidal insanity is a family trait and begins laughing maniacally before the credits roll.

More violent than these is the protagonist of Jay Lee's 2011 horror film, *Alyce*. Like *Resident Evil*, Lee's film is neither a continuation nor a retelling of Carroll's novels, but, once again, a potential connection is hinted at by the use of "Wonderland window dressing": the ubiquitous white rabbit is an ornament on the heroine's dressing table, a bartender waves a drink in Alyce's face repeatedly saying, "Drink me!" and a cover version of *White Rabbit* blasts out of Alyce's car stereo in the opening scenes. However, it is in the characterization of Lee's Alyce that we see the strongest indication that, despite the "y" in her name, the heroine of this film is to be read as an Alice. Her story begins, like

Sucker Punch, with the accidental death of a loved one. The socially awkward heroine causes her close (female) friend Carroll Lewis to fall from a roof and receive serious injuries. Terrified that Carroll will reveal her involvement in the "accident," Alyce smothers her in the hospital. Guilt leads Alyce to seek solace in drug use, which in turn leads to her killing more people and disposing of the bodies in increasingly gory ways. While Alyce's murder spree begins while she is under the influence of drugs, doubts are thrown on her mental health prior to the death of Carroll. When Alyce and Carroll go to a bar near the beginning of the film, a male acquaintance states that "[t]here's something not right about that one there." And Alyce's "joke" push that causes Carroll to fall is in retaliation for the latter's taunting about the obsessive "single white female" attachment Alyce has for her friend. In many ways, Lee's Wonderland is a mental landscape that exists within the heroine. This is signposted early in the film when Carroll refers to Alyce's previous "not right" behavior as being a consequence of her living "[d]own the rabbit hole." Much of what Alyce experiences in the film is psychological: she repeatedly "sees" the decaying corpse of Carroll and hallucinates further murders of her erstwhile friend. However, Wonderland is also an external threat to which Alyce responds with violence. Her guilt leads her to the drug dealer Rex (with his companions, March and Mouse), who forces Alyce to perform degrading sexual acts in return for drugs. Even Alyce's murder and dismemberment of Carroll's ex-boyfriend Vince, though ostensibly an act of retaliation for his betrayal of her friend, is facilitated by overbearing sexual advances and threat. When Alyce finally confronts Rex, baseball bat in hand, the man asks her what the weapon is for: "Finding control" is her succinct answer.

Alyce's drink- and drug-induced Wonderland superficially bears little resemblance to that in *Resident Evil*; however, the idea of a heroine using violence as a way to "find control" in a threatening world is common to both. The lack of empathy shown by both Alice and Alyce to the creatures/men that they kill reveals a disengagement from Wonderland that resonates through a tradition of violent and mad Alices, and echoes (albeit in a distorted, exaggerated form) scenes from Carroll's nineteenth-century novels. Like Alyce, *Resident Evil*'s Alice also exhibits some guilt over her role in creating the nightmarish Wonderland in which she has to fight. Her flashbacks in the first film suggest some complicity in the release of the T-virus from the Hive. In *Afterlife*, when she believes that she is the last survivor of the viral apocalypse, she reflects: "This is my punishment for letting all this happen." But, like Lee's Alyce, Alice cannot and does not allow guilt to prevent her from continuing to fight and kill; she presses ahead on her journey through Wonderland, with military training and an ever-expanding battery of weapons as her "vorpal sword."

Goodbye Mister Dodgson

One of the most violent, disengaged and mentally ill Alices—though the majority of her malevolence is narrated rather than shown—can be found in the first series of the U.S. television show *Warehouse 13*. In the episode entitled "Duped" (1:8, 2009), the team of supernatural custodians discover "Lewis Carroll's mirror" in which "Alice Liddell" appears to be trapped. After some research, Artie reveals to other team members that this is the "real" Alice Liddell, stating: "Lewis Carroll's Alice. So sweet. So innocent. So not ... true. This woman was mad as a hatter." Alice was a serial killer who was imprisoned in the mirror to prevent further crimes. Artie continues: "And Charles Dodgson (aka Lewis Carroll) was not writing books. He was chronicling this young woman's descent into a sociopathic madness." Due to a mishap at the warehouse, Alice Liddell escapes and takes control of the body of one of the agents (Myka), before attempting to continue her career of homicidal violence—in one scene picking up a hammer and gazing at it with interest, murmuring the not entirely unexpected words "curiouser and curiouser."

In "Duped," though Alice is mad, her violence follows a different pattern to that of the Alices discussed in the previous section. In this text, Alice's disengagement and lack of empathy is not a defense mechanism against a hostile world, but a symptom of a "descent into a sociopathic madness." It is perhaps futile here to determine where a lack of empathy ends and sociopathic madness begins, but *Warehouse 13*'s Alice Liddell's insistence that "[h]urting is half the fun" seems at odds with *Resident Evil*'s portrayal of violence as a strategy of survival or revenge. Nevertheless, some aspects of the presentation of a violent Alice in "Duped" find a clearer parallel in the *Resident Evil* series. Specifically, the introduction of "Charles Dodgson" as a character and the concomitant naming of Alice as "Alice Liddell" points to a problematic tradition of reflecting the "authorship" of the *Alice* novels within fictional texts inspired by them. While there is no "Charles Dodgson" character as such in the *Resident Evil* films, Alice's relationship to her creator(s) is not only a continual site of conflict, but is in fact the central focus of the climactic confrontation in all five films in the series to date.

As noted above, the 1930s saw the first psychoanalytic readings of Carroll's *Alice* novels; this decade, from the 1932 centenary of Carroll's birth, also saw the first attempts to build a narrative around the stories' authorship that scrutinized the relationship between the Rev. Charles Dodgson (who wrote under the pseudonym Lewis Carroll) and Alice Pleasance Liddell, the young daughter of the Dean of Christ Church, Oxford, for whom Dodgson wrote *Alice's Adventures Under Ground* (to be published as *Alice's Adventures in Wonderland*). Dodgson's friendship with the Liddell girls—Alice, Edith and

Lorina—was first questioned in this period, with suggestions of an "obsession" on the clergyman's part fuelled by newspaper articles featuring stories from other girls who had known him, the circulation of photographs of nude children taken by Dodgson, and supposedly mysterious missing diary pages that may (or, as is now clear, may not) have recounted a marriage proposal to an eleven-year-old Alice Liddell.

As the twentieth century progressed, so too did the portrait of Dodgson, developing into the image of a virginal Victorian clergyman who shunned the company of adults (particularly women) in favor of pseudo-pedophilic attachments to prepubescent girls, a man who immortalized the object of his repressed desires in a tale conceived as a result of an opium addiction. It is not my purpose here to repeat or debunk all the insinuations that have been made regarding Dodgson's relationship to Alice Liddell over the past eighty years; Karoline Leach's *In the Shadow of the Dreamchild* provides a thorough examination and presentation of evidence on which much of this overview is based.

This introduction to what is known as the "Carroll Myth"—divorced as it is from the reality of Dodgson and the Liddell family—may seem to have little relevance to a reading of the *Resident Evil* films. It may seem unimportant that the figure of "Lewis Carroll" or "Charles Dodgson" (and, at the same time, "Alice Liddell") has been so thoroughly mythologized that the "facts" of his pedophilia and obsession are now treated as received wisdom. However, this "received wisdom" informs numerous contemporary texts inspired by, or responding to, the *Alice* novels. It also has a significant and consistent impact on the characterization of an "Alice" in the texts, which can be seen in an echoed (but still recognizable) form in the *Resident Evil* films.

Though some responses to the *Alice* novels have sought to address the relationship between Dodgson and Alice Liddell directly—for example, Katie Roiphe's *Still She Haunts Me* and Melanie Benjamin's *Alice I Have Been*—by offering a fictional account of the two "real" people that lie behind the famous novels, other texts incorporate the Carroll myth in a more tacit fashion. Though Dodgson's supposed sexual deviancy and drug addiction are implicitly referenced in the numerous Alice-texts that employ what Brooker identifies as recurring "motifs of psychedelia and paedophilia" (177), this is not the focus for all *Alice*-inspired texts. In the films under consideration in this chapter—and particularly, for *Resident Evil*—it is not psychedelia and pedophilia that come to the fore, but authorship and control. These aspects of the Carroll myth are not exclusive, and depend on an "axiom upon which the entire analysis of Carroll's life and literature depends," which is, as Leach argues, "the assumption that the girl-child was more or less the single outlet for his emotional and creative energies in an otherwise lonely and isolated life" (12). This axiom has incredible potency, and we can see its power in the near ubiquity of "Charles Dodgson" characters in contemporary Alice-texts.

In the *Warehouse 13* episode discussed above, Charles Dodgson is neither a pedophile nor a drug addict. He is rather a demon-hunter, determined to imprison the sociopathic Alice Liddell and prevent further murders. Though the episode reveals no attempt to encourage the audience to identify or sympathize with Alice Liddell, the character's intense desire to escape and subsequent enjoyment of freedom allow us to briefly consider the situation from the other side of the looking-glass. Here we have a child—the glimpses we have of Alice Liddell's true face is of a ghostly Victorian child-woman—trapped forever by a man who is obsessed with her and who "chronicles" her life.

Charles Dodgson as benign obsessive also appears in other contemporary Alice-texts. In one chapter of Jeff Noon's *The Automated Alice*, a "trequel" to Carroll's *Alice* books, the protagonist opens a cottage door to find a kindly old man waiting for her. "Have you forgotten me so easily, Alice?" the man asks. Alice then realizes it is "Mister Dodgson!" (220). After some discussion about Alice's current adventures, Mister Dodgson reveals to her that he "was a real person who once upon a time naturally died," but that Alice is "both a *real* and an *imaginary* character" whose story can continue. Alice expresses a desire "to escape, unlike [...] Mister Dodgson," and the old man begins to cry: "I was rather hoping we could spend some time together, Alice" (222). The girl kisses him goodbye and leaves. This final exchange possibly carries with it some echoes of the imagined pedophilic relationship so prevalent in popular discourse surrounding Dodgson, but the references to "story" and "narrative" in this passage also underline the man's *authorship* of the girl, which is emphasized by the appearance of "Zenith O'Clock" (an avatar of Noon himself) elsewhere in the novel. Though the Alices are ostensibly very different, the Dodgson-author of *The Automated Alice* has much in common with the Dodgson-chronicler of *Warehouse 13*, not least in the fact that both have "naturally died," while their Alices' stories have continued.

The relevance of this analysis to the *Resident Evil* films may not be initially clear. There is no "Charles Dodgson," benign or deviant, in any of the installments of the series to date. However, *Resident Evil's* Alice *is* a created product, and confrontations with her "authors" appear at the climax of each film. As Alice's memories begin to return in *Resident Evil*, she recalls some details of her married life with Spence. This, as One reveals, is actually a story invented by Umbrella as part of a covert operation. At the end of the film, when Alice believes she has survived the Hive, she is confronted by Umbrella operatives who take control of her once more. She is rendered unconscious, and when she recovers she is in quarantine, naked (save a minimal square of material), with sensors attached to a partially shaved head. She is a blank slate ready to be rewritten. In subsequent films, Alice's "author" is individualized. In *Apocalypse*, it is revealed that, during the time she was unconscious at the end of the previous film, Alice was mutated through exposure to the T-virus. Major Cain assumes the role of creator here, pitting Alice against his other creation, the Nemesis Project, and encouraging her to accept that the latter and she are "like brother and sister." The reference to sibling relationship between Alice and the Nemesis Project situates Cain as a pseudo-father figure to the two, which is evidenced in both his praise and condemnation of Alice. He refuses to accept the term "mutation" to describe what has been done to her: "You're evolution. With my help, just imagine what you can achieve." When she refuses him, he responds: "You're such a disappointment to me." Unlike the Charles Dodgson characters of *Warehouse 13* and *The Automated Alice*, Cain does not "naturally" die; Alice kills him. However, her activation as "Project Alice" in the final moments of the film reveals that she is still under the obsessive authorship of a controlling creator.

In *Extinction*, it is Dr. Isaacs who assumes the Charles Dodgson role. Manufacturing clone after clone with limited success, Isaacs reveals a fascination with the activities of the "real" Alice. He describes her as "magnificent," and only "shuts her down" with reluctance. In the inevitable final showdown, a now–Tyrant Isaacs defiantly states: "You can't kill me!" Alice manages to do so, but only with the assistance of a clone–Alice also created by her "author." Isaacs is then replaced in *Afterlife* and *Retribution* by Wesker, who continues the role of Alice's controller. Significantly, Wesker's role moves from malevolent (in *Afterlife*) to benign (in *Retribution*), despite being "killed" by Alice on more than one occasion. The reformed Wesker's final act at the end of *Retribution*, after everything Alice has survived, destroyed and overcome, is to inject her with a serum to modify her once more. This reading of Cain, Isaacs and Wesker as Charles Dodgson characters relies on two strands of the Alice tradition. Firstly, it refers to an understanding of Wonderland as an externalized and menacing threat that can only be overcome through Alice's agency-through-madness and violence. Secondly, it reflects the continued shadowing of Alice texts by the "sinister twins, warped looking-glass reflections" of Charles Dodgson/Lewis Carroll and Alice Liddell (Brooker xvii). These strands come together to produce texts in which Alice's amnesia/madness and descent into Wonderland is effected through the obsessive machinations of an unwholesome "author." *Resident Evil* resembles other Alice-texts in this respect, and we might compare it to the portrayal of Clara and Alice's dysfunctional relationships to their respective fathers in *Beyond the Glass* and Simon Fellows's *Malice in Wonderland*, Dr. Stringer's questionable hypnosis in *The Ward*, and Babydoll's lobotomization in *Sucker Punch*.

To understand Cain, Isaacs and Wesker as "Charles Dodgson" requires some examination of Alice as "Alice Liddell." Invocations of the Carroll myth necessarily rely on an understanding of "Alice Liddell" as a girl who never moves beyond the age of eleven. However, fictions inspired by the *Alice* novels have increasingly presented audiences with Alices who are far older. Pilinovsky argues that, in contemporary fictions, "the once innocent young child heroine is now commonly depicted as a physically mature young woman, and the Wonderland that surrounds her is more commonly employed as a place of experience than as a place of innocence" (175). She accounts for the maturation of Alices by suggesting that it is "based in an uneasy fascination with the circumstances surrounding the composition of her original story and the myth of her relationship with Lewis Carroll, and that in many retellings Alice is aged in order to excuse that interest" (176). Pilinovsky's intention here is to explore the presentation of Alice in Alan Moore and Melinda Gebbie's *Lost Girls*, a graphic novel in which the character of Alice is presented as an older woman who takes laudanum and has sexual relationships with underage girls; however, her exploration of the maturation of Alice has resonance with the presentation of post-pubescent heroines in films such as *Malice in Wonderland, Alyce, Sucker Punch* and *The Ward*.

Resident Evil's Alice is also much older than either the heroine of the *Alice* novels or the mythologized "Alice Liddell"; nevertheless, she is, in many ways, closer to her child-forebears than many of the other Alices discussed in this chapter. While *Lost Girls'* Alice is constructed through her sexual desires and encounters, and *Malice in Wonderland's* Alice finds herself physically and emotionally attracted to Whitey, a time-obsessed taxi driver played by Danny Dyer, *Resident Evil's* Alice is resolutely asexual. Though her character, as played by Milla Jovovich, is clearly intended to be *desirable* (to the audiences, though not specifically to characters within the films), Alice reveals no indication of being *desiring*. Notably, the only potential relationships shown for Alice, her faux-marriage to Spence in *Resident Evil* and the suburban home-life of clone–Alice and clone–Carlos at the beginning of *Retribution*, are based in either shadowy espionage or domesticity and parenthood, rather than attraction or desire. Moreover, though the Alices of *Sucker Punch* and *The Ward* are similarly devoid of any sexual desire, and Lee's Alyce exhibits only autoerotic and necrophiliac desire (revealed in her masturbating to traumatic news footage and molesting Carroll's corpse), their texts imply that this is the result of previous or ongoing abuse by men. In the filmic universe of *Resident Evil*, Alice has no such traumatic past. Any hint of attraction between Alice and Matt in *Resident Evil* is rewritten as the sibling relationship of Alice and the Nemesis Project in *Apocalypse*, and Alice is able to reproduce asexually from *Extinction* onwards.

Alice's lack of sexual desire is not enough alone to point to her as a childlike character. However, the films further contrast Alice to other adult women, suggesting that she is somehow different from her ostensible peers. The fierce self-sacrificing loyalty of Rain Ocampo (*Resident Evil*), the protective nature of Jill Valentine (*Apocalypse*) and Claire Redfield (*Extinction*), and these women's connection and empathy with those around them highlights Alice's distance from the "norm" of survivalist femininity that surrounds her. Instead, Alice is aligned with child characters in each of the films.

Child-avatars for Alice appear in four of the first five films of the series. *Resident Evil* and *Retribution* feature the Red Queen, an AI computer whose "personality" manifests as a school-aged child. *Apocalypse* introduces Angela Ashford, the daughter of the computer's programmer and inspiration for its appearance. *Extinction* offers the White Queen, a benign version of the Red Queen, also apparently modeled on a young girl (perhaps Angela again, though this is not made clear). Finally, *Retribution* sees Alice faced with a cloned child, Becky, who has appeared in simulation experiments as a clone–Alice's daughter. Each child-avatar is explicitly the product of "authorship" by a (literal, in some cases) father figure. And each film makes an explicit connection between Alice and the child—in the Red Queen's acquiescence to Alice's requests in *Resident Evil*, Angela's direct insistence that she is the product of T-virus experimentation just like Alice (in *Apocalypse*), and in Becky's assumption of the role of Alice's "daughter" in *Retribution*. These girls (most of whom have English accents, and some of whom are dressed in Victorian-style clothing) function as Alice's doubles, suggesting that it is they, rather than Rain, Jill and Claire, to whom Alice should be compared.

Project Alice

Resident Evil is neither a retelling nor a continuation of Lewis Carroll's *Alice's Adventures in Wonderland*. The visual references to Carroll's work in the first film of the series can be dismissed as superficial nods to the "strangeness" and "otherness" of the world. However, the heroine of the series, a namesake of Carroll's child-heroine, can be read alongside an eighty-year tradition of imagining and reimagining Alice.

The model of Alice's agency-through-madness (or, in some cases, agency-through-amnesia) outlined here can be traced through Bedlam narratives to video games and contemporary films. That a common thread in texts of this type is evocation of, and identification with, Carroll's *Alice* novels suggests that Alice is more than simply an archetypal character: the Alice tradition reveals an idiosyncratic model of femininity that is both recognizable and contradictory.

The externalization of Alice's relationship to a hostile Wonderland, and the determination with which she fights, presents an alternative characterization of female madness to feminist psychoanalytic models of nonsubjectivity and fragmentation. While undoubtedly fragmented, Alices in the texts described here weaponize this rupture and turn it outwards onto the brutal world that menaces them. Near—and sometimes actually—sociopathic in their lack of connection to Wonderland, violent Alices can only survive by accepting the absurdity of the world they are in and facing it on their own terms. The "vorpal sword" of Carroll's Alice-avatar in "Jabberwocky" has expanded into an arsenal of technologically advanced weapons and military fighting skills.

And yet, despite her (madly) defiant stand against the brutality and cruelty of Wonderland, *Resident Evil*'s Alice, like many other contemporary Alices, is shadowed by her looking-glass twin. "Alice Liddell" resurfaces in the Red and White Queens, Angela Ashford and the clone–Becky, reflecting Alice's own descent from this mythologized figure. No matter how many times she kills "Charles Dodgson," he returns to exert his obsessive, controlling authorship over his "dreamchild." *Resident Evil*'s protagonist might be separated from Carroll's heroine by time, medium, genre and narrative, but she is an Alice nonetheless. And at the conclusion of *Retribution*, having come to the end of that particular adventure in Wonderland, her "creator" stands beside her once more and injects her with a serum that will only serve to continue her story.

Works Cited

Brooker, Will. *Alice's Adventures: Lewis Carroll in Popular Culture*. New York and London: Continuum Books, 2004.

Carroll, Lewis. *Alice's Adventures in Wonderland* and *Through the Looking-Glass*. Ed. Robert M. Hopper. N.P.: Doublethumb Press, 2011. Kindle file.

Falconer, Rachel. "Underworld Portmanteaux: Dante's Hell and Carroll's Wonderland in Women's Memoirs of Mental Illness." *Alice Beyond Wonderland: Essays for the Twenty-First Century*. Ed. Cristopher Hollingsworth. Iowa City: University of Iowa Press, 2009. 3–22.

Hancher, Michael. "Alice's Audiences." *Romanticism and Children's Literature in Nineteenth-Century England*. Ed. James Holt McGavran, Jr. Athens: University of Georgia Press, 1991. 190–207.

Leach, Karoline. *In the Shadow of the Dreamchild: The Myth and Reality of Lewis Carroll*. London and Chester Springs, PA: Peter Owen, 2009 (orig. pub. 1999).

Noon, Jeff. *The Automated Alice*. London: Black Swan, 2000 (orig. pub. 1996).

Pilinovsky, Helen. "Body as Wonderland: Alice's Graphic Iteration in *Lost Girls*." *Alice Beyond Wonderland: Essays for the Twenty-First Century*. Ed. Cristopher Hollingsworth. Iowa City: University of Iowa Press, 2009. 175–98.

White, Antonia. *Beyond the Glass*. London: Virago, 1979 (orig. pub. 1954).

Thank You for Making Me Human Again: Alice and the Teaching of Scientific Ethics

Kristine Larsen

Introduction

One of the most persistent tropes in science fiction and horror films is the character of the "mad scientist," the quintessential Dr. Frankenstein, who oversteps the bounds of what is considered "natural" and falls into the trap of playing God. Unfortunately, this often cartoonish stereotype is not without its real-world counterparts. Modern marvels such as genetic engineering, nuclear energy, and nanotechnology further the mistrust of science in the average person's mind, as they see them as the modern equivalent of a genie released from its bottle with little thought as to the possible outcomes. The public rightly questions why the U.S. military stockpiles smallpox and anthrax in high security laboratories, and worries about the wisdom of changing the genetic structure of bacteria, crops, and livestock. The general public is also concerned by the military industrial complex and the increasing emphasis on profit and patents in the realm of scientific research (especially in the biological and medical fields). Stories of scientists genetically modifying extremely virulent strains of avian flu explode on the internet at the same time that the scientific community is reeling from a series of scandals involving eugenics and unethical human experimentation perpetrated upon those of racial minorities and lower socio-economic classes.

Given this environment, scientists in the early 21st century are therefore automatically examined with a suspicious eye by the same public that once lauded scientific achievements and thought scientists to be heroes in lab coats who landed humans on the moon and conquered polio. To a general public that surveys have perennially demonstrated is woefully ignorant of both the methodology and content of science, every scientist has the potential to become a mad scientist hell-bent on destroying the world (National Science Board 7–17). Therefore it can be argued that what Henry Greely calls ELSI— the ethical, legal, and social implications of science—should be taught along-side the scientific method, not only in courses meant for students majoring in the sciences, but all students, as part of their general education/liberal arts requirements (474). In this essay I will argue that herein resides one of the largely untapped yet central messages of the *Resident Evil* series, and demonstrate its usage in two zombie-centric courses that focused on controversial topics in 20th century science.

Resident Evil *and Science Ethics*

The number of zombie films that feature archetypal mad scientists is legion. Some works openly embrace the Frankenstein comparison, as in the case of the third installment of George Romero's famed trilogy, *Day of the Dead* (1985). Here the mentally unbalanced Dr. Logan is openly referred to as "Frankenstein" by both his fellow scientists and the military personnel sharing a bunker turned research facility. In the novel *Brains: A Zombie Memoir*, former English professor turned zombie, Dr. Jack Barnes, refers to Dr. Howard Stein, developer of a zombie-creating biochemical agent, as "my creator. Our father, Mad Scientist Extraordinaire" (Becker 4). Like Shelley's protagonist, Howard Stein openly rejects his creation, explaining to Jack that he and his band of special still-cognizant zombies are "a mistake. Something out of *Frankenstein*" (Becker 178). Perhaps the most (in)famous mad scientist of zombie films is Herbert West of the *Re-animator* series (loosely based on a short story by H.P. Lovecraft). In the first film, *Re-animator*, West conducts experiments with his re-animating reagent on both animals and humans without seeming concern for either his subjects' basic rights, or the unpredictable and unstable results of these experiments. "I've conquered brain death," he boasts to room-mate and fellow medical student Dan Cain. "We can defeat death. We can even achieve every doctor's dream and live lifetimes."

The mad scientist label can certainly be applied to Dr. Isaacs and the other scientists of the *Resident Evil* series. In the original film, Spence is killed by the mutant creature known as the Licker, called one of the Hive's "early and unstable experiments." When Matt is scratched by the Licker, he too begins to mutate, and the Umbrella Corporation Clean Team takes him away to become part of the "Nemesis program," their code name for a secret bio-weapon program. In *Resident Evil: Extinction* Isaacs continues to experiment on the T-virus and the zombies it creates, under the guise of domesticating them for the Umbrella Corporation. His true motivations are to recapture Alice at any cost, and to use his serum and her DNA to create a species of super-zombies under his control. As he explains to an Umbrella bureaucrat who questions the aggression of his zombies, "some aggression has its uses." When Alice clone number 87 momentarily appears to successfully reach the final stage of the "test" (the rather sadistic maze that the Alice clones are forced to negotiate like lab rats), Isaacs gloats that his research "will change the face of everything." Isaacs is bitten by one of his super-zombies, and injects himself with an overdose of the anti-virus; afterwards he mutates into a monstrous physical form reflecting his inner monstrosity, and taunts Alice with the fact that even though he used to think she was the future, he has come to realize that his new form is the true realization of his goal. In the end, Frankenstein has become his own monster.

The fictional Umbrella Corporation is itself clearly a rather dangerous parody of the huge conglomerates that are all-too-common in our real world. Like Frankenstein's monster, some have come to power by being stitched together from many pieces through corporate mergers. Others have developed proprietary technologies that they have convinced many of us we cannot possibly live without (the so-called "evil empire" of Microsoft being a classic example). In the *Resident Evil* series the intersections of science, power, and profit play a central role, with Umbrella's unethical commercial/military monopoly being responsible for the creation of the zombies. The original *Resident Evil* (2002) begins with a confidential file on the Umbrella Corporation, describing the impressive and rather frightening scope of its influence. It is described as a commercial enterprise funded by the military that not only produces commercial products found in 90 percent of all homes, but also specializes in genetic experimentation and viral technology. As Alice regains her memory throughout the film, the viewer learns that she had planned to steal the Umbrella Corporation's bio-engineered T-virus from the subterranean Hive laboratory in order to bring down the all-powerful corporation (whose trademark can be found throughout the film on everything from bullets to wedding rings). Spence (like Alice, an Umbrella Corporation security guard) nearly succeeds in stealing the virus and anti-virus for his own personal monetary gain, and spawns the zombie outbreak in the process.

Despite the damage the T-virus wreaks once it escapes from the Hive, the remaining executives of the Umbrella Corporation continue their business plan for world domination in the remaining films in the series. A less overtly evil (but equally manipulative) science-based corporation is *Fido*'s ZomCon. The film opens with a black and white newsreel extolling the virtues of ZomCon and its role in winning the Zombie Wars, as well as its centrality in securing the safety of the suburban way of life. ZomCon controls not only the zombies, but every aspect of society, from burials to school curriculum, and the ZomCon logo appears on items from cars to caskets.

When an organization—whether it be corporate or political—achieves such ubiquitous power, individual human rights are endangered. In such an atmosphere, members of minority and/or dissident groups are especially at risk. One specific class of real world scientific atrocities is particularly well-illustrated in the *Resident Evil* series, namely human experimentation. The most well-known examples in the real world are of course the barbaric experiments perpetrated by Nazi scientists on concentration camp victims, and included the intentional infliction of gangrene and mustard gas wounds, infecting victims with malaria and typhus, freezing experiments, forcing victims to drink sea water, and Josef Mengele's infamous experiments on twins. As horrific as these were, they were unfortunately not isolated cases in the twentieth century. For example, between 1937 and 1945, Japan's Unit 731 studied the effects of plague and other diseases on the human body through the vivisection of both living and dead Chinese victims (Baader et al. 221).

Nor was the United States above conducting human experiments without the informed consent of the participants. For example, between 1950 and 1975 the U.S. Army conducted experiments on nearly 7000 human subjects to study the effects of nerve gas, psychotropic chemicals, and pain killers as incapacitating agents for use in warfare (Moreno 251). But by far the most infamous example of American human experimentation is the "Tuskegee Study of Untreated Syphilis in the Negro Male," a forty-year study conducted by scientists associated with the U.S. Public Health Service of the effects of syphilis on over 400 African American men in Alabama who were not even told that they had syphilis. What is perhaps most alarming about this event is that it was not concealed, but in fact was openly discussed in medical journals and conferences. It was not until the media discovered the study that it was quickly ended in the 1970s (Jones 7).

The Tuskegee experiment was an alarming and unusual example of the breakdown of the peer review process, wherein the scientific community self-polices itself not only for standards of intellectual integrity, but also adherence to proper procedures (including ethics). It is the power of the peer review process that drives mad scientists underground—both figuratively and literally—away from the prying eyes of their peers. As Robert Park noted in *Voodoo Science*, "Scientists engaged in questionable research consciously or unconsciously seek to isolate themselves from critics.... Not only does secrecy contribute to scientific blunders, it allows those blunders to remain hidden" (189). Unless, of course, if your blunders include a zombie-creating virus that leaks out of your subterranean fortress, as is the case of the Umbrella Corporation's Hive.

The idea that scientists could treat fellow human beings in such a callous manner as in the Tuskegee experiment is hard to wrap one's mind around. Psychological studies have shown that in order to act in such a manner, the scientist views the victim as being a subhuman animal, or even an object—literally as a "thing." For example, Japanese researchers in Unit 731 not only viewed the Chinese prisoners as intrinsically inferior to Japanese citizens, but in documents referred to the Chinese prisoners as "research material," "monkeys," or even "logs." Similarly Nazi scientists viewed the concentration victims (Jews, Roma, homosexuals, and other marginalized and oppressed groups) as less than human (Baader 223; 330).

In zombie films, the differences between humans and zombies are accentuated, labeling the creatures as "other" and thus inhuman; this in turn opens the door to all manner of gruesome scientific experimentation on zombies (and even living humans). In the *Resident Evil* series, Alice is clearly viewed as a commodity; she is alternately referred to as Umbrella Corporation property, a project, and a program. In *Resident Evil: Extinction*, Dr. Isaacs experiments on a series of Alice clones which all die in various experimental battle scenarios. When one particular clone fails, Isaacs instructs his assistants to "get rid of that," and the clone is unceremoniously dumped into a cement ravine along with innumerable other clones. The visual similarity to photographs of the callous disposal of concentration camp victims is certainly intentional. The Alice clones are expendable, subhuman, and therefore unworthy of even the most basic human respect.

Similarly, much of George Romero's *Day of the Dead* centers around Dr. Logan's experiments on the zombies. While Logan explains that "they are us," his treatment of his specimens is less than humane. In one experiment he has severed all the vital organs in a zombie's torso, leaving it basically just limbs and a brain. In another he has removed the face and skull, leaving a completely exposed brain. A fellow scientist, Sarah Bowman, criticizes Logan for what she considers pointless experiments, and she is further horrified to learn that the zombie in question is not a "wild" zombie but in fact the recently deceased former military commander of the facility.

While the experiments conducted on zombies in these works reflect the general inhumanity of human experimentation in the twentieth century, a number of these experiments have a particular goal—to domesticate and control the zombies as one might an animal or a slave. The potential for zombies to serve as a slave underclass harkens back to the original Haitian zombie, who lost his or her will and personality under the complete control of the voodoo master. Early zombie films relied heavily on this archetype, for example *White Zombie* (1932), generally considered the first film of the genre. *Day of the Dead*'s Dr. Logan justified his experiments as searching for a way that a zombie could be "domesticated. It can be conditioned to behave, the way we want it to behave." Indeed, he succeeds in getting the zombie he nicknames Bub to mimic shaving and telephone usage, and even fire a gun. However, Bub performs much like a circus animal for Logan, motivated by a desire to get his reward—in this case a piece of human flesh.

As previously noted, the domestication of zombies is also the stated goal of some of Dr. Isaacs' experiments in *Resident Evil: Extinction*. Isaacs injects zombie subjects—his personal lab rats—with a special serum which is meant to return some intelligence and memories to the zombies and suppress their desire for human flesh. He explains to the Umbrella Corporation Board that the zombies are "animals, essentially. We can train them; if we can take away their baser instincts. They'll never be human,"; however, they would provide the "basis for a docile workforce." He successfully tests the intelligence and problem-solving skills of zombie subjects, such as through using a camera and cellphone; unfortunately, one becomes frustrated by the task of trying to fit a square peg into a round hole and attacks the lab technicians. As previously noted, Isaacs' true intention, however, is to create his own elite force of super-zombies, presumably under his personal control. Similarly the ultimate plan of Herbert West's nemesis Dr. Hill in *Re-animator* is to steal West's reagent and partner it with his own laser lobotomy procedure to create an army of zombies who will give him "undreamed-of power."

Zombies are successfully exploited as menial laborers in *Fido* (2004). Here the ubiquitous ZomCon Corporation uses science and technology to solve the zombie problem through the domestication collar, which contains the zombies' desire for human flesh, "making the zombie as gentle as a household pet." The objectification of zombies (and the accompanying loss of basic human rights) is also a central theme in the novel *Breathers: A Zombie's Lament*, in which zombies not only lose their social security numbers, but the rights to surf the internet, ride public transportation, and be seen alone in public. The main zombie character, Andy Warner, spends much of the novel being picked up and caged by Animal Control for his civil disobedience, and is frequently threatened by his mortified parents with being given to zoos, medical schools, "plastic surgery chop shops," or crash test dummy facilities (Browne 81; 181). Once again, the comparison between zombies and lab animals is intentional.

Neither the zombies, nor the human subjects, in any of the aforementioned works' experiments have given informed consent for the experimentation done upon them.[1] They are merely masses of tissue deemed to have no inherent rights whatsoever. Linda Badley (73–4) notes that *Re-animator* and similar works reflect the idea of the body as commodity, an increasingly real yet troubling development in this Brave New World of organ transplantation, stem cell research, and assisted reproductive technologies (such as surrogate pregnancies). Scientists have successfully patented new DNA sequences and genetically engineered organisms, and the California Supreme Court case *Moore v. Regents of the University of California* struck down a patient's right to receive monetary compensation for a cell line grown from his tumor that was patented and afterwards sold to other research facilities without his informed consent (Greely 488).

The possible loss of rights over one's own body is a politically charged issue, with examples ranging from reproductive rights to black market organ transplants. But the possibility of cloning humans unifies many in the general public in their viewpoints against such technology, as it nearly unanimously raises alarm bells in the mind of the average person. For example, in a 2004 Opinion Research Corporation poll, 84 percent of those surveyed opposed the commercial cloning of pets ("Animal and Pet"). The National Science Board's *2010 Science and Engineering Indicators* surveys found that 78 percent of Americans opposed genetically engineering or cloning humans (7–41). In addition to the charge that such experiments are tantamount to "playing God," opposition to cloning centers around such ethical and theological issues as whether clones have souls, whether they deserve the same basic rights as other humans, whether clones could be used as organ banks for the wealthy, and if such technologies could be used to develop a race of perfect soldiers. A number of countries, including the United States and United Kingdom, have banned the cloning of adult humans, and bioethicist Arlene Judith Klotzko (xxi) notes that "any scientist who actively engages in cloning humans in order to create a new human being risks being branded a 'mad scientist.'" One of the (non-ethical) reasons why humans have not yet been cloned is that it is just plain difficult.

For example, the successful birth of Dolly, the world's first cloned sheep, only came after 276 failures (A. Park). This is certainly reflected in the case of Dr. Isaacs and his experiments in *Resident Evil: Extinction*. Isaacs admits to the Umbrella executives that his project is behind schedule, hindered by his reliance on clones of Alice rather than Alice herself. "It's laborious. The results unpredictable."

While one can argue whether or not the general public's fear of possible military misuses of genetic engineering and cloning are well-founded or not, there is no doubt that the possibility of biochemical agents being used either against soldiers or civilians is a very real threat in the twenty-first century. In the years since the end of the Cold War, information has slowly come to light concerning the United States and Soviet biological warfare programs, including the possible genetic engineering of bacterial strains which are antibiotic resistant and target specific ethnic groups (Committee on Homeland Security 22). In addition to these artificial biological weapons, the Centers for Disease Control has identified approximately sixty pathogens which have the potential for use in biological warfare, including anthrax, typhoid fever, plague, Ebola, and smallpox.

Any thoughts that biological warfare or bio-terrorism could be prevented in the United States were squelched in 2001, when anthrax-laden letters killed five people and sickened seventeen others. After a lengthy investigation, the attacks were traced back to a Fort Detrick, Maryland bio-defense scientist, Dr. Bruce Ivins, who committed suicide before he could be indicted for the crime ("Amerithrax"). Recalling that the bio-engineered T-virus was the source of the infection in the *Resident Evil* series, it is clear that the series can be seen as a warning against the dangers of such research, especially in the hands of all-too-human scientists who—in life as well as literature—can fall victim to greed, hubris, megalomania, and all manner of mental illness. As we have seen, the *Resident Evil* series has obvious connections to a number of controversial aspects of 21st century science and to the emerging field of ELSI. Therefore the series provides excellent source material for courses that explore such issues.

Zombies and Science Education

At this point in the essay, the astute reader will have noted that I have only included examples from two of the *Resident Evil* series films, the original and *Resident Evil: Extinction,* despite the fact that myriad examples of the topics discussed can also be found in the other series films. This was purposefully done to motivate the main thrust of my argument, namely that *Resident Evil* and its sequels can be successfully used in the teaching of these and other ELSI-related topics, even if only certain films are included. The use of popular culture in the teaching of science is certainly not new. The academic literature is filled with examples of works that have been used in the teaching of science, such as Kurt Vonnegut novels (Liberko), *Star Trek: The Next Generation* television episodes (Dubeck and Tatlow), and fantasy works such as *The Lord of the Rings*, the *Harry Potter* Series, the *Chronicles of Narnia*, and Pullman's *His Dark Materials* series (Larsen and Bednarski). Such strategies are often used to combat student fear and apathy concerning scientific concepts. Zombies have also been used as a thematic hook in a number of college courses, with several of these garnering considerable press coverage (e.g. Cohan; Gordon). Since zombie outbreaks are often blamed on mad scientists in films and literature, using zombies to teach topics of science, especially ELSI and science, seemed to me to be a natural fit (Larsen, "Vampires"; Larsen "Zombies"). Fortunately, my fellow faculty and administrative colleagues at Central Connecticut State University have allowed me to test this hypothesis. This section will describe two recent zombie-themed courses with a scientific core.

In late 2009, art Professor Ronald Todd (a long-time attendee of the Burning Man festival and SantaCon flash mob) and I committed to team-teaching a zombie-based sophomore level course for the university's interdisciplinary Honors Program the following Autumn semester. The course, HON 210 Western Culture II, is expected to cover cultural and literary (defined loosely) themes from the 20th century as selected by the instructors. It was decided that zombies were the perfect foil to discuss issues of human rights, issues of beauty and ugliness in the arts, and ELSI in late 20th century science (defined as starting with the Cold War). The course proposal—"Seeing the 20th Century Through Undead Eyes"—was accepted (with a raised eyebrow) by the new director of the program, and Ron and I submitted a University Curriculum Development Grant, asking for summer stipends to develop the course and funds to buy DVDs for the library's lending library. The proposal openly noted that "The applicants acknowledge that the subject of this course is rather untraditional," and the course "pushes the envelope of what is considered to be 'academic.'" While the stipends were not approved, the DVDs were funded, and word of the course spread across campus, in part thanks to head-shaking comments by members of the grant review committee. The course sold out in one minute during the online course registration period, and a number of Honors students pleaded for entrance into the course above the set class limit.

The scientific content I taught (as is true of much of the science contained in most zombie films) naturally divided itself into three components: death (including definitions, treatment and mistreatment of corpses, and pandemics); medical issues involving ownership of the body (including euthanasia, transplantation, cloning, life extension, and genetic engineering); and controversies in modern science (such as nuclear power and weapons, biological and chemical weapons, and space exploration). For each scientific topic, both the basic science and the ELSI were emphasized, and students made connections between this material and the assigned DVDs and readings (through written assignments and in-class discussions). Topics covered by Ron Todd include the shifting definitions of beauty and horror in modern culture, civil rights movements, mob mentalities, propaganda, consumer culture and fads.[2]

The DVDs which the students were assigned to watch (and which were discussed at length in class) were *White Zombie* (generally considered the first zombie film), the classic George Romero trilogy, *Re-animator* (for its depiction of mad scientists), *Resident Evil* (for its secret bio-warfare/pandemic focus), *Resident Evil: Extinction* (for its portrayal of mad scientists and cloning), and *Fido* (for its discussion of zombie rights). In addition, the original and remake of *The Fly* as well as the original short story were assigned in order to discuss the process of film adaptations, and the classic horror film *The Cabinet of Dr.*

Caligari (1920) and excerpts of *Freaks* (1932) were viewed during class time as part of a discussion of societal definitions of beauty and horror. In addition, S.G. Browne's zombie novel *Breathers* was assigned, due to its focus on zombie rights. Course assignments included four reflection essays, viewing/reading questions for each assigned work, a short group project on a specific type of organ transplant, and a final paper and presentation in which each student analyzed a zombie film, novel, or graphic novel for depictions of the topics covered in the course. In addition, the class took a field trip to New York City to visit the World Trade Center site and the controversial *Bodies: The Exhibition* display of preserved and artistically displayed corpses. Written reflections handed in the class period after the field trip, as well as class discussions, demonstrated the important impact both aspects of the NYC trip had on these students.

While HON 210 was being taught, plans were already in the works for a first year student science seminar class, focusing on just the science and ELSI content, to be offered the following Autumn semester. FYS 104: The Undead Ate My Science Homework: Zombies and 20th Century Science, had no difficulty being certified for general education science credit by the University Curriculum Committee, based on the strength of the proposed syllabus and the sensitizing of (at least some of)[3] the campus culture to the scholarly nature of zombie studies.

The proposed content included all of the scientific topics taught in HON 210 (although expanded to include assisted reproductive technologies) as well as an introductory unit on the scientific method, mad scientists, and science and religion (topics that at least half of the students in HON 210 had already covered in an earlier honors course I had taught). In addition, there was a discussion of general disaster preparation and a three class periods devoted to scientific debunking skills (using astrology and the 2012 apocalypse hysteria as examples). Ironically, the section on disaster preparation became far more than a theoretical exercise when the course was actually taught, as the freshman orientation date and first day of classes were cancelled that semester due to Tropical Storm Irene (and the then record-breaking 760,000 electric customers without power across the state). Less than two months later, a late October snow storm cancelled four days of school as falling trees caused more than 830,000 power outages in Connecticut. For five days, the only sections of campus with power (self-generated by the university) were the dorms and cafeteria. Students received a valuable lesson in disaster relief as the majority of the commuting students lived without heat or electricity for days, and the residential students witnessed their professors flocking to campus for hot meals and to use the electrical outlets to charge phones and access the internet for updated information on the storm clean-up.[4]

Because the audience was freshmen rather than sophomores, and it was not an honors-level course, the out-of-class work was limited to viewing *Re-animator*, the Romero trilogy, *Resident Evil* and *Resident Evil: Extinction*, and *Fido*. *Breathers* was replaced by Robin Becker's *Brains*, due to its shorter length and its focus on mad scientists and issues of zombie reproduction. The viewing questions, reflection essays, and final project were all kept, as was the transplant assignment, and augmented with the writing of a living will, 5-minute in-class prompted writing, and take-home midterm and final essay exams that focused on the scientific topics covered. A description of the class (including a disclaimer) was included on the freshman registration survey and students self-selected. In fact, according to anecdotal evidence from the registration staff, about half of all incoming freshmen requested the course.

In both HON 210 and FYS 104, students were given open-ended assignments in which they could hone their critical thinking and writing skills as well as demonstrate their mastery of the course material. For example, when asked in what ways Umbrella robs Alice of her humanity and how despite their actions, she still retains it, one student wrote, "By creating these replicas, Umbrella has stolen Alice's identity. She retains it because she is able to operate independently of Umbrella. To Umbrella she is an experiment, but as long as she is able to override that she still retains her humanity." Another student offered:

> Umbrella has taken from Alice part of what makes humans human: her individuality. By cloning her, they have removed the uniqueness of her personal self.... They have also combined her DNA with the T-virus, which gives her some kind of psychic powers rather than actually infecting Alice as it would "normal" humans. Alice is still incredibly humane. Despite all she has been through, Alice is still very sympathetic towards her fellow humans.

When asked to consider in what ways Isaacs is more of a monster than his zombies, one student replied "he becomes more of a monster because he can think. His actions are not derived from fulfilling a need to feed...." Another student opined:

> Isaacs not only created the zombies, but he treats other people (like Alice and his underlings) as specimens to experiment on. He has no respect for human life or for nature, and he feels the need to push the limits of his creations despite the detrimental effects it has on the rest of the world. Isaacs cares for nothing but the progression of his experiments, He pays no heed to the consequences of his actions, and doesn't care who or what it harms.

Students were also asked to consider whether or not Alice was a monster. One student offered:

> She is not a zombie and does not have the characteristics of a zombie or whatever Isaacs turned into. She is human with her ability to speak, think rationally, express

emotions and die like a human. Alice also wants to help humanity by saving them.... It can be argued that she is a monster because Isaacs could do all of those things and he was a monster but there is a difference; she was not a destructive, manipulative, crazed person gone bad.

In all these responses we can see students connecting the films to the issues of science and ethics discussed in class and thinking far more deeply about these issues than any standard multiple choice exam could elicit.

In the reflection essays, students were free to make whatever connections they wished between the films and the course material. Speaking of the H1N1 (so-called "swine flu") outbreak that caused a near hysteria a few years ago, one student wrote "Since it was believed that it was caused from swine thousands of pigs were slaughtered, just like in *Resident Evil*, everyone in the Hive was killed by [the] Red Queen because she felt that the entire complex was infected." Another student drew connections between *Resident Evil: Extinction* and the hypothetical rights of clones: "There has been no human clone yet, except for Alice in *Resident Evil 3*.... In this movie Alice's clones did not have any rights, They were puppets. If we were able to clone humans they should have the same rights as their original and they should be considered human."

Other students took a broader viewpoint when situating the films within the course material. After completing the course content on the Cold War and Space Race, one student warned:

> In *Resident Evil*, the hive is a top secret, underground research facility for Umbrella Corporation. When a virus is released into the environment, all the scientists are quarantined but consequently are mutated into zombies. It is only a movie, but it is a message as well. In the early 1940's, Los Alamos, New Mexico, was a top secret research facility for the federal government. It tested and researched the capability of an atomic bomb, a weapon of mass destruction. These scientists were never the same: psychologically damaged by what horrors they had created and even physically affected from the radiation they had been exposed to. This was not a movie.

While discussing the possibility of using genetic engineering to eradicate hereditary diseases, another student pondered:

> When do we stop doing it for science and research and do it for personal, selfish reasons in an attempt to reach perfection? Dr. Isaacs draws this line and is out of control in *Resident Evil: Extinction*. His initial reasoning to domesticate the zombies went too far because even then he was trying to change their behaviors and instincts. And later on in the film, his way of thinking just becomes progressively worse: he wanted to create his own race of Super Zombies. To relate this to everyday life and what ways people draw the lines between science and morality could be associated with reproduction and children. We all have preferences of what kind of hair color, hair texture, eye color, head shape, etc. we would like our children to have, but who would actually create their child to be what they view to be perfect?

The use of personal reflection essays therefore also allows faculty to get far deeper inside of a student's brain (no pun intended) than standard test questions.

Without the pressure to produce the singular "right answer," students are free to make their own connections to the course material, as well as connections to their everyday lives. This process was evident throughout student work in both courses. For example, one student wrote in a reflection essay, "I have learned more than I realized I would learn in a zombie class. Also, I did not realize how throughout history any event, tragedy, invention, etc. could be so easily related to zombies." Another reflected on how "I found myself talking about these things to my friends and thinking about the class during my own time. I would say you guys were successful in showing the evil in the world as well as how zombies can actually relate to everything." Another interesting source of informal student feedback in regards to the class was an extra credit question on the FYS 104 final exam in which the students were asked to explain the most important thing they learned in the class. The most common answers focused on skepticism, the importance of ethics, information on historical events (such as the Space Race and the Holocaust), and stereotypes of scientists. A number of students simply explained that the entire course was important because it forced them to face how much they have left to learn.

Focusing on student opinions of the two *Resident Evil* films included in both classes, students in both courses generally enjoyed them, although a significant number had never seen them before. For example, one student wrote of the original film, "I liked the film more than I thought I would.... The overall plot brought up a lot of controversial issues again, like illegal/unethical experiments, uncontrollable experiments, company monopolies, etc." Another noted, "A movie I would never watch if I didn't have to, *Resident Evil* surprised me as being appropriately violent mixed with strong messages against the power of dangerous scientific experimentation." A third student explained that, "The best thing they did, in my opinion, is that the whole thing feels real. It's caused by a virus that mutates the human genetics so that corpses can walk and feast on flesh. It's plausible. Admittedly in the later films when Alice gets psychic abilities the story gets a little far-fetched, but for the duration of the first film it's a very plausible story." However, not all students were unanimous in their positive opinion of *Resident Evil*. One student criticized its "lack of character development.... I think the zombies were well portrayed, but the living humans were just generic people to kill."

That same student (a science major) panned the "predictable plot" of *Resident Evil: Extinction*, but was "a little intrigued by the experimenting on the Alice clones, but the fact that Alice was a weird bio-weapon and could be turned on and off was very disturbing." Again, the majority of both classes enjoyed *Resident Evil: Extinction*. For example, one student wrote:

I liked the film. I enjoyed the fact that Isaacs changed so that he physically resembled the monster that he is.... The movie in general was also really scary because of the fact that we as a collective specie seems ridiculous[ly] close to doing something like this, and wiping ourselves out. Whether it be by bio-weapon, or nuclear, or whatever we think of next, it almost seems an inevitable fate.

Several students have kept in touch with me after the conclusion of both courses and occasionally send me links to zombie-related items in the news. I was even able to reinforce one of the lessons taught in both classes—the proper way to conduct human research—when I emailed the students from both classes to secure informed consent for their written work to be anonymously quoted in this paper. Faculty may talk about life-long learning in the traditional classroom, but nothing beats modeling it for students in a real-world context.

Given the general excitement generated by the topic and evidence from these assignments to show that students were engaged with the course material, as well as anecdotal evidence from in-class discussions, it is not surprising that the student evaluations for both courses were overwhelmingly positive. For HON 210, 64 percent rated the course as excellent and 32 percent termed it very good. In FYS 104 100 percent of the students surveyed strongly agreed that the class meetings were intellectually stimulating and 83 percent agreed that class often presented them with "challenging, thought-provoking ideas" (the remaining 17 percent noted this occurred "sometimes"). The class even got a positive rating on my www.ratemyprofessors.com page: "This class was awesome and the proffesor was really cool. Its alot of work but about really cool and controversial issues" (errors original). I wholeheartedly concur with this synopsis from my vantage point of instructor of the course as well.

"I Thought You Were the Future": The Next Iteration

While both courses were highly successful in the eyes of faculty and students alike, there is no such thing as a perfect course (or a perfect zombie). In the time since the development of FYS 104, there have been a number of important developments in both science and popular culture that afford the opportunity for a serious revamping of the course, including the very real possibility that the entire course could be largely based on the *Resident Evil* series. These include the success of AMC's *The Walking Dead* television series, the publication of Steven Schlozman's novel *The Zombie Autopsies*, and the publication of two controversial scientific papers that explain how the avian flu could be transformed into a form that passes from human-to-human with just a few mutations. In a nutshell, the first of these both reflects current interest in zombies and has itself been responsible for introducing zombies to new audiences, thereby making zombie-based courses even more popular. It is the other two developments that will receive detailed treatment in the last section of this essay.

Penned by Harvard Medical School child psychologist Dr. Steven Schlozman, *The Zombie Autopsies* juxtaposes the stark scientific method used by desperate scientists trying to understand and control an air-borne zombie pandemic with international treaties that struggle to define life, death, and what it means to be human. In the process, those in the final stages of "Ataxic Neurodegenerative Satiety Deficiency Syndrome" (ANSD) are stripped of their basic human rights, including the right to be administered pain medication or anesthesia during exploratory surgery. However, acts of unnecessary violence against those deemed "No Longer Human" (NLH) is considered a criminal offense. As the protagonist, Dr. Stanley Blum, uneasily admits, "We don't even afford the same rights to zombies that we do lab rats—not because we want to hurt them, but because time is short and enacting those rights and safeguards takes time" (Schlozman 34).

As previously noted, the Umbrella Corporation's disrespect for basic human rights and the commoditization of Alice plays a central role in the film series. The inclusion of the entire *Resident Evil* series within the course would allow for the use of additional examples from films previous omitted from the curriculum. For example, in *Resident Evil: Afterlife*, Umbrella Corporation chief Albert Wesker injects Alice with a serum that neutralizes the T-virus, thus neutralizing her physical and psionic powers. "Umbrella Corporation is taking back its property," he sneers. "You didn't work out, so you're being recalled." Although Alice is clearly being reduced to the commodity which Umbrella has repeatedly claimed her to be in the previous films, she actually thanks Wesker for returning her humanity to her. This refers back to various statements Alice has made in the earlier films, especially the second, including "They did something to me. I barely feel human anymore" and "I became a freak." Later in the fourth film, we learn that Wesker cannot control his exposure to the T-virus, and, unlike Alice, mutates into a monstrous form as the virus runs rampant through him. He seeks to "injest" Alice in order for his body to regain control over the virus. In keeping with the Umbrella Corporation's patent (pun intended) disregard for human dignity, the tanker ship Arcadia sails up and down the Pacific coastline kidnapping uninfected survivors in order to have fresh specimens for Wesker's scientific experiments. The actions of Wesker, Isaacs, and Cain in these films can be set in sharp contrast with the careful and sometimes agonizing decisions made concerning zombie experimentation and containment of the disease in *The Zombie Autopsies*. Here we read of scientist Blanca Gutierrez's struggles to accept the "No Longer Human" designation of zombies in a letter to her childhood parish's pastor: "Is someone born with a genetic malformation human?... Those born without limbs, without speech, without the capacity to feel.... Someone born even without a brain is still one of us. You taught us that. We are all God's children, all created in His image" (Schlozman 185–6).

The other recent development of relevance is the long-delayed publication of two scientific papers in the prestigious peer-reviewed science journals *Science* and *Nature*. These two papers detail separate studies in which the avian flu H5N1 (which currently cannot pass from mammal to mammal through airborne droplets, i.e., sneezing,) was intentionally mutated until it took on such a form in ferrets, the leading animal model in human flu research. These papers demonstrated for the first time that a worldwide pandemic on the scale of the infamous 1918–9 Spanish flu (that killed between 20 and 40 million people) could result from natural mutations to the current virus (Herfst et al.; Imai et al.). It also opens up the possibility for bio-terrorists or rogue scientists to create deadly mutations of their own; for this reason, publication of the papers was delayed for almost a year, and leading members of the international flu research community took part in a self-imposed sixty-day moratorium on flu research while ELSI and regulatory issues were explored by international organizations (Malakoff 387). This research is considered the seminal example of "dual-use research of concern" or DURC, defined as biological research that has the reasonable possibility to be misused and could "pose a significant threat" to society (Fauci and Collins 1523). The T-virus is a similar DURC agent, one in which the possibility became a reality. Originally developed to prevent his daughter Angela from developing a hereditary degenerative disease, Dr. Ashford's genetically engineered virus was stolen by the Umbrella Corporation and further experimented upon, with dire consequences. The T-virus has other parallels to the mutated H5N1 virus, in that it can infect various species (including dogs and birds), and it can change from being airborne to blood-borne depending on the conditions.

Clearly there is much more science and ELSI content within the *Resident Evil* series to be exploited in future iterations of both courses. Therefore I will make the seemingly heretical statement that, to paraphrase Cain's words comparing Nemesis to Alice in *Resident Evil: Apocalypse*, our society has not mutated but rather evolved to such a point where the anti-war and anti-consumerism messages of Romero's trilogy are less powerful than the ELSI messages of the *Resident Evil* series. Therefore, the next iteration of FYS 104 will focus on the *Resident Evil* series, with selected scenes from *Night of the Living Dead*, *Reanimator*, and *Day of the Dead* shown during class to spark comparisons and discussions. The assigned reading will be *The Zombie Autopsies*, and students will be directed to contrast the scientific methodologies and ethical considerations voiced in this book to those of the Umbrella Corporation's scientists.

In addition, significant class time will be devoted to the controversy surrounding the publication of the avian flu mutation papers, again, with an eye to comparing and contrasting the actions of real world scientists, governments, and review bodies to the Umbrella Corporation. All in all it should make for interesting discussions.

Conclusion

As a student in HON 210 mused in one reflection paper, "When do we set limits on science? Is there really a point in which ethics can completely prevent people from advancing with risky subject matter? I believe the answer is that humans will never stop wanting to go further." She is not alone in her concern. Consider the following excerpt from a recent editorial in *Science*:

> The life sciences have reached a crossroads. The direction we choose and the process by which we arrive at this decision must be undertaken as a community and not relegated to small segments of the government, the scientific community, or society. Physicists faced a similar situation in the 1940s with nuclear weapons research, and it is inevitable that other scientific disciplines will also do so [Berns et al. 661].

Zombie films such as the *Resident Evil* series echo these concerns in a far more graphic and gut-wrenching manner than the classical cautionary tales of general science fiction, such as *Jurassic Park*. In a zombie apocalypse, the monster is no prehistoric beast; more disturbingly, he is us, we humans, and, in the case of the Umbrella Corporation, he is the dark underbelly of what the scientific community can become.

According to one HON 210 student, zombies are:

> A manifestation of all things mankind fears and does not understand.... They are the thing that goes bump in the night; they are the lurking shadows around the corner. They are everything wrong with society; they are the heavy breathing over your shoulder that you pray you've imagined. The living dead keep us on our toes.... When mankind no longer has anything to fear, then we are truly damned. Fear keeps us in check and it ensures our survival.

Perhaps in the end it is this fear—along with a scientific establishment and greater society that pays close attention to the ethical, legal, and social implications of scientific research—that will prevent a true apocalypse (zombie or otherwise) from occurring. This is why the general public must be literate not only in the scientific method, but in the ELSI of scientific research as well. Isaacs, Wesker, Alice, and her clones therefore have the potential to play a valuable role in our science curriculum.

Notes

1. An interesting counterpoint to this occurs in Season One of *The Walking Dead*, where Jenner's scientist wife gives permission for her "zombification" to be studied in the name of science.

2. Unbeknownst to us, an article that paralleled much of Todd's content in HON 210 appeared while the course was ongoing. See Do Vale.

3. There is at least one science colleague who gets angry whenever I bring up the course, muttering with clenched teeth that zombies don't exist.

4. For more information on the impact of these storms on the Northeast United States, see Barnard and Nir.

Works Cited

"Amerithrax Investigative Summary." United States Department of Justice, 19 Feb. 2010. Web. 3 Jun. 2012.

"Animal and Pet Cloning Opinion Polls." Center for Genetics and Society, 1 Jun. 2011. Web. 4 Jun. 2012.

Baader, Gerhard, Susan E. Lederer, Morris Low, Florian Schmaltz, and Alexander V. Schwerin. "Pathways to Human Experimentation, 1933–1945: Germany, Japan, and the United States." *Osiris* 20 (2005): 205–31. Print.

Badley, Linda. *Film, Horror, and the Body Fantastic*. Westport, CT: Greenwood Press, 1995. Print.

Barnard, Anne, and Sarah Maslin Nir. "Cleaning Up After Nature Plays a Trick." *New York Times*. 30 Oct. 2011. Web. 2 Jun. 2012.

Becker, Robin. *Brains: A Zombie Memoir*. New York: Eos, 2010. Print.

Berns, Kenneth I., et al. "Adaptations of Avian Flu Virus Are a Cause for Concern." *Science* 335 (2012): 660–1. Print.

Browne, S.G. *Breathers: A Zombie's Lament*. New York: Three Rivers Press, 2009. Print.

Committee on Homeland Security. *Engineering Bio-Terror Agents: Lessons from the Offensive U.S. and Russian Biological Weapons Programs*. Washington D.C.: U.S. Government Printing Office, 2005. Print.

Day of the Dead. Dir. George A. Romero. Perf. Lori Cardille, Terry Alexander, Joe Pilato, and Jarlath Conroy. Anchor Bay Entertainment, 2003. DVD.

Do Vale, Simone. "Trash Mob: Zombie Walks and the Positivity of Monsters in Western Popular Culture." *At the Interface/Probing the Boundaries* 70 (2010): 191–202. Web.

Dubeck, Leroy W., and Rose Tatlow. "Using *Star Trek: The Next Generation* Television Episodes to Teach Science." *Journal of College Science Teaching* Mar/Apr 1998: 319–23. Print.

Fauci, Anthony S., and Francis S. Collins. "Benefits and Risks of Influenza Research: Lessons Learned." *Science* 336 (2012): 1522–3. Print.

Fido. 2006. Dir. Andrew Currie. Perf. K'sun Ray, Billy Connolly, and Carrie-Anne Moss. Lionsgate, 2007. DVD.

Gordon, Jill. "The 15 Strangest College Courses in America." *Online Colleges*. 25 Feb. 2009. Web. 10 Jun. 2012.

Greely, Henry T. "Legal, Ethical, and Social Issues in Human Genome Research." *Annual Reviews of Anthropology* 27(1998): 473–502. Print.

Herfst, Sander, et al. "Airborne Transmission of Influenza A/H5N1 Virus Between Ferrets." *Science* 336 (2012): 1534–41. Print.

Imai, Masaki, et al. "Experimental Adaptation of an Influenza H5HA Confers Respiratory Droplet Transmission to a Reassortant H5HA/H1N1 Virus in Ferrets." *Nature*, digital object identifier: 10.1038/nature10831. 22 May 2012. Web. 15 Jun. 2012.

Jones, James H. *Bad Blood*, rev. ed. New York: Free Press, 1993. Print.

Klotzko, Arlene Judith. *A Clone of Your Own? The Science and Ethics of Cloning*. Cambridge: Cambridge University Press, 2000.

Larsen, Kristine. "Vampires, and Zombies, and Ghosts, Oh My...Run! The Undead in the College Classroom." *NEFDC Exchange* 22.2. (2011): 7–9. Web. 3 Jun. 2012.

_____. "Zombies ~~Ate~~ Are My Science Homework: Enticing Reluctant Science Students with the Undead." *Connecticut Journal of Science Education* 48.2 (2011): 11–13. Web. 3 Jun. 2012.

_____, and Marsha Bednarski. "Muggles, Meteoritic Armor, and Menelmacar: Using Fantasy Series in Astronomy Education and Outreach." *Preparing for the 2009 International Year of Astronomy*. Eds. M. G. Gibbs, J. Barnes, J.G. Manning, and B. Partridge. San Francisco: Astronomical Society of the Pacific Press, 2008. 82–90. Print.

Liberko, Charles A. "Using Science Fiction to Teach Thermodynamics: Vonnegut, Ice-nine, and Global Warming." *Journal of Chemical Education* 81.4 (2004): 509–11. Print.

Malakoff, David. "Flu Controversy Spurs Research Moratorium." *Science* 335 (2012): 387–9. Print.

Moreno, Jonathan D. *Undue Risk*. New York: W.H. Freeman, 2000. Print.

National Science Board. *Science and Engineering Indicators: 2010*. Washington, D.C.: National Science Foundation, 2010. Jan. 2012. Web. 4 Jun. 2012.

Re-animator. Dir. Stuart Gordon. Perf. Jeffrey Combs, Bruce Abbott, Barbara Crampton, and David Gale. Anchor Bay Entertainment, 2007. DVD.

Park, Alice. "The Perils of Cloning." *Time*. 5 Jul. 2006. Web. 10 Jun. 2012.

Park, Robert. *Voodoo Science*. Oxford: Oxford University Press, 2001. Print.

Resident Evil. Dir. Paul W.S. Anderson. Perf. Milla Jovovich, Michelle Rodriguez, and Colin Salmon. Sony Home Entertainment, 2008. DVD.

Resident Evil: Afterlife. Dir. Paul W.S. Anderson. Perf. Milla Jovovich, Ali Larter, and Wentworth Miller. Sony Home Entertainment, 2010. DVD.

Resident Evil: Apocalypse. Dir. Alexander Will. Perf. Milla Jovovich, Sienna Guillory, and Eric Mabius. Sony Home Entertainment, 2008. DVD.

Resident Evil: Extinction. Dir. Russell Mulcahy. Perf. Milla Jovovich, Ali Larter, and Oded Fehr. Sony Home Entertainment, 2008. DVD.

Schlozman, Steven C. *The Zombie Autopsies*. New York: Grand Central Publishing, 2011. Print.

Zombies, Cyborgs and Wheelchairs: The Question of Normalcy Within Diseased and Disabled Bodies

JL Schatz

The cultural currency of science fiction films in general and zombie flicks in particular should not be understated. Oftentimes in movies the origin of the infectious disease can be traced to a corporation or a clandestine government organization.[1] In the *Resident Evil* series the origin of the T-virus comes from the Umbrella Corporation. As a catch-all conglomerate, it has its hands in household goods and services just as much as it does in paramilitary and biological research. In reality, corporations that conduct chemical and biological experiments to produce household goods often also have ties to governmental weapons programs.[2] The fact that current corporate research has not caused a "zombie apocalypse" yet is irrelevant. "What emerges from recent research into ... science fiction is that writers ... foresaw nearly every horror ... before it materialized and that ... every horror yielded a profusion of tales developing its implications ... for the future of humankind. Fiction anticipated truth and truth provoked more fiction" (Wagner 448). Films like *Resident Evil* demand rigorous investigation because such fictions both construct and are constructed by reality. No doubt, "the zombie has become a scientific concept by which we define cognitive processes and states of being.... The ubiquity of the metaphor suggests the zombie's continued cultural currency ... as an ontic/hauntic object that speaks to some of the most puzzling elements of our sociohistorical moment" (Lauro and Embry 85–86).

What is of particular interest in zombie films like *Resident Evil* is the way the living dead are constructed as not only (un)dead but also simultaneously not human—even though they are certainly to some extent alive and were at least once fully human. The way these films demarcate the boundaries of life and humanity form the basis for justifying the slaughter, enslavement, and genocide of those that threaten a restricted definition of what constitutes human.[3]

186

In the films this leads the Umbrella Corporation to reduce Alice to her capitalist utility in order to clone, experiment, and kill her repeatedly without a second thought. In reality once living creatures are determined less than fully conscious they are justifiably imprisoned, killed, and consumed in the instance of factory farms and vivisection labs with a similar wanton disregard. Beyond this ready parallel with animal oppression, Alice's infusion with the T-virus and subsequent technologies in her evolution makes her not only (un)human but also part machine. As such, Alice embodies a cyborg politics that can transform the current sociopolitical moment ushered in by the quickening pace of biotechnological progress. By examining how Alice interacts with others in the films it is readily apparent that she exists as part of a hybrid identity that envisions a future free from apocalypse, which means much more than a world without zombies.

Alice's embodiment follows the notion of cyborg politics, which was coined in the 1990s by Donna Haraway. She claimed that "by the late twentieth century ... we are all ... hybrids of machine and organism; in short, we are cyborgs. The cyborg is our ontology; it gives us our politics ... [because] is the condensed image of both imagination and material reality ... which we need to understand for our survival" (150). Since the 1990s the field of transhumanist studies has grown as exponentially as the advancement of science and technology itself. The central tenent of transhumanism is that the synthesis between biology and technology can undermine the most central dichotomies in contemporary politics. "Chief among these troubling dualisms are self/ other, mind/body, culture/nature, male/female, civilized/primitive, reality/ appearance, whole/part, agent/resource, maker/made, active/passive, truth/ illusion," among countless others (Haraway 177). Transhumanists claim humanity will go extinct unless we embrace the hybridity the cyborg represents because new evolutionary merges with technology will fundamentally change what it means to be *Homo sapiens*. Unless humanity can cognitively evolve as it confronts a new species of *Homo technicus*, which exists in the in between, *Homo sapiens* will be left to the margins of history as inconsequential as the dodo.[4] Put simply, the essence of a cyborg politics is the fusion of opposites that undoes hierarchal configurations between the seemingly distinct parts that currently enframe the world. While I will return to this point later when examining the calculative logic of binary thought, it will here suffice to say that trying to cling to old dualistic divisions that separate human from zombie, animal, or machine is to ensure an apocalyptic end.

In opposition to the cyborg politics of hybridity stands a quest for purity that is embodied by both the Umbrella Corporation's desire to create the perfect living being and the American military's attempt to create the perfect soldier.[5] In both cases the end result is the same. Those who are deemed imperfect and who threaten the established order must perish or be enslaved. In the second film we learn that the T-virus was created by Dr. Ashford in order to help his daughter overcome a genetic abnormality and live a "normal" life. Shortly thereafter the positive potential of the virus became co-opted by its paramilitary applications in order to secure power for those who owned the patent rights. Time and time again the Umbrella Corporation uses Alice, her friends, other humans, animals, and zombies as a standing reserve absent intrinsic value.[6] Everyone outside Umbrella's executives are reduced to the potential profit they represent, even when seeking such profit risks destroying the world. This is similar to the military's concept of collateral damage. William Spanos points out, "What is astonishing in the typical discourse of the Rand Corporation report ... is its unquestioned reduction of living human beings ... who are being killed, mutilated, unhoused, imprisoned, tortured, by a foreign invading and occupational force (a horror it calls 'collateral damage') to 'targeted' 'consumers' of 'branded' products" (200–201). This is exactly what the Umbrella Corporation does in its reports marketing the bioweapon application of the T-virus to the very populations they test it on. In either case we find that people are turned into the living dead long before they become zombies. They are all merely waiting for hegemonic institutions to determine that their death or modification would be beneficial for the greater good. Fortunately, Alice represents an alternative possibility as she increasingly evolves into an almost "consciousless being that is a swarm organism ... and the only imaginable specter that could really be posthuman" (Lauro and Embry 88). Such an organism places the individual as part of a larger collective instead of a stand-alone autonomous subject, vastly expanding what matters in the construction of the Self.

There are a few differences between cyborgs and zombies that must be highlighted even if difference carries no real meaning anymore. To clarify, to see past difference is not to erase diversity and affirm a purified singularity. Rather it appreciates difference as part of our hybrid selves that are no longer prioritized in relation to the Other. Quite clearly, not everything is the same and not everything can be treated the exact same way. Hence, to say there is no difference between a cyborg and a zombie is to oversimplify the relationship between the two. At the same time to say they are entirely different is inaccurate as well.

> For Haraway ... becoming cyborg is not purely a material experience but involves a discursive transformation: we become cyborgs when we decide to be cyborgs. Haraway thus requires a moment of cognition, a moment of consciousness, that always insists upon subjectivity. The zombie may entail a material collision of living and dead tissues ... or it may merely be a symbolic or figurative construction[.] ... Regardless, in the zombii's purest form as an ontic/hauntic object, transformation

must be created outside the body, proclaimed by others. The zombii cannot see itself as such, much less claim a zombie identity for itself [Lauro and Embry 105].

Therefore, while one might speak of learning to become zombie, this becoming must transcend the very notion of what "becoming" currently means. We must not identify. We must simply be. This means that, even if people are already cyborgs consciously, they must give way to their unconscious impulses in order to be guided by more than their individual body alone. Only then can the space of the zombie be inhabited productively. To give this space a name reduces it to a mere utility of Being. Such lack of identity demands a rethinking of thinking itself since it must be divorced from any notion of consciousness that demarcates the difference between humans and other (un)dead animals. Put simply, we must (un)identify unconsciously.

Alice stands in stark contrast to the villains in the films, who declare themselves as the final stage of evolution due to their post-mutation genetic superiority. Much of this contrast is due to Umbrella Corporation's inability to deal with the uncertainty that comes with truly being a zombie. In the third and fourth installments of the film series, the Umbrella Corporation obsesses over finding the original Alice since all their clones and alternative subjects are inadequate for their research needs. To them the matter of zombies is purely about potential profit, cures, and the quest for immortality. Ultimately, Umbrella's style of thinking not only wasted the potential of countless clones—left in a mass grave witnessed in a horrifying scene in the third movie—but also caused them to militarize themselves in order to capture a single individual. This allowed the Umbrella Corporation to write everything else off as nothing more than collateral damage. Meanwhile, once Alice took over Umbrella's underground installation she immediately treats all her clones as equal. By the end of the fourth film it is unclear which Alice is the original or if the "original" even exists anymore because every sacrifice she makes is a sacrifice of the self. As a result, Alice's refusal to understand cloned life as subordinate opens up new evolutionary potentials far greater than Umbrella could ever imagine. It is precisely this lack of individualization that holds Alice's most transformative potential because it enables her to be more powerful than any single individual alone. Alice is more than just the property or genetic and financial future of the Umbrella Corporation, despite being born out of their technology. Instead she remains unanswerable to such a structure of ownership. This position breaks down any attempt to take control and reproduce her biologically or symbolically in a structured way. In the end, it was not that the clones were less capable than the original but that to understand them as separate parts already renders them powerless when nothing could be further from the truth. In short, Alice is always already every Other because every Other always already is Alice. This is why in the fifth film, when Alice's clone daughter asks her, upon seeing Umbrella's warehouse full of clones, "Are you my mommy?" Alice answers, "I am now."

What sets *Resident Evil* apart from other horror films is that at the end of each one the problem is not solved, the virus is not contained, and there are future obstacles to overcome. Alice never fully emerges victorious even when she is triumphant. For instance, for her to triumph at the end of the second film, she is forced to fight the Nemesis Project against her will despite recognizing how they are intimately connected. In order to imagine any of the installments as a happy ending the viewer must (un)identify as Alice and resign themselves to living in a world of zombies. From this perspective

> the zombie speaks to humanity's anxiety about its isolation within the individual body, and ... call[s] ... into question [that] which is more terrifying: our ultimate separation from our fellow humans, or the dystopic fantasy of a swarm organism. What we see in examining the historical trajectory of the zombie's evolution is that our fears ... are narratives informed by the material conditions of society. If the zombie articulates anxiety about the division of body and mind/soul, through history this narrative takes on various trappings of political and social crises. The zombie is not purely an expression of the pressing social concerns of the historical moment ... but, rather, it is given structure by these historical events ... concerning the mortality of the flesh [Lauro and Embry 101].

The 2012 news coverage of mentally afflicted people eating human flesh and surviving numerous gunshot wounds stands testament to this fact. While some news outlets played up the sensationalism of the events, and others noted how they occurred as a result of the lack of basic services for the mentally ill, official government channels promoted steps for zombie preparedness while simultaneously issuing statements that zombies were, in fact, not real.[7] In each instance how one approached their material conditions was informed by the evolution of fear that surrounds zombie narratives. Likewise, these narratives arose out of the very social crises that brought them into the popular imagination in the first place. As a consequence it is always already impossible to separate the fiction from fact concerning zombie outbreaks and the sociopolitical conditions that enframe such events.

One crucial difference between the films and reality is that "*Resident Evil* simply assumes a world in which genetic research is already controlled almost entirely by corporate interests" instead of one that's still in the process of evolving (Mitchell 142). It is precisely that difference that makes fiction so potent insofar as it allows society to think through potential futures before they happen. Further, it is not the accuracy of *Resident Evil*'s mirroring of the status quo that is important but rather the ontological figuring of its discourse. More than any other sci-fi genre, the spread of zombies in the media has become as infectious as the zombie itself.... The contagious nature of the zombie is reflected in this serial, intertextual structure of filmmaking. With this proliferation, the political and symbolic connotations of the zombie have similarly expanded to the extent that films ... do not use the zombie as a metaphor, but serve as explicit, self-reflexive explorations of zombie-as-metaphor [Boluk and Lenz 135].

By re-envisioning what it means to be a zombie at any moment this endless evolution of zombie narratives causes its form to bring about its content.[8] This enables one to move beyond a world of either human or zombie in order to "reveal ... much about the crisis of human embodiment, the way power works, and the history of man's [*sic*] subjugation and oppression of its 'Others'" (Lauro and Embry 87). Once this happens it is inconsequential if it is the brains of zombies that are getting blown out on the screen or the brains of soldiers on the battlefield. The symbolic power of both shapes the psychological conditions upon which fiction and reality co-evolve.

From this vantage point one may wonder why the *Resident Evil* series is categorized as horror films, despite its science fiction implications. Part of the reason for this categorization is due to the very presence of zombies. For the Motion Pictures Association, zombies are so horrifying that they cannot possibly be real despite the scientific facts provided throughout the movies that explain the progression of the disease. Whereas science fiction often requires a subject,

the zombie is an antisubject, and the zombie horde is a swarm where no trace of the individual remains. Therefore, unlike the vampire, the zombie poses a twofold terror: There is the primary fear of being devoured by a zombie, a threat posed mainly to the physical body, and the secondary fear that one will, in losing one's consciousness, become a part of the monstrous horde. Both of these fears reflect recognition of one's own mortality and ultimately reveal the primal fear of losing the "self" [Lauro and Embry 89].

As a result, zombie movies cannot traditionally be understood as science fiction since any such fiction conventionally imagines a world where there is a conscious self to navigate the future.[9] With zombies there can be no such self because in the future all humans have evolved into animals—something ironically they already are. Relegating zombie films to horror allows society to disassociate from the movies without questioning what it means to be an animal in reality today. Throughout *Resident Evil* the protagonists would rather die than become a zombie because to be a zombie is to be less than human, which is a state that might as well already be dead. From the first film, characters like Rain Ocampo ask to be put down at the first sign of losing their humanity. For all the animals confined against their will in laboratories waiting to be slaughtered when the research grant is complete they are already zombies and the fiction is already real.[10] Understanding Alice's uprising against the Umbrella Corporation as more than just a tool for fancy special effects is the first step in understanding how even a zombie's life isn't without value even if it's already (un)dead.

To escape the anthropocentrism inherent to human value systems that privilege the conscious self above all else is no easy task. However, the notion of the conscious self as uniquely autonomous from all other agents is a distinctly Western concept. This way of approaching identity uses a very limited "definition of intelligence [that] is so anthropocentric as to be next to useless for anything else ... [because] the more a thing resembles ourselves ... the more intelligent we think it" regardless of how smart it might actually be (Clark 188). The fact that non-human animals' response to pain is understood as mere instinct while human response is considered cognition stands as testament to this fact. In the *Resident Evil* films the Umbrella Corporation violently clings to the notion of a singular self despite the swarm uprising all around them. This violence plays out in the second installment when they obsess over whether Alice or Nemesis is the perfect singular evolutionary creation by pitting them against each other. "In *Resident Evil: Extinction* ... Alice herself is cloned multiple times ... [with] each disposable 'self' reflecting the devaluation of the durable that ... is now almost exclusively linked in the West to ... sites of social stability" (Vint 117). In the fourth installment it plays out the same way as in the third, with Albert Wesker declaring himself as the final stage of evolution only to be defeated by Alice. In the fifth it enables Wesker to go to extraordinary lengths to obtain Alice to re-infect her with the T-virus in order to create the perfect weapon to save humanity, regardless of how many had to die in the process. What matters here is that time and time again privileging the self, as well as neat divisions over what constitutes consciousness, results in a calculable logic that allows for everyone outside a privileged center circle to be expendable. This is not to say that the world was perfect before the outbreak, nor is it to say that humanity should seek to return to what once was. The Umbrella Corporation existed with immense power before the apocalypse. The only thing that changed afterwards was that there was now someone powerful enough to challenge them.

Yet, to willingly give oneself over to the uncertainty of living with zombies is simpler said than done. Even Dr. Ashford feared for Alice's life once Raccoon City was quarantined in the second film, despite having willingly infected her with the T-virus. More telling is the way Dr. Ashford was utilized and valued by the Umbrella Corporation during this time. At the onset of the movie, they go great lengths to save both him and his family because of his worth to the company. They ensure his survival even as they leave the rest of Raccoon City to the die within the quarantine zone by the hands of corporate security officers, military authorized nuclear strikes, and zombies. However, Dr. Ashford eventually becomes expendable to the Umbrella Corporation once they decide that testing the success of the Nemesis Project is their top priority. It is not coincidental that Dr. Ashford is portrayed as paralyzed from the waist down and has to use a wheelchair, nor is it coincidental that his daughter had a genetic defect that caused him to research the T-virus in the first place. It is their very so-called disabilities that mark them as viable test subjects and pawns in Umbrella's larger plans for profit and power. It is also no accident that what was at first a benign scientific breakthrough led to a paramilitary invention that caused the whole of humanity to mutate. In fact, this linkage between disability, disease, and genetic deficiency is all too common in medicalized approaches to human biology. Such approaches partake in a quest for purity by policing the borders of what constitutes the normal progression of human evolution insofar as they eliminate those genes that stray from the path. Indeed, "most critics note that the concept of monstrosity is deeply associated with disabled bodies. The same should, of course, be said of zombies. The mentally ill historically have been portrayed as having a consciousness that is morally suspect" if they are seen as having any consciousness at all (Lauro and Embry 103).

Because parts of the disabled body are already perceived as (un)dead, people with disabilities are often understood as being unable to live a normal life. Nowhere is this confusion over cyborg politics, zombiehood, and disability clearer than in contemporary debates that surround brain dead patients. Take for instance the case of Terri Schiavo.

> Her parents, who opposed their son-in-law's desires to remove Terri's feeding tube, released video of Schiavo blinking and appearing to smile. The issue of whether the outward appearance of cognition reflects an internal awareness of one's circumstances directed the argument. This alludes to the larger discussion that rages in cognitive neuroscience, concerning the various "zombie" agents that comprise what we call consciousness.... This kind of court case pronounces cognizance the determining factor of what constitutes life. If consciousness is found to be illusory, the person in question is decided not to be a "person" at all ... [and] are considered legally dead [Lauro and Embry 104–105].

The elevation of the brain as the marker of personhood enables society to pull the plug on all those who cannot display the expected signs of being conscious. On the flip side, people whose bodies are entirely paralyzed are recognized as fully human if their minds are active and can communicate thoughts assisted by technology—take for instance Stephen Hawking. However, neither Schiavo or Hawking, or any number of other people with more mundane enhancements like pacemakers, would be able to survive if it were not for artificial means. They are all zombies, they are all cyborgs, and they are all slaves to their machines. Despite this fact, due to a lack of communication in a way humanity deems valuable, zombies, non-human animals, and the brain dead are approached as not fully alive even though they are clearly not fully dead.

While Alice and the many disenfranchised populations throughout history can unquestionably communicate, when their utterances are outside the calculative logic of the hegemonic order such communication remains utterly unintelligible, and hence meaningless.[11] In turn, Alice is always already doomed to fail when she speaks and offers her body as a sacrifice to save those around her. Yet, her continual sacrifice challenges the Umbrella Corporation in order to reshape the hegemonic order of her world. But this sacrifice that results in her capture or death in almost every film is never fully a sacrifice because she extends beyond her biology alone and therefore can never die.

> The reconfiguration of information in *Resident Evil* enables the film to move beyond the sacrificial paradigm[.] ... While the question of sacrifice is central to *Resident Evil*, the film does not seek to isolate the good from the bad sacrifice, but instead reveals the concept of sacrifice as a limited, and limiting, understanding of the conditions for innovation ... [since] the reanimation of the dead as zombies ... undercuts the possibility of understanding worker deaths as "sacrifices." As a species of living dead, zombies are animated by what Giorgio Agamben calls "bare life," a form of vitality that precludes the sacrificial paradigm: one can kill, but not murder, and destroy, but not sacrifice, a zombie [Mitchell 148–149].

The real threat, however, is not becoming a zombie but forgetting that value continues to exist even in bare life. What Alice represents then is not so much a voice for the unspoken but a call to arms to displace the hierarchy of value that renders test subjects and zombies as (un)dead in the first place. This leaves room for a new understanding that can enact a form of "democracy [that] is about 'the power of those who have no qualification for exercising power.' It is 'the count of the uncounted—or the part of those who have no part' ... [who in] exercising rights that they do not have ... turn ... bare life into political life" (Lee 64). In other words, for Alice to save humanity she does not have to find the cure or thoughtlessly kill zombie after zombie. Rather it requires her to help humanity appreciate living life as the already (un)dead even while still being alive. Once the viewer recognizes how Alice is at once already part-zombie and part-machine, while simultaneously being human, they can understand that there is more to being a person than being an individual breathing body that sees itself as conscious.

Fortunately, in reality, just as in the films, there is no reason why society can't approach Others in the same way Alice does. Her approach is one that outlines a divergent evolutionary path where the self is a mere construction and where difference in intelligence, genetic makeup, and bio-technological composition is not used to determine value. This approach can subvert the

Umbrella Corporation's use of evolutionary discourse to demarcate value to life. In reality, it is possible to subvert the dominant discourse that relegates all those beyond the bounds of humanity as more than just mere animals. No doubt,

> Darwin himself believed that evolutionary history is no basis for deciding "who is better than whom." Evolution occurs as the result of genetic mutations and there is no moral basis for declaring that the mutated form is better than the unmutated ancestral form.... The more we learn about the earth's environment, its ecosystems, and the creatures who live here, the more we see the absurdity in the concept of ranking species against one another. All life on earth is inextricably bound together in a web of mutual interdependence [Spiegel 21–22].

In the films this is why Alice finds strength in those around her and never devalues their lives even if she is their evolutionary heir. In each instance, even though she is stronger and smarter, she never calculates the value of her companions for her own good. Instead the connections she forms with those around her are what matters because they are part of her collective self. When she is told that her life is more valuable than the clone of her daughter in the fifth installment Alice simply responds, "That's where you're wrong." Alice then goes on to rescue the child despite the clone not being biologically connected to Alice in a literal sense. In reality, just because humans have opposable thumbs does not mean that they're any better or more valuable than any other species on the planet. In both instances we must learn to expand what it means to be a living person in the current cybernetic world of zombie politics. To a large extent this is what is happening as groups like PETA push for legal personhood for non-human animals in order to afford them rights despite not being human.[12]

Beyond our shared environment with other species, the individual human self is not a stand-alone unit. As early as 1999, roughly 10 percent of the American population were cyborgs in a technical sense, living with artificial enhancements, while a much higher percentage were cyborgs in a metaphoric sense, living beyond the conceptual bounds of their biology (Hayles 115). No doubt, these percentages have increased because

> the human brain is ... biologically and technologically posed to explore cognitive spaces that would remain forever beyond the reach of non-cyborg animals.... What matters most is our obsessive, endless weaving of biotechnological webs ... [that] transform our sense of self, of location, of embodiment, and of our own mental capacities.... [Ultimately,] in embracing our hybrid natures, we give up the idea of the mind and the self as a kind of wafer-thin inner essence, dramatically distinct from all its physical trappings [Clark 197–198].

As technology advances, and internet access becomes more instantaneous and streamlined into the brain, it is feasible to imagine a world where a collective consciousness is built off of separate indistinct parts in much the same way as Alice and her clones are connected. By understanding these mergers as part of the self and not as distinct pieces it becomes possible to reshape what it means to be human, conscious, and alive. Once society recognizes that the non-human animals around them are also intimately part of humanity—whether it be from their consumption or shared environment—there can be space for a hybrid understanding that would make it impossible to inflict untold amounts of violence upon the world. From here it becomes infeasible to use difference as the basis for discrimination since there is no stable "I" to base such difference upon.

Despite all of the above, some may claim that what works for Alice in the movies is irrelevant since it still doesn't say anything about the real world. After all, zombies aren't real. To this end, three things should be kept in mind. First, as Katherine Hayles explains, technology and biological identity is "best approached ... by looking not only at the scientific content of the programs but also at the stories told about and through them. These stories ... constitute a multilayered system of metaphoric and material relays through which 'life,' 'nature,' and the 'human' are being redefined" (224). The way one approaches such stories frames the way one approaches the material world. If one's approach is merely to look for differences between oneself and Alice then they have already ontologically ordered themself within the same utilitarian calculus that justifies paramilitary research and corporate greed in the first place. "Insofar as modern technology aims to order and render calculable, the objectification of reality tends to take the form of an increasing classification, differentiation, and fragmentation of reality. The possibilities for how things appear are increasingly reduced to those that enhance calculative activities" (Sawicki 59–60). Michael Dillon, who serves as Professor of Politics and Director of the Institute for Cultural Research at the University of Lancaster, explains how "once rendered calculable ... units of account are necessarily submissible not only to valuation but also, of course, to devaluation. Devaluation, logically, can extend to the point of counting as nothing" (165). Placing the science fiction of *Resident Evil* as less relevant than news coverage of drug-induced zombies not only devalues characters like Alice but also upholds a very limited view of the world, which is then violently policed.

Second, while the movies obviously aren't real, they are still clearly based off a reality where the events that take place are hardly impossible to foresee as coming true. In fact, what Dillon describes in his theorization of devaluation is based firmly on his understanding of reality, not the silver screen. He writes, "there is nothing abstract about this: the declension of economies of value leads to the zero point of holocaust. However liberating and emancipating systems of value-rights may claim to be, for example, they run the risk of counting out the invaluable." (165). Such calculative logic can clearly be witnessed in things like the Holocaust, which utilized extermination to engineer a master race, and in systems of enslavement that reduced people of color into economic units. It can still be witnessed through

> the suffering animals currently endure at the hands of human beings in laboratories, on "factory farms," as pets, and in the wild ... [that] sadly parallels ... [the fate] endured by black people in the antebellum United States[.] ... Both humans and animals share the ability to suffer from restricted freedom of movement, from the loss of social freedom,... from their ... capacity to be terrified by being hunted, tormented, or injured [Spiegel 31].

The very reason why animals can be skinned alive for their fur, made to be utterly immobile for their entire lives, and have their bodies dissected and experimented upon is because they are not human. Indeed, it is this very identity of being outside of humanity that allows for corporations to clone, patent, and conduct virtually any operation they want on non-human animals in the name of profit or progress. In *Resident Evil: Retribution* it is what allows the Umbrella Corporation to sacrifice hundreds of cloned lives every time they simulate an outbreak to sell the T-virus to another country and further a biological arms race. In reality it was the branding of people of color, Jews, Gypsies, and an endless list of other people as somehow sub-human that led to the same devaluing logic that ended in extermination and enslavement. Thus, there is very little abstract or merely symbolic when the Umbrella Corporation clones, massacres, and willingly sacrifices whole populations to advance their own agenda at the risk of apocalypse. While one may be fiction, these very fictions give rise to the social imaginations that shape reality.[13]

Lastly, even if the outcome of science fiction never becomes fact, such films structure the technological innovations humanity decides to advance. And even when attempts at progress "fail ... we learn a little more about what really matters in the ongoing construction of our sense of place and personhood" (Clark 114). The reality of high speed smartphones, advances in science, life expectancy, and genetics were unimaginable less than one-hundred years ago and only became possible once science fiction imagined them. Hence, one should never assume that anything society can imagine is impossible since much of what is unimaginable currently can very possibly become reality as quickly as it's dreamed. By looking to the imaginative fictions of today humanity can be better suited to deal with the unexpected when it happens in reality tomorrow. The fact that *Resident Evil* has such strong parallels with reality is all the more reason to interrogate its characters and plot because it reflects what the current political moment is and could evolve to become. And while not every one of Alice's lessons may translate into reality, many will. By expanding what it means to be part of humanity, Alice is humanity's evolutionary heir in this new era of cybernetic zombie politics because she outlines a way to live life meaningfully, even when one is neither human nor alive.

Notes

1. Movies such as *Outbreak*, *28 Days Later*, *Contagion* and *Warning Sign* are among a long list of films that feature science gone astray. In each instance what starts out as a cure or a biological weapon meant to provide global security results in a deadly virus that risks wiping out the world.

2. Procter & Gamble serves as one of any number of ready examples. On its face the company is "the world's largest maker of consumer packaged goods ... [for] Beauty and Grooming and Household Care.... [Yet, as early as] 1940 Procter & Gamble's packaging expertise was given military applications when ... [they] operated as a subsidiary and filled government contracts for 60-millimeter mortar shells. Glycerin also became key to the war effort for its uses in explosives and medicine, and Procter & Gamble was one of the largest manufacturers of that product" (Hoover Company Profiles).

3. While this point will be returned to later, it is worth mentioning how concepts of life and death parallel notions such as Marx's concept of "undead labour," as well as Focault's notion of "docile bodies," and Heidegger's concept of a "standing reserve." In each instance, the way populations are defined forms the basis of their treatment by creating boundaries over which lives are worth living and which are expendable for the greater good.

4. For more on transhumanism from a scientific perspective see Gregory Stock's *Redesigning Humans*, as well as Andy Clark's *Natural-Born Cyborgs*. For an overview of transhumanist thought from both a scientific and theoretical perspective see Joel Garreau's *Radical Evolution*.

5. In but one example, the U.S. Defense Advanced Research Project Agency, in conjunction with the U.S. military, has already started working on developing soldiers that "are unstoppable[, immune from] ... pain, wounds, and bleeding" through advanced genetic engineering, giving "new dimension" to "the old Army slogan 'Be All You Can Be'" (Garreau 25–26). Expectedly, these genetic advancements are made at the cost of countless lives lost in vivisection labs across America in order to make human soldiers more effective killing machines.

6. "Looking at the well-heeled, bureaucratic discourse of 'human resource management' and 'personnel resources,' the challenging forth of human beings into standing reserve is fairly evident. Factory-farmed cows, pigs, and chickens obviously have it far worse than people, but in both cases the purpose is to harness resources for maximum efficiency and profit.... It is precisely the ... metaphysics of technical control and capitalist exploitation ... [that] will always lapse back into the false and oppressive hierarchy of 'man' over 'nature' and 'man' over animals with attendant effects of technological, disciplinary control over humans, nonhumans, and the Earth" (Best & Nocella 82).

7. "Mention Miami ... and the first people will talk about is the 'zombie' attack.... The Police are blaming it on a synthetic drug called 'bath salts,' while the Twitterverse is blaming it on a looming zombie apocalypse.... But the sensationalism and the sick jokes do make sense. It is easier to stock up on supplies and firearms ... while preparing for a zombie apocalypse ... than it is to really look at what would make a man like Rudy Eugene ... do the things he did[.] ... It is also easier than admitting that there were plenty of warning signs in Eugene's life indicating that he needed help. Unfortunately for him, those warning signs went off in a city where the early warning systems and institutions are constantly crumbling ... when it comes to funding mental health services" (Kateel). For

more information on official steps on how to prepare for a zombie outbreak visit the CDC's blog at http://blogs.cdc.gov/publichealthmatters/2011/05/preparedness-101-zombie-apoc alypse/.

    8. This is particularly the case for the *Resident Evil* collection since they are constantly being replicated for both the big screen and the video game console. While the games are beyond the scope of this essay, it will here suffice to point out how in the game "the lighting, camera angles, and music of *Resident Evil* ... draw ... upon the conventions of the horror movie genre ... using the language of film" in order to bring the user further into its fiction (Clarke & Mitchell 1).

    9. While there has recently been an influx of zombie films, such as *Wasting Away*, which have humanized zombies by creating them as more than unconscious entities, by and large they are filmed as parodies. The 2013 film *Warm Bodies* takes this a step further by focusing on a zombie that can experience love. In the movie, when zombies experience love and emotion they stop being cold dead bodies and start becoming warm, turning back into humans and helping fight those zombies who are even further (un)dead than themselves. While these films begin to complicate the question of the zombie they ultimately reaffirm the belief that the traditional zombie is without consciousness because once they begin to obtain consciousness they are somehow more than just a zombie. This is why the preview of *Wasting Away* tells viewers that the movie allows them to see the world through the "eyes of a monster and see how human the undead can be."

    10. "Right now, millions of mice, rats, rabbits, primates, cats, dogs, and other animals are locked inside cold, barren cages in laboratories across the country. They languish in pain, ache with loneliness, and long to roam free and use their minds. Instead, all they can do is sit and wait in fear of the next terrifying and painful procedure that will be performed on them" (PETA). Worse still is the fact that "'One major finding is that ... researchers ... [do] not show that they tried to find an alternative to painful experiments on animals.' ... Unfortunately, this kind of treatment happens so frequently in university labs that it is almost routine" (Bennett).

    11. Judith Butler elaborates, "The media's evacuation of the human through the image has to be understood, though, in terms of the broader problem that normative schemes of intelligibility establish what will and will not be human, what will be a livable life, what will be a grievable death. These normative schemes operate not only by producing ideals of the human that differentiate among those who are more and less human" (146).

    12. For more information in regards to the battle over personhood and rights see Eric Johnson's article "The Case for Non-Human Personhood Rights" as well as Brandon Keim's article "Whales Might Be as Much Like People as Apes Are."

    13. As put by Jean Baudrillard, "an unreal event ... is merely the expression of a— neither good nor bad, but quite simply immoral—collective will.... And we are not passive spectators of this fatal episode, but full-blown actors in it, playing our part in a lethal interactivity for which the media provide the interface.... There are no longer either actors or spectators; all are immersed in the same reality, in the same revolving responsibility, in a single impersonal destiny which is merely the fulfillment of a collective desire" (137–138).

Works Cited

Baudrillard, Jean. *Impossible Exchange*. London: Verso Press, 2001.

Bennett, Karin. "Government Inspectors Condemn Animal Laboratories at UW–Madison." *The PETA Files*. January 5, 2010. http://www.peta.org/b/thepetafiles/archive/ tags/USDA+vivisection+laboratory+/default.aspx, last accessed 7/1/2012.

Best, Steven, and Anthony Nocella. *Igniting a Revolution: Voices in Defense of the Earth.* Oakland, CA: AK Press, 2006.

Boluk, Stephanie, and Wylie Lenz. "Infection, Media, and Capitalism: From Early Modern Plagues to Postmodern Zombies. *Journal for Early Modern Cultural Studies.* Vol. 10. No. 2 (Fall/Winter 2010): pp. 126–145.

Butler, Judith. *Precarious Life: The Powers of Mourning and Violence.* New York: Verso Press, 2006.

Clark, Andy. *Natural-Born Cyborgs: Minds, Technologies, and the Future of Human Intelligence.* New York: Oxford University Press, 2003.

_____, and Grethe Mitchell. "Film and the Development of Interactive Narrative." http://www.transformreality.com/downloads/papers/Virtual%20Storytelling.pdf, last accessed 7/1/2012.

Dillon, Michael. "Another Justice." *Political Theory.* Vol. 27, No. 2. April 1999: pp. 155–175.

Garreau, Joel. *Radical Evolution: The Promise and Peril of Enhancing Our Minds, Our Bodies—And What It Means to Be Human.* New York: Doubleday, 2005.

Haraway, Donna. *Simians, Cyborgs, and Women: The Reinvention of Nature.* New York: Routledge, 1991.

Hayles, Katherine. *How We Became Posthuman: Virtual Bodies in Cybernetics, Literature, and Informatics.* Chicago: The University of Chicago Press, 1999.

Hoover Company Profiles. "The Procter & Gamble Company." http://www.answers.com/topic/procter-gamble, last accessed 7/1/2012.

Kateel, Subhash. "It's Bigger Than 'Bath Salts' and 'Zombie Apocalypses.'" *Huffington Post.* June 6, 2012. http://www.huffingtonpost.com/subhash-kateel/its-bigger-than-bath-salts_b_1562014.html, last accessed 7/1/2012.

Keim, Brandon. "Whales Might Be as Much Like People as Apes Are," *Wired Magazine.* June 6, 2009. http://www.wired.com/wiredscience/2009/06/whalepeople/, last accessed 12/25/2012.

Johnson, Eric. "The Case for Non-Human Personhood Rights." *Huffington Post.* March 12, 2012. http://www.huffingtonpost.com/eric-michael-johnson/non-human-personhood_b_1336480.html, last accessed 12/26/2012.

Lauro, Sarah, and Karen Embry. "A Zombie Manifesto: The Nonhuman Condition in the Era of Advanced Capitalism." *Boundary 2* (Spring 2008): pp. 85–108.

Lee, Charles. "Bare Life, Interstices, and the Third Space of Citizenship." *WSQ: Women's Studies Quarterly.* Vol 38, No 1/2 (Spring/Summer 2010): pp. 56–76.

Mitchell, Robert. "Sacrifice, Individuation, and the Economies of Genomics." *Literature and Medicine.* Vol. 26, No.1 (2007): pp. 126–158.

PETA. "Animals Used for Experimentation." http://www.peta.org/issues/animals-used-for-experimentation/default.aspx, last accessed 7/1/2012.

Sawicki, Jana. "Heidegger and Foucault: Escaping Technological Nihilism." *Foucault and Heidegger: Critical Encounters.* Eds. Alan Milchman and Alan Rosenberg. Minneapolis: University of Minnesota Press, 2003, pp. 55–73.

Spanos, William. "Global American: The Devastation of Language Under the Dictatorship of the Public Realm." *Symploke.* Vol. 16. Nos. 1–2 (2008): pp. 172–212.

Spiegel, Marjorie. *The Dreaded Comparison: Human and Animal Slavery.* New York: Mirror Books, 1996.

Vint, Sherryl. "Review of Zygmunt Bauman, *Liquid Fear.*" *Science Fiction Film and Television.* Vol. 2. No. 1 (Spring 2009): pp. 115–119.

Wagar, Warren. "Truth and Fiction, Equally Strange: Writing About the Bomb." *American Literary History.* Vol. 1 No. 2 (Summer 1989): pp. 448–457.

"I barely feel human anymore": Project Alice and the Posthuman in the Films

Margo Collins

Despite their resounding box-office successes, the live-action *Resident Evil* movies have generally been met with critical disdain—they are often considered, at best, "videogame-inspired action schlock" (Maio 192). The first movie, for example, is described as having "proved surprisingly popular, cuing a sequel that raised the stakes and increased the body count" (Leydon 88). The second film, *Resident Evil: Apocalypse*, is decried as "calamitously uninspired and borderline incoherent," a "new pic [that] lacks even those fleeting pleasures (namely, a sense of humor) that made the first film a passable popcorn attraction" (Foundas 41). In *Extinction*, "the final face-off between the Millas and a tentacle-armed, latex-buried Iain Glen is as disappointingly rote as the lumbering appearance of the Frankensteinian nemesis at the end of *Resident Evil Apocalypse* [*sic*]" (Newman). *Afterlife*, according to one reviewer, "isn't just bad. It's so abysmal that it manages to transcend 'bad' and become hysterical" (Adams). Indeed, the best any critics could muster about any of the films was that *Extinction* "sustains a reasonable degree of narrative consistency while advancing a mythos that, with each new episode, has grown more expansive in scope" (Leydon 88)—though virtually every review does acknowledge that each of the movies offers up some form of adrenaline-inducing action scenes featuring Milla Jovovich as the lead character, Alice.

Scholars have been as reluctant to engage in critical discussion of the films as have movie critics. They almost all seem to agree, as Maitland McDonagh claims, that

> while it could be argued that Alice's journey from Umbrella pawn to self-appointed savior of the world adds depth to a series of shoot-'em-up set-pieces, that would be wishful thinking. Despite the revolving parade of decent actors who've traipsed through the franchise, *Resident Evil* movies are more or less zombies versus hot

babe packing serious heat, aided [in some cases] by an exceptionally handsome 3D process that makes the most of glinting shuriken and splattering blood [118].

The critics are all right, to some degree—the movies do highlight the "zombies versus hot babe" aspect of video games. As one critic asks about *Extinction*, "What does it say when the top-grossing female-led film of 2007 is little more than a violent fanboy fantasy?" (Markovitz 14). But the continuing popularity of these films (and the video game that spawned them) illustrates an enduring cultural fascination with the monstrous in society, and the *Resident Evil* movies focus increasingly intently on examining the possibilities of existence in a postapocalyptic, posthuman world. Ultimately, the movies offer a variety of options for posthumanity, but delimits each of those options as inherently unviable. In the end, it is not enough to be a human, a corporation, a clone, a cyborg, a mutation, or a zombie. In order to function effectively in the posthuman world as depicted in these films, Alice—or rather, Project Alice—must become all of these: cyborg, corporation, clone, mutation, revenant. In doing so, she becomes the answer to the question of what it means to be humane in a posthuman world.

The Posthuman and the Monstrous

That the *Resident Evil* movies are explosively popular should come as no surprise in an era that has been hailed as something of a zombie renaissance. In fact, depictions of monsters in general continue to abound, even if, as Peter J. Dendle claims, "in a largely secular and self-conscious age, the forms of monstrous past are infantilized, commoditized, and incorporated into the kitsch icons of leisure and entertainment" (438). The monsters of the *Resident Evil* films are all of those things—hence the critique that the fourth movie crosses into the "hysterical"—but the movies are indicative of our cultural concerns about monstrosity, as well. Asa Simon Mittman writes,

> Monsters do a great deal of cultural work, but they do not do it nicely. They not only challenge and question; they trouble, they worry, they haunt. They break and tear and rend cultures, all the while constructing them and propping them up. They swallow up our cultural mores and expectations, and then, becoming what they eat, they reflect back to us our own faces, made disgusting or, perhaps, revealed to have always been so ... all "monsters" are our constructions ... through the processes by which we construct or reconstruct them, we categorize, name, and define them, and thereby grant them anthropocentric meaning that makes them "ours" [1].

Part of the cultural work at hand for the *Resident Evil* movies is an examination of the various possibilities of existence in a posthuman world. That these possibilities should range from the viral to the corporate, include the living and the dead, and slip into the monstrous and the mutated is unsurprising, given that "literary and scientific works which theorise the posthuman sometimes blend the discourses of the primitive, technology and horror to explain or explore various accounts of the posthuman condition" (Campbell and Saren 172). The *Resident Evil* movies explore the possibilities of posthumanity as they follow Alice's transformation from blank slate waking in a house, to survivor of a zombie outbreak, to cybernetically enhanced human, to leader of a group of other survivors searching for a mythical land free of zombies, and finally, to the proposed savior of that group, and perhaps all humankind.

The critical idea of posthumanism has been increasingly discussed by theorists in the last two decades. N. Katherine Hayles succinctly describes the importance of the posthuman when she writes:

First, the posthuman view privileges informational pattern over material instantiation, so that embodiment in a biological substrate is seen as an accident of history rather than an inevitability of life. Second, the posthuman view considers consciousness ... as an epiphenomenon, as an evolutionary upstart trying to claim that it is the whole show when in actuality it is only a minor sideshow. Third, the posthuman view thinks of the body as the original prosthesis we all learn to manipulate, so that extending or replacing the body with other prostheses becomes a continuation of a process that began before we were born. Fourth, and most important ... the posthuman view configures human being so that it can be seamlessly articulated with intelligent machines. In the posthuman, there are no essential differences or absolute demarcations between bodily existence and computer simulation, cybernetic mechanism and biological organism, robot teleology and human goals [2–3].

Thus the posthuman is that which acknowledges the lack of primacy of the purely human. Patricia MacCormack notes that "Posthuman theory developed as a result of the deconstruction of meta-discourses such as science, history, and transcendental philosophy that had worked to attain and maintain the meaning, truth, and status of what defines the human" (293). Donna Haraway's cyber-feminist theories of the techno-posthuman create a connection between "woman" and "technology" as both separated from the norms of "human" and "man." In "A Cyborg Manifesto," she writes "Cyborg monsters in feminist science fiction define quite different political possibilities and limits from those proposed by the mundane fiction of Man and Woman" (150). More recently, the idea of connections between the posthuman and the monstrous have begun to take hold. Indeed, though Haraway focuses on the cyborg without considering it monstrous, the cyborg's potential monstrosity exists in its lack of humanity. At this point, the monstrous and the posthuman are quickly becoming inextricably intertwined. Karin Myhre claims that monsters "bridge ordinarily stable categories in thought and language. Not only are the bodies of monsters hybrid and complex, the very process of identifying uncommon beings may put pressure on the stability of documents, human powers of classification, and the possibilities of language" (222). The instability of meaning, of language, of classification, also calls into question the issue of what it means to be human, what it means to be monstrous, and what might constitute ethical posthumanity. Each of the posthuman options offered in the *Resident Evil* movies explores the potential deconstruction of an essential dichotomy—living/dead, monster/human, machine/human, corporation/person—and finds the results lacking. Ultimately, the movies illustrate, the only possible answer to the dilemma of living as an ethical posthuman is to elide all distinctions, to embrace all possible elements of these dichotomies.

Posthuman Options in Resident Evil

ZOMBIES

Deborah Christie and Sarah Lauro, in the introduction to their collection *Better Off Dead: The Evolution of the Zombie as Post-Human*, suggest that the zombie also functions as a symbol of the posthuman; they write that "the zombie has not just evolved within narratives—it has evolved in a way that transforms narrative" (2). Zombies function as the return of what should be the ultimate end of narrative—the mindless revenant rising to consume that which it helped create. Steve Zani and Kevin Meaux have claimed the characteristic zombie fear is that "the institutions holding our culture together, specifically law, family, and belief in the sacred, will break down or reveal themselves to be false in the face of catastrophe." In the *Resident Evil* movies, these institutions, in the form of the Umbrella Corporation that developed the zombie-creating T-virus, reveal themselves to be not only false, but ultimately culpable.

Nowhere is this as obvious as in the zombies that the T-virus creates. Yet even these failed human elements of the corporation become part of the posthuman condition. As Elson Bond and I have argued elsewhere, "zombies function as monstrous placeholders for potentially dangerous human interactions in an anomic society used to instant communication with virtual strangers—thus zombies become a kind of anonymous, amorphous threat that replaces individual conscience and volition with a collective but uncalculating malice" (Collins and Bond 187). This collective behavior thus becomes one posthuman option: to join the ranks of the walking dead, consuming and destroying what is left of humanity. Jeff May notes that

> There is an integral moment in many zombie films when living characters realize zombies are something to be feared. This moment presents a key crisis of identity.

Identity differences (based on race, gender, family, etc.) undergo rapid transitions to the new divide between undead and living. The othering process forces characters to make hasty delineations between "us" and "them," which leads to some powerful discursive formations [291].

This distinction between "us" and "them" leads to what May calls the "familiar zombie," i.e., the newly zombified character whose existence threatens all those around her. In zombie form, then, the posthuman is a threat, an "other" to be eradicated. The distinction of living versus dead might come into question (how does one "kill" something that is already dead?), but as the zombies in the *Resident Evil* movies have, at best, only "some memory" of their former lives, their continued existence becomes untenable. The creation of zombies through the T-virus in the *Resident Evil* series leads to a posthuman reality with no room for the individual—perhaps the least ethical or attractive of the posthuman options offered by the films.

MUTANTS

The mutants in the movies represent a second posthuman option. The mutations offer bestial power, an exploration of the dichotomy between human and animal. The first iteration of these mutations shows up in the films in the form of skinless, bloody Dobermans, a commentary on animal testing and its perhaps inevitably horrific results. But more importantly, the mutations also bond with humans. In the first movie, the monstrous creature released when the Red Queen is shut down attacks Spence Parks (James Purefoy) and feeds on his DNA. In the process, the creature becomes stronger. The animal benefits from the addition of the human. The reverse is not true; in a forced show-down, Alice beats Nemesis in *Apocalypse*, largely because his human intellect and emotion—left over from his days as Matt (Eric Mabius)—overcome the monstrous instincts the mutations have created in him. The balance between human and animal is continuously refined over the course of the movies, but is never fully stabilized. In *Extinction*, Dr. Isaacs (Iain Glen) injects himself with an overdose of the T-virus antidote in order to become stronger after being bitten by a zombie. This strength is monstrous, as is his transformation, but the strength (and tentacles) granted to him by the mutations he undergoes allow him to survive much longer than he would have otherwise, and he manages to keep a greater degree of his personality and intellect intact than did Matt/Nemesis. By *Afterlife*, the T-virus mutation gives Umbrella chairman Albert Wesker (Shawn Roberts) the ability to survive a fiery helicopter crash and continue to run the Umbrella Corporation experiments—and also gives him tentacles that sprout from his mouth. Yet he states that living with the T-virus is a struggle: "The T-virus brought me back. But it's so strong. It fights me for control."

Thus, the most obvious problem with mutations in the films is that the combination of human and animal is unstable; those mutants with the ability to exercise human compassion and loyalty are easily overpowered, whereas those mutants without those abilities are unable to coexist with others. Indeed, in an attempt to overcome the T-virus, Wesker plans to consume Alice, saying "I thought if I ingested fresh human DNA, I could redress the balance.... You were the only one who successfully bonded with the T-virus. Your DNA is stronger than the others. I ingest you, I gain control" (*Afterlife*). In the end, the mutants' physical hybridity and moral deformity are coequal, and thus the mutants, like the zombies, offer a dead end for posthumanity. Karl Steel notes that historically, monsters were "on the edges of ... the civilized world, where nature becomes unrecognizable" (261). In the case of the mutants in *Resident Evil*, that place where nature becomes unrecognizable is in our midst, and the possibilities that hybridity offers do not extend to a viable posthuman existence.

CYBORGS

Cyborgs are, in many ways, the traditional posthuman. As Pramod K. Nayar points out, "Literary imaginations, especially after Mary Shelley's cult text, Frankenstein (1817), have been concerned with questions of techno-bodies" (30). The initial cyborg form in the *Resident Evil* movies is slightly less embodied than one might generally consider "cyborg," showing up first as the Red Queen (Michaela Dicker), the artificial intelligence program in control of the Hive in *Resident Evil* (and again in *Retribution*). The Red Queen's holographic body is in the form of a child, a young girl designed to seem doubly horrific when juxtaposed with the calculating intelligence behind the form. Nayar notes that "modified and enhanced cyborg bodies ... or posthumans are not simply techno-bodies. Cyborg bodies are a congeries of hardware (computers), software (codes and computer programs) and wetware (organic bodies). They are located within particular social, cultural and economic contexts, where a cyborged, networked body leads (also) to questions of identity" (31). In this case, the identity of the Red Queen is also tied to issues of motivation, as she is the instigator of the Hive lockdown after the T-virus is released and thus the initially apparent cause of the death of all of the humans living and working in the Hive. But the Red Queen's begging not be shut down and her proclamation that "You're all going to die down here" become less sinister when the first movie reveals that the AI program is the only thing that keeps the T-virus, the mutants, and the zombies locked away from the rest of humanity. Alice might rightly call the Red Queen "a homicidal bitch" (*Extinction*), but the cyborg's homicide has a purpose. That this kind of calculating, disembodied posthumanity cannot prevail becomes clear in *Extinction*, when the White Queen

(Madeline Carroll), AI controller of another research facility, can manage only to keep the mutant Dr. Isaacs contained; she cannot, in her disembodied state, prevail against the embodied posthumans. Moreover, the White Queen defends the Red Queen by saying, "My sister computer was merely following the most logical path for the preservation of human life." Alice's dismissive response of "Yeah, kill a few, save a lot" indicates that the Red Queen's logical path was less than ideal. Logic, the movies suggest, must be tempered by compassion and backed up by physical strength, and the AI programs have neither.

THE UMBRELLA CORPORATION

Ultimately, though, the zombies, mutants, and cyborgs in the *Resident Evil* series all stand in for the Umbrella Corporation. As Dana Oswald notes, "Those monsters occupied by excessive, particularly cannibalistic, consumption, often serve as metaphors for human greed or poor governance, but they also exhibit a kind of masculine tyranny and need for possession or inclusion" (347). If the monsters themselves are occupied by consumption, the Umbrella Corporation is consumed by the desire for power and thus illustrates both this need for possession and the possibility of a posthuman reality that is comprised of, but not reducible to, humans. In a world where corporate personhood is a legal reality, the Umbrella Corporation becomes a viable option for posthumanity. Like the other posthuman options, the corporation is a hybrid, and in its hybridity, inherently monstrous. In the *Resident Evil* films, the corporation is the scientific urge made manifest, but in a way that is almost insectile in its function. The Umbrella Corporation is represented by the artificial intelligences of the Red Queen and the White Queen and by the scientists who do their bidding, as worker ants in the Hive. One potential problem with the corporate posthuman is that it is, in part, made up of humans—but the scientists are part of the corporate whole, not individuals. Like the AI programs, the leaders of Umbrella most often appear as holograms in their meetings with one another and are therefore relatively disembodied; unlike the Queens, the men have military might to back them up. Moreover, in its continuing production of clones (particularly as seen in *Retribution*), the Umbrella Corporation shows that it does not value human life. It is as lacking in individualism as the zombies, as inhumane as the mutants, and as coldly calculating as the cyborgs—it has all of the flaws and none of the redeeming qualities of the other posthuman options offered by the films.

ALICE AS POSTHUMAN

Alice, on the other hand, is the perfect posthuman—or rather, Project Alice is. The point at which the person who thinks of herself as "Alice" becomes "Project Alice" is not entirely clear—there are some indications that she has been little more than another Umbrella Corporation project all along. It is important to note that she is given no name at all until the beginning of the second movie. At this point, the character says in voice-over that "my name is Alice," but the audience repeatedly sees an Umbrella Corporation medical monitoring screen with the words "Project ALICE" on it, and the Umbrella Corporation employees, including Dr. Isaacs, never use the simpler moniker; she is always called "Project Alice." This distinction is significant in that it highlights Alice's position as a posthuman; she is not a person, but a project.

Alice is set up as posthuman from the beginning. Like the zombies, she has little memory. In the first scene in which she is shown, she wakes naked in the shower with no memory. Though we are told that this is a temporary condition, the audience never sees more than a few flashback glimpses of Alice's life before. The Red Queen says that the zombies have "perhaps a little memory," but nothing more, a comment that directly connects Alice to the zombies.

Also like the zombies, Alice is a revenant. At the end of *Apocalypse*, Alice dies in a helicopter crash. As she dives forward to intercept a metal rod headed for Angie, the child she has just saved from Raccoon City, she is impaled and falls back, eyes open. That she is dead is clear—the next scene shows a scattering of smoking helicopter remains with a single body, covered by a sheet. When Dr. Isaacs lifts the sheet off the body's face, Alice's eyes stare blankly out of a burned face. Isaacs' response to the body of "fetch the medical team" might seem to indicate that she lives, but the fact that the body has not been treated yet implies that the initial respondents did not resuscitate her. Moreover, a soldier says to Isaacs that there were "no other bodies found, sir," indicating that what we are seeing is Alice's corpse—she is a body, not a person.

But of course Alice does not stay dead. Like the zombies, she revives because of the T-virus infection. Unlike the zombies, though, she revives with her mental faculties intact. Kevin Alexander Boon argues that "The reanimated dead are not proper zombies unless they lose some essential quality of self" (36). Thus Alice is not a zombie, exactly—but she is a revenant. The scene immediately following the discussion of Alice's body shows her floating in a tank, and a female voice that sounds suspiciously like the Red Queen's says "Alice, wake up." After giving her a few moments to recover—she shakes and shivers and moans in ways reminiscent of the zombies—Isaacs asks her if she remembers her name. We see flashbacks as Alice regains at least part of her memory and identity, and she says "My name is Alice and I remember everything." This act of remembering herself after being revived is what makes Alice a successful revenant. Like the zombies, she might have only "perhaps a little memory" (as the Red Queen said), but unlike the zombies, neither her body nor her memory are in a state of decay. She is herself and she is a revenant.

Alice is also a mutant, albeit on a cellular level rather than the gross physical level of the other mutants in the movies. We see the beginnings of this change in *Apocalypse*: after Alice leaves the hospital and is in the process of gathering clothing and weapons, she falls to the ground and convulses while something crawls up her arm, under the skin. That the change is going to be beneficial becomes clear when she saves Jill Valentine's group, hiding in a church—Alice's new skills are remarkable, as Valentine indicates:

VALENTINE: Those were some pretty slick moves back there. I'm good, but I'm not that good.
ALICE: You should be grateful for that.
VALENTINE: What do you mean?
ALICE: They did something to me. I barely feel human anymore.

As a result of the cellular mutations, Alice's senses are heightened, as well— she recognizes Nemesis's presence without any overt signal, and when she fights against him, her superhuman strength becomes clear. And as the newly revived Alice leaves the Umbrella facility at the end of *Apocalypse*, she uses psionic powers to disable the cameras and kill the security guard watching her. By *Extinction*, these skills have developed fully, and she uses her psychic powers and physical strength to protect those around her. The White Queen tells her "Your blood has bonded with the T-virus. Dr. Isaacs correctly deduced that it could be used to destroy the biohazard for good." Thus Alice's mutations have the potential to benefit those around her.

Alice is also a cyborg—but unlike the Red and White Queen, she is a fully embodied cyborg. The films begin to hint at this techno-humanity at the beginning of *Apocalypse*, when the audience sees a close-up of one of Alice's eyes opening, much like the early scene of the first film. But in this case, Alice's iris is in the shape of the Umbrella Corporation. The scene shifts immediately to a series of computerized images with Alice's voiceover, thereby connecting Alice to the corporation and to computerized, mechanized imagery.

Her cyborg nature becomes fully realized in *Extinction* when Dr. Isaacs and his crew use their satellites—hitherto employed only in tracking Alice— in an attempt to control her. As Alice and the convoy led by Claire Redfield (Ali Larter) and Carlos Olivera (Oded Fehr) attempt to find fuel in a desert-ravaged Vegas strip, the point of view shifts from Alice's eyes to a screen showing Alice's view to Dr. Isaacs. This shift is of course in part a nod to the first-person shooter games that spawned the films, but it also highlights Alice's status as part machine—Dr. Isaacs has the ability to see what she sees because her eyes transmit the view back to him. Isaacs says "Satellite in position? ... Then shut her down," again pointing to Alice's position as mechanical object to be controlled. At this point, Alice's eyes again flash to the Umbrella Corporation logo, and she freezes.

However, one of the benefits of being only partly machine is that Alice is also still partly human—she is posthuman, but still maintains a connection to humanity. The fight continues around her and as various members of the convoy die, Claire screams in anger. The scream reaches Alice, whose eyes flash again. One of the soldiers in the control tent says "She's fighting conditioning" and Isaacs replies "Boost the signal." But Alice is also a mutant with psychic powers, so she uses those powers to short out a chip in the satellite itself. As the only fully realized posthuman in the movies (and, of course, as the heroine), Alice is ultimately uncontrollable by any outside forces.

Finally, Alice is also the Umbrella Corporation, as both her "branding" by the corporation (in the form of the logo that appears in her eyes) and her clones illustrate. If to be part of the Umbrella Corporation is to be lacking in individualism, then to be a clone is to be the ultimate corporate functionary. *Extinction* opens with a repeat of much of the imagery from the first movie: Alice wakes in a shower, finds a red dress, attempts to make her way through a laser-protected hallway. But this Alice dies, and Umbrella Corporation employees take her body to the surface, where it is dumped on top of a number of other Alices—eighty-six of them, we discover later. Each of these clones, however, is a failed Alice; none of them are able to replicate the posthuman survival that the original Alice effects, which begs the question: Is "Project Alice" different from the original Alice—or did "Alice" ever exist at all? The other clones apparently don't work the same way she does, though they have at least some of her memories. We see the clone's memories of Alice's experiences, so she is clearly capable of much of the same activity as the Alice who is the heroine of the films—but to be a clone is to be incomplete, the movies suggest. Ultimately, though, one of the clones also moves into the territory of fully realized individual. At the end of *Extinction*, one of the clones wakes up (after apparently having died) and saves the heroine. Thus the clones have the chance to move into viable posthumanity, as well—but only by separating themselves from the Umbrella Corporation. Similarly, Umbrella might, as Wesker tells Alice in *Afterlife*, consider her its "property," but she has already distanced herself from the corporate conglomerate. In fact, *Retribution*, the fifth movie of the series, indicates that Project Alice is also a clone. After a long series of scenes showing Alice as a housewife—married to Carlos and mother of a deaf child—Project Alice awakens in a cell in Umbrella Corp's headquarters; the housewife sequence reads as a dream at that point, marking a connection between Alice and the clones (similar to the connection illustrated in *Extinction*, when Alice twitches in her sleep as another clone dies). Later, when Alice comes across the dead body of the housewife version, Ada Wong (Li Bingbing) tells her that she is one of fifty base models populating Umbrella Corp's mock cities. Wong's comment that Alice could be a housewife in one version and a soldier for Umbrella in another reinforces the idea that Alice is a clone—after all, she was a soldier for Umbrella—as does the fact that Alice uses sign language to communicate with the deaf child left behind; as Ada notes, the clones are imprinted with basic memories, and Alice's easy use of sign language illustrates that she, too, was imprinted with this information. Therefore, it's Alice's ability to separate herself from the Umbrella Corporation that makes her different from the other Alice clones.

Finally, Alice's posthumanity is permanent. Although Wesker claims in *Afterlife* to be returning Alice to her former human self, it is clear that she has moved so far into the realm of the posthuman that a full return to humanity is impossible. After all of the clones from Dr. Isaac's laboratory have died in an attack on Wesker's Umbrella facility, Wesker flees in a helicopter, where Alice attacks him. Wesker manages to inject her with a serum. This scene makes it clear that both Wesker and Alice believe that the process will restore Alice to her previous human condition:

> WESKER: How nice to finally meet the real you. Hurts, doesn't it? That's just the start of the bad news. All those powers of yours? Speed, strength, accelerated healing; you can kiss all those goodbye.
>
> ALICE: What have you done?
>
> WESKER: The serum I've injected you with is neutralizing the T-cells in your body. Put simply, the Umbrella Corporation is taking back its property. You just didn't work out, so you're being recalled.... I'm what you used to be, only better ... (points a gun at Alice).
>
> ALICE: Please wait.
>
> WESKER: Last words?
>
> ALICE: Thank you.
>
> WESKER: For killing you?
>
> ALICE: For making me human again.

However, Alice does not become fully human again, as is instantly obvious when she is first engulfed in flames when the helicopter crashes into a mountainside and then walks away from the smoldering wreckage. Further, she continues to fight well above normal human ability. She may have lost some of her powers, but she remains posthuman. Wesker's reinfection of Alice in *Retribution* is ultimately redundant; it may aid in the fight to save the remaining people, but it does not affect her posthuman status.

Also, by the end of *Afterlife*, virtually all of the humans Alice is attempting to protect are some form of posthuman. Having found siblings Claire and Chris Redfield, Alice boards the Umbrella Corporation ship *Arcadia*, where she finds a mutant Wesker continuing to experiment on the survivors of the

T-virus-induced zombie apocalypse. Thus, the remaining on-screen humans have become Umbrella Corporation experiments, making them all "posthuman." Indeed, even those who have not been experimented on, such as the model/athlete Luther West (Boris Kodjoe) are living in a posthuman world. The final scene of *Retribution* reinforces this fact, as the few remaining humans stand in a devastated Washington, D.C., surrounded by zombies and mutants tearing at the gates. The only question remaining is how to continue to be humane and ethical in that posthuman world.

Conclusion

Many discussions of the female combatant in video games and the movies derived from them—including Alice's role in the *Resident Evil* movies—focus largely on the heroine's gender. That this should be true seems particularly odd, given how asexual Alice's behavior is portrayed as being. However, in a discussion of the video game character Lara Croft, Claudia Herbst writes:

> The gratification and pleasure of the gaze in the context of war and eroticism are closely related. The female is sought after with the intent of procreation (or the act leading up to it); the enemy, inversely, is chased with the intent of destruction. Possibly that is why the new images of women currently permeating popular culture are a composite of sexualized aggression; in computer games and films today, the continued objectification of women is the offspring of the process of visualizing sex and death, humanity's most frequently depicted spectacle. The visually stimulated objectification of women in Western, male society takes on new forms when coupled with contemporary, war-based imaging technologies. In the countless virtual worlds of military-inspired computer games, the representation of the female body is pushed to new extremes. Hyper-realistic productions of sex and death reduce the female to a territory of lust and deadly menace. Based on Lara Croft's appearance, actions, and equipment, she is a fine example of this trend [21].

Alice, too, becomes an example of the trend. The only sexual activity we see is in a flashback to her fake marriage in the first movie. Once she moves from being the unnamed character to being Project Alice, she is the object of the gaze, but only the gaze—to touch her is to invite death, as we see in *Extinction*. In one of the early scenes in the movie, Alice enters a radio station broadcasting a request for help. Once there, she is captured by a stereotypical backwoods family. The adult sons of the family hold her down and one of them prepares to rape her by spreading her legs and flicking a knife at the straps holding her weapons. She warns him, saying "I wouldn't do that," but he ignores her; she responds by kicking out and sending a spike into his chest, thus impaling him in a violent reversal of gender roles. Sherrie Inness writes that "popular culture's tough women—no matter how traditionally feminine and beautiful they might appear—offer insights into how women are fighting to escape conventional gender role expectations that, in the past, have kept them from being aggressive, whether in real life or the media" (7). In Alice's case, this escape is one that precludes sexuality, in large part because Alice's lack of overt sexuality is important in order to contain her monstrous possibilities. To be both sexually active and violent is to transgress against what culture considers "feminine." Indeed, in *Apocalypse*, her fight with Nemesis is a gendered fight as well as a cyborg/mutant fight; the character of Matt must be removed as a potential sexual partner. It's not enough to turn him into the Nemesis mutant; he must also be completely removed from the sexual arena.

This lack of sexuality further cements the case that Alice is herself the perfect posthuman. As a cyborg-mutant-revenant, she is unable to procreate in human ways. But Alice as Project Alice also underscores our fear of the unseen, the monster within ourselves. According to Abigail Lee Six and Hannah Thompson, "a monster stands as a visible symbol of something important and usually ominous, collapsing two Latin derivations in the popular imagination: monere 'to warn' and monstrare 'to show'" (237). Our society's continuing fascination with the monstrous as seen in the *Resident Evil* movies highlights our concern about what, precisely, monsters can show us about ourselves—and whether they can warn us of our own potentially destructive acts in time to prevent our collapse into a postapocalyptic landscape of horrors of our own making. Jeffrey Weinstock notes that "when the 'monster' becomes the protagonist and culture becomes the antagonist, ideas of normality and monstrosity must be reconsidered" and that "the contemporary disconnection of monstrosity from physical appearance" means that "looking different is no longer sufficient to categorize a creature as monstrous" (276). Project Alice offers the answer of a normality that incorporates the monstrous. Alice looks human, but she is not. She is monstrosity contained. She is posthuman, and must remain so in order to fight and save what is left of humanity in a posthuman world.

Works Cited

Boon, Kevin Alexander. "Ontological Anxiety Made Flesh: The Zombie in Literature, Film and Culture." *At the Interface/Probing the Boundaries, Volume 38: Monsters and the Monstrous: Myths and Metaphors of Enduring Evil*. Ed. Niall Scott. Amsterdam: Editions Rodopi, 2007. 33–44. Print.

Campbell, Norah, and Mike Saren. "The Primitive, Technology and Horror: A Posthuman Biology." *Ephemera: Theory & Politics in Organization*. 10.2 (2010): 152–176. Print.

Christie, Deborah, and Sarah Juliet Lauro. Introduction. *Better Off Dead: The Evolution of the Zombie as Post-Human*. Ed. Deborah Christie and Sarah Juliet Lauro. New York: Fordham University Press, 2011. 1–4. Print.

Collins, Margo, and Elson Bond. "Off the Page and into Your Brains! New Millennium Zombies and the Scourge of Hopeful Apocalypses." *Better Off Dead: The Evolution of the Zombie as Post-Human*. Ed. Deborah Christie and Sarah Juliet Lauro. New York: Fordham University Press, 2011. 175–186. Print.

Dendle, Peter J. "Conclusion: Monsters and the Twenty-first Century: The Preternatural in an Age of Scientific Consensus." *The Ashgate Research Companion to Monsters and the Monstrous*. Ed. Asa Simon Mittman and Peter J. Dendle. Farnham, Surrey, England: Ashgate, 2012. 437–448. Print.

Foundas, Scott. Rev. of *Resident Evil: Apocalypse*. *Daily Variety*. 10 September 2004: 8–14. Print.

Haraway, Donna. "A Cyborg Manifesto: Science, Technology, and Socialist-Feminism in the Late Twentieth Century." *Simians, Cyborgs and Women: The Reinvention of Nature*. New York: Routledge, 1991. 149–181. Print.

Hayles, N. Katherine. *How We Became Posthuman: Virtual Bodies in Cybernetics, Literature and Informatics*. Chicago: University of Chicago Press, 1999. Print.

Herbst, Claudia. "Lara's Lethal and Loaded Mission: Transposing Reproduction and Destruction." *Action Chicks: New Images of Tough Women in Popular Culture*. Ed. Sherrie A. Inness. Gordonsville, VA: Palgrave Macmillan, 2004. 21–46. Print.

Inness, Sherrie A. "Introduction: 'Boxing Gloves and Bustiers': New Images of Tough Women." *Action Chicks: New Images of Tough Women in Popular Culture*. Ed. Sherrie A. Inness. Gordonsville, VA: Palgrave Macmillan, 2004. 1–19. Print.

Leydon, Joe. Rev. of *Resident Evil: Extinction*. *Variety*. 1 October 2007: 88. Print.

Maio, Kathi. "Films: Mission Accomplished at the Zombie Jamboree." *Fantasy & Science Fiction*. 13.4/5 (2007): 192–196. Print.

MacCormack, Patricia. "Posthuman Teratology." *The Ashgate Research Companion to Monsters and the Monstrous*. Ed. Asa Simon Mittman and Peter J. Dendle. Farnham, Surrey, England: Ashgate, 2012. 293–310. Print.

Markovitz, Adam. "A Woman's Worth." *Entertainment Weekly*. 26 October 2007: 14. Print.

Mason, Adam. "*Resident Evil: Afterlife*—Review (F, as in F-Off)." *Movie Moron: Movie News and Humor*. Web. 3 Sept. 2012.

May, Jeff. "Zombie Geographies and the Undead City." *Social & Cultural Geography* 11:3 (2010), 285–298. Print.

McDonagh, Maitland. Rev. of *Resident Evil: Afterlife*. *Film Journal International*. 113:11 (2010), 118. Print.

Mittman, Asa Simon. "Introduction: The Impact of Monsters and Monster Studies." *The Ashgate Research Companion to Monsters and the Monstrous*. Ed. Asa Simon Mittman and Peter J. Dendle. Farnham, Surrey, England: Ashgate, 2012. 1–16. Print.

Myhre, Karin. "Monsters Lift the Veil: Chinese Animal Hybrids and Processes of Transformation." *The Ashgate Research Companion to Monsters and the Monstrous*. Ed. Asa Simon Mittman and Peter J. Dendle. Farnham, Surrey, England: Ashgate, 2012. 217–236. Print.

Nayar, Pramad K. "Wetware Fiction: Cyberpunk and the Ideologies of Posthuman Bodies." *ICFAI Journal of English Studies*. 3.2 (2008): 30–40. Print.

Newman, Kim. Rev. of *Resident Evil: Extinction*. *Sight & Sound*. 17.11 (2007): 71.

Oswald, Dana. "Monstrous Gender: Geographies of Ambiguity." *The Ashgate Research Companion to Monsters and the Monstrous*. Ed. Asa Simon Mittman and Peter J. Dendle. Farnham, Surrey, England: Ashgate, 2012. 343–364. Print.

Resident Evil. Dir. Paul W. S. Anderson. Impact Pictures, Davis-Films, and Constantin Film Produktion, 2002. Film.

Resident Evil: Afterlife. Dir. Paul W. S. Anderson. Impact Pictures, Davis-Films, and Constantin Film Produktion, 2010. Film.

Resident Evil: Apocalypse. Dir. Alexander Witt. Screen Gems, Impact Pictures, and Davis-Films, 2004. Film.

Resident Evil: Extinction. Dir. Russell Mulcahy. Impact Pictures, Davis-Films, and Constantin Film Produktion, 2007. Film.

Resident Evil: Retribution. Dir. Paul W. S. Anderson. Impact Pictures, Davis-Films, and Constantin Film Produktion, 2012. Film.

Six, Abigail Lee, and Hannah Thompson. "From Hideous to Hedonist: The Changing Face of the Nineteenth-Century Monster." *The Ashgate Research Companion to Monsters and the Monstrous.* Ed. Asa Simon Mittman and Peter J. Dendle. Farnham, Surrey, England: Ashgate, 2012. 237–256. Print.

Weinstock, Jeffrey Andrew. "Invisible Monsters: Vision, Horror, and Contemporary Culture." *The Ashgate Research Companion to Monsters and the Monstrous.* Ed. Asa Simon Mittman and Peter J. Dendle. Farnham, Surrey, England: Ashgate, 2012. 275–292. Print.

Zani, Steve, and Kevin Meaux. "Lucio Fulci and the Decaying Definition of Zombie Narratives." *Better Off Dead: The Evolution of the Zombie as Post-Human.* Ed. Deborah Christie and Sarah Juliet Lauro. New York: Fordham University Press, 2011. 98–115. Print.

"Six Impossible Things Before Breakfast": Living Memory and Undead History

Simon Bacon

"My name is Alice... There was an incident, a virus escaped. Everybody died. Trouble was ... they didn't stay dead!"—(*Resident Evil: Afterlife* 2011)

Introduction

These opening lines from the fourth installment of the *Resident Evil* films succinctly encapsulate what the continuing series of movies is not about. For the character of Alice, played by Milla Jovovich, does not know who she is and resultantly is continually trying to discover her real identity. This struggle for self-knowledge by Alice is then manifested, allegorically, as her battle against the hordes of the undead. Although, as the above quote suggests, they are monstrous because they refuse to remain dead, what they actually configure is the more horrifying death of memory and identity; not being the dead made alive but the alive made dead. Consequently, the cinematic versions of *Resident Evil* are predicated upon identity and memory, and that Alice's, and indeed humanity's, ongoing struggle with the zombie horde represent the continuing battle between individual or "living" memory and reified, or "undead" history. This configuration sees living memory as something that is not fixed but in a continual state of change or becoming,[1] and undead history, as that which, although giving the appearance of life, remains fixed and unchangeable. This fixing of memory can then also be seen as a means of control and so the T-virus, created by the Umbrella Corporation, which turns those which it infects into zombies, signifies an attempt to control memory and shape it to the Corporation's own ends. The T-virus becomes an ideological infection that spreads through the population, making them forget who they are so that they become the undead monsters that the Umbrella Corporation desires (where the corporation represents a version of homogeneity enforced through globalization). As such, their actions embody the kind of reification of history, where individual memory is lost to an all encompassing global notion of what constitutes the past and what human identity can be.

In opposition to this, Alice is constantly in motion and continually discovering who she is and who she may become: from the first film *Resident Evil* by Paul W. S. Anderson (2002), where she has to re-discover who she is, through *Resident Evil: Apocalypse* (Witt 2004) and *Resident Evil: Extinction* (Mulcahy 2007), where she is evolving into a "new" being. From this she goes on to *Resident Evil: Afterlife* (Anderson 2010), where she becomes human again and then *Resident Evil: Retribution* (Anderson 2012), within which she once again "becomes" herself; Alice's identity is constantly in motion. She then embodies the fluidity of individual memory that cannot be contained by an over-arching ideology or an imposed notion of what history is or should be. Even the new forms of mutation that the Umbrella Corporation creates— Nemesis in *Apocalypse*, the mutant Dr. Isaac's in *Extinction* and Wesker in *Afterlife* and *Retribution*—are still held in a present that they cannot escape, and so are defeated by Alice's "multi-directionality" or ability to live beyond the moment of her creation.[2]

In this essay I shall first look at the construction of the undead zombie as the physical embodiment of undead memory and examine how texts such as Richard Matheson's seminal novel in the genre, *I Am Legend*, begins this process and how the zombie horde is a necessary consequence of this. Following this, I shall look at Alice's search for identity and how the processes of cloning, used within the films, act on a very different level to the means of "undead" reproduction that are an inevitable consequence of the T-virus used by the Umbrella Corporation. For this I shall use the example of an earlier film where individual identity and becoming are specifically achieved through the control and evolution of individual memory, and that is *Alien Resurrection* by Jean Pierre Jeanet from 1997. Finally, I shall consider the different uses of mutation and evolution, both genetically and memorially, to example how the films represent what Sarah Nuttall calls the "entanglement" of time and memory which expresses the continuing and continual fight between individual becoming and societal control.

The Eternal Moment

In *Resident Evil* we already see a differentiation between those who work for the Umbrella Corporation and those who do not. Those who "do not" are the rest of humanity who live on the surface of the Earth and largely depend upon the products and services provided by the Corporation for their everyday lives, and those who do exist in an artificial world beneath the ground buried deep beneath Raccoon City. This immediately sets up certain configurations around notions to do with memory and undead-ness. In terms of memory it instantly relates to memory as something buried in the past, as something hidden from sight, and as something separate from the present, which is represented as the passing of time on the surface. This separation is graphically shown when we see the pictures of the city skyline during the day shown on the walls of the underground facility. This camouflaging then emphasizes the fact that all those that see the "view" are actually entombed under the earth; a point that sees it linked to more gothic imaginings of memory, such as the "[d]ark subterranean vaults" (Botting 29) of Fred Botting but also seen in Carl Jung's idea of the oneiric house, which Gaston Bachelard sees as a "topography of our intimate being" (Bachelard xxxii). Here memory, identity, and being are inherent within the structure of a building which is both metaphorical and actual. As he comments: "In the cellar we discover Roman foundation walls, and under the cellar a filled-in cave, in the floor of which stone tools are found and the remnants of glacial fauna in the layers below" (Bachelard, xxxiii). As such, the Umbrella facility beneath the ground becomes not just the memory of the city above, but a memory that is frozen in time and held in place. In a certain way then, the workers who inhabit this space are already differentiated from the present and the "life" that goes on above them, a differentiation that is further emphasized by the ownership of the workers by Umbrella itself. While Umbrella can be seen to create the world above the ground through the various products and services that they provide, the underworld of their Hive facility is totally under their control. Such a complete ownership of both an environment and its inhabitants encourages a Marxist reading of such "controlled" labor. Here the actions of the Umbrella Corporation would seem to conform to Karl Marx's notion where, "Capital is dead labour which, vampire-like, lives only by sucking living labour, and lives the more, the more labour it sucks" (Marx 342). Umbrella feed off their workforce, making their living "work" into undead capital and infecting them with this same undead need for the consumption of labor. The workers then become creations of the Corporation, no different in fact than the T-virus that is also being manufactured in this under laboratory.

This ownership is further seen when the workers are "disposed" of by the Corporation when the virus is first released. Franco Moretti, in his book *Signs Taken for Wonders*, sees this same process being undertaken in Mary Shelley's novel *Frankenstein*. Here, as Moretti explains, the monster "belongs wholly to his creator (just as one can speak of a 'Ford worker'). Like the proletariat, he is a collective and artificial creature. He is not found in nature, but built" (85). This last part in particular relates very strongly to the mutations caused by the release of the T-virus and the subsequent use of the zombie horde by their creators, the Umbrella Corporation. But it can also be seen that the conditions of the workforce, already as partially created and controlled, make their change into actual mindless zombies if not inevitable then at least not so unexpected.

This theme of a mindless proletariat, a mindless capitalism, and mindless consumerism is seen as underpinning many zombie films, from George Romero's *Night of the Living Dead* (1968) onwards. Beneath Raccoon City, the situation can be seen to be very similar as it is the product of capitalism, the T-virus, which then causes the workers trapped underground to change from living zombies to re-animated undead ones. It is at this point that memory, or its lack of change, becomes central to the configuration of the zombie, for it is unable to make new ones and so becomes fixed within the present that it exists in. This idea becomes stronger as the series of *Resident Evil* films develops, and it is possibly more innate in the construction of the zombie in them than in Romero's conception of it embodying an all consuming consumerism. This idea of memory held in time, in a never-ending present, is central to Richard Matheson's 1954 novel *I Am Legend*, and so it is to that I turn now, and while it does not directly equate to specific scenes and plot devices of the *Resident Evil* series, this slight detour will explain the nature of how the idea of undead memory works in relation to Alice and the Umbrella Corporation.

The novel is seminal to the current configuration of the zombie at the start of the 21st century, and as Romero himself has confessed, "The *Night of the Living Dead* thing, though, I basically ripped off from Richard Matheson's *I Am Legend*."[3] The zombies in *I Am Legend* are actually constructed as vampires: they have an aversion to crosses, garlic and sunlight, but their behavior marks them out as what we would call mindless zombies.[4] The main character in the novel, Robert Neville, describes them thus: "None of the three was speaking to either of the others. *They* never did. They walked and walked about on restless feet, circling each other like wolves, never looking at each other once, having hungry eyes only for the house and their prey inside the house." (Matheson 55, my emphasis) This sees the earlier configuration of the zombie as an individual under the control of a voodoo curse changed into a far more menacing horde that has no master other than its own insatiable appetite.[5] These zombies created by magic had no mind of their own, and although capable of violence if directed to do so, could not spread their affliction themselves but, very much like Marx's earlier configuration of undead labor, were at the command of their masters. In Matheson's hands they become a flesh-eating horde that is driven by an overwhelming desire to devour every living human left alive; under the control of no one but the all consuming hunger. Interestingly, no one knows what caused the plague to start, though it is intimated that is the result of "the bombings" that are "causing the dust storms ... that are causing a lot of things" (Matheson 45). Coming after America's testing of nuclear weapons, the association is clear and indeed informs many such "Cold War" narratives where military or scientific experiments have gone wrong, producing life-threatening mutations: giant ants in *Them* (1954) by Gordon Douglas, and a reptilian sea monster in *Godzilla* (1954) by Ishirō Honda, to name but two.

This idea of scientific mutation forms the basis of *Resident Evil* of course, though the level of intention on behalf of the Umbrella Corporation is far higher than that seen in relation to the as then unknown effects of nuclear radiation in the 1950s. In line with this, Robert Neville's immunity is equally the product of chance, as indeed is Alice's later cellular bonding to the T-virus in *Resident Evil*. While all around him succumb to the mystery virus he remains unaffected, possibly due to a bite from a vampire bat he received during the war when stationed in Panama. Oddly though, his continued humanity does little to differentiate him from the vampire zombies that surround him as they both seem locked in time. The zombies, as exampled by Neville's former neighbor, Ben Cortman, seem unable to leave the environs of the areas they inhabited during life. Cortman, who was friends with Neville and lived in the same neighborhood, continually returns to the house into which Neville has now barricaded himself, an occurrence which is seen within the first three *Resident Evil* films where the infected often stay in the buildings they inhabited during life.[6] Once there, Cortman always calls for Neville to "come out," which of course he never does. This sense of inevitable return is echoed in the way that Cortman looks almost exactly as he did in life, as Neville observes, "Ben hadn't changed much. His hair was still black, his body inclined to corpulence, his face still white. But there was a beard on his face now; mostly under the nose, thinner around his chin and cheeks and under his throat. That was the only real difference" (Matheson 54). Neville too seems not to have developed, only grown further into himself, fortifying his house and never venturing from it after dark. Cortman's and Neville's actions, somewhat uncannily, mirror each other in that they are not able to leave the places they lived in before the plague began, as though they are trapped in the memory of their previous lives. Zombie-ism here is distinguished as much by its similarities to humanity as its differences and it is those unchanged qualities that make it that much more sinister. As Kyle Bishop notes in his book *American Zombie Gothic*:

> Yet while they might look like "us," their unnatural state makes them a poignant representation of mortality itself, an uncanny memento mori that threatens the hapless living with either death or transformation to undeath. Furthermore, such

creatures accomplish what Freud calls the return of the repressed and force us to face our deepest, our most primal fears [Bishop 108].

In *Resident Evil*, this doppelganger aspect of the zombie happens mainly at the point when the newly infected are about to "turn." However, in regard to *I Am Legend* this is interesting as, if Cortman is a remembrance of the death that awaits Neville, he is also representative of the dead life that he leads now—he is the repressed knowledge that Neville himself is also no longer "alive."[7] Alive in this sense is not so much his biological condition as a living, breathing human, but as a being that inhabits the present within which he lives, for both Neville and Cortman stopped doing that a long time ago. The narrator in *I Am Legend* describes Neville's state as follows:

> The past had brought something else, though; pain at remembering. Every recalled word had been like a knife blade twisting in him. Old wounds had been reopened with every thought of her. He'd finally had to stop, eyes closed, fists clenched, trying desperately to accept the present on its own terms and not yearn with all his very flesh for the past [Matheson 48].

Even though it pains him, Neville cannot will himself to escape the past—the memories of his wife and the life he used to live. As such, he remains literally held in time and fixed in the memories of a present that was long ago. His attempts to fortify his home from the zombies then become an attempt to keep the present at bay, and to hold his memories of his past fixed in the former present, in which they occurred, forever.

This action relates directly to ideas on how memory can remove itself, or stand outside of time, and become an undead thing in its own right—neither alive, as in changing, or dead, as in forgotten. Ludwig Wittgenstein, after noting that the living cannot live to experience death, observes that, "if we take eternity to mean not infinite temporal duration but timelessness, then eternal life belongs to those who live in the present" (Wittgenstein 87). Such an eternal present, that remains unaffected or changed by new experience, belongs to those that live, or are forced to exist, outside of both time and history. Neville does this in his attempts to hold the past in his house and the zombies do this through their inability to escape the moment of their deaths. We see this in Ben Cortman's "eternal" return to Neville's house and also his strangely unchanged appearance.[8] More so we see this in Cortman's reactions to the other vampire/zombies around him, because they all share the same "moment" of death or undead memory. They mean nothing to him as they are the same as him; it is his mirror image that consumes him and that he wants to consume. Marina Warner, talking more of the individual zombie than the rampaging horde, observes, "The zombie has been robbed of all the qualities that made up personhood—feelings, sentience, reflexivity, memories—but survives under a sense of immortality.... Unlike angels and daimons ... the zombie is a spectre still tormented by the carnal condition of being" (Warner 359). In this configuration the mirroring of Cortman and Neville shifts in perspective for it is not the zombie that is the uncanny reflection of the human, but the other way round—Neville's continued existence literally haunts Cortman. Within this it is the quality of the eternal present and its relation to memory that defines the differences between them: Neville actively reifies and protects the past moment that he refuses to leave, but Cortman has no choice, not even death will release him from the moment that created him. The fact that both Neville and the zombies are locked out of the present is shown at the end of Matheson's novel, when a new hybrid species of human captures him. Unknowingly, while killing zombies he has also been killing members of this mutated species who are winning the battle with the virus through their own intervention. As such, Neville is representative of the past that still sees the world in black and white and refuses to accept human hybridity. He also then becomes the manifestation of the memory of a violent past that caused the infection in the first place, a past violence that Neville continually reenacts and refuses to leave. Consequently, he is no different from the vampire zombies, a point he realizes just as the new species are about to execute him. The book's narrator observes, "Robert Neville looked out over the new people of the earth. He knew he did not belong to them; he knew he was like the vampires, he was anathema and black terror to be destroyed" (Matheson 161). Both Neville and the vampires are similarly creations of the past and the memory of an ideology that lives on in them. The world that made them froze them in the moment of that creation: a memory fixed in time, and outside of history, forever.

Similarly then, this then can be seen to be the basis of the zombies in *Resident Evil*, they too are created by a very particular ideology which then locks them in the moment of their creation. More importantly one can say that this is the moment that they became "owned" by Umbrella and under their absolute control. In the case of the first film this is literally true, for the Red Queen computer locks down the underground complex in an attempt to contain the virus. This scene at the start of the film means that no one can escape that moment, and they in fact spend the rest of the film trying to do so. Similarly, the school children in *Resident Evil: Apocalypse* seem trapped in the school where they were infected. However, slightly differently to Matheson's novel, as the series of films develop the zombies no longer remain solely attached to the memory of the places that they once inhabited. It is as if the strength of the memory of the moment that created them is locked within their bodies so that they cannot move beyond the boundaries of their former lives. Yet they still embody individual moments locked in time, not interacting with each other or having any sense of a past or a future, just driven by the specter of the humans that still inhabit the world and the all-consuming ide-ological moment of the Umbrella Corporation. Not unlike Romero's vision of the zombie as all consuming consumerism that is corporately driven, the Umbrella Corporation represent an ideological moment where all memory is controlled by them; the Corporation does not just signify consumerist desire, but also the memories that create that desire. This control of memory does not allow for any variety or difference but infinite similitude. Consequently, the almost unstoppable reproductive capability of the T-virus means that it infinitely replicates the moment of its creation and when all memory became fixed and identical. And so the zombies then come to represent the control and annihilation of living memory, beyond any that the Umbrella Corporation does not make itself. This is of course the moment when Alice became such a fly in their undead ointment.

Me, Myself, I

Unlike Robert Neville in *I Am Legend*, Alice is constructed as an oppo-sitional force to the zombies; if they remain fixed in time and inescapably the same forever, she is constantly trying to discover who she is and remains in a state of constant flux. The first film in the series begins with her collapsed on the floor of a shower in the bathroom of a large house, which we later discover is the gateway between the underground complex and the world above. The house configures a liminal space between the past and the present, empty but somehow full of memories of what has previously occurred there. Alice is naked and as she awakes, disoriented and confused, it is as though she is being born, or re-born, not unlike the "re-animations" that are unknowingly hap-pening beneath here, in the Hive below. The representation of the moment of birth, or re-birth, is central to Alice's character and it always revolves around the idea of memory: either in trying to remember who she was or what she actually is. The idea of what she "is" becomes increasingly important as the narrative of the series continues, as it centers upon the notion of memory developing into the future, or what we might call becoming memory. But returning to the first film, Alice's awakening in the shower marks the beginning of her quest to remember who she is, or as it becomes increasingly clear, who she was. This distinction is quite important for as the narrative unfolds, she begins to realize how implicit she is in the horrific events that have occurred in the underground complex.

As her memory begins to return she says "I'm not sure I want to remember what went on down here" (*Resident Evil* 2002). Her quest in the first film is very similar to that undertaken by another central female character from a long running series of science fiction films, that of Ellen Ripley from the *Alien* quadrilogy, and in particular, *Alien Resurrection*. Released in 1997 and directed by Jean Pierre Jeunet, *Alien Resurrection* sees lieutenant Ellen Ripley reborn as a clone of herself. Her ongoing battle with the Company, now replaced by the equally faceless and ubiquitous United Systems Military, has seen her DNA harvested from her dead body, and cloned to try and reproduce the Alien Queen that was growing inside of her at the moment she committed suicide, diving into a vat of molten lead. When we first see the "fully-grown" Ripley in the film, she too is awakening as if from a deep sleep, and like Alice, unsure of who or where she is (here Ripley is actually the 8th clone of herself, so a granddaughter seven times removed as it were). As Ximena Gallardo and Jason Smith observe, "she takes her first gasps of air and slowly writhes out of the bag [protective sac]. The effect is that of a chrysalis in a cocoon struggling to get free and, at points, of a body emerging from its death shroud" (166). And as the scene continues, "appropriately, the as yet unnamed clone does not seem to know herself and looks up, as if the answer to her identity lies somewhere above herself" (ibid.).

Alice's birthing is very similar, as she awakes in the shower wrapped in the white shower curtain that had been hanging around it. She too, and not unlike the zombies underground, shakes off her death shroud and emerges into a new life. And like Ripley, she looks around herself to try and discover from her surroundings just who she is. Alice, at least at this stage of the story, is not a clone, but this re-birth, as indicated by her emergence from the death shroud of her former life, signals that she can never return to what she once was but it will be her "remembering" or "re-owning" of her memory that will pose the greatest threat to the intentions of the Umbrella Corporation. As Gallardo and Smith point out in regard of Ripley's amazingly quick learning of language skills through "inherited memory," "General Perez's [the representative of United Systems Military] greatest fear, the fear of all totalitarians, is that the Ripley clone will remember" (167). Memory becomes Alice's greatest weapon, and, as the story progresses and she is trying to escape from the underground complex, it is the remembrance of her former life as a security operative that saves her from various re-animated corpses, both human and canine. What is also interesting at this point, and again relates her to Ripley, is that she is already effectively the property of the Umbrella Corporation. As an employee, as noted above in relation to the other workers, she is already a creation of their ideological intent, and so it is not so surprising at the end of the film when, like Ripley, she is reborn once again, but this time totally engineered by Umbrella.

In a scene reminiscent of her initial awakening in the shower, she now opens her eyes to find herself naked and lying on a hospital gurney.[9] She has a cloth draped over her, as a partial gown but also not unlike the shroud from the earlier shower scene. She is umbilically linked to monitoring machines arrayed around her signifying that they, and by extension the Umbrella Corporation, are now her new "mother" and responsible for bringing her into this third life.[10] Again Alice is disoriented but her relationship to the mother, the Umbrella Corporation, has subtly changed. Whereas before she existed under the controlling gaze of her parent, seen in the constant camera surveillance that took place in the house and the underground complex, now she is part of that in that they can now "see" through her eyes too. This is made explicit at the start of the second film, *Resident Evil: Apocalypse*. Here, we see the film begin with the close up of Alice's eye, as we also saw at the end of *Resident Evil*, but this time it has the telltale insignia of the Umbrella Corporation—an octagon divided into eight sections, overlaid on top of her iris. This again creates some interesting links with Ripley in *Alien Resurrection*. Alice, like Ripley, is almost a "meat by product" (Gallardo & Smith 167) of the original experiment and it is only later that the "Company" becomes interested in what she is capable of. She then supersedes the monsters, that were the original focus of the company's representatives, and consequently her re-birth at the start of *Apocalypse* is then re-configured as the beginning of "Project Alice." At this point her search for her past becomes a search for herself; not a quest for the memories of the life she once lived but for the ones that will tell her what she is now.

This then begins to describe how Alice is the embodiment of living memory; it is not about trying to retrieve a past but a way to understand the future she is heading toward. In *Apocalypse*, although she is still trying to grasp who she was in her earlier life, she is now more focused on trying to understand what she is capable of. This is not a past that is stuck in a moment unable to escape, but one that is continually moving into the future. As *Apocalypse* moves into the next film, *Resident Evil: Extinction*, what we increasingly get is the sense of Alice being the product of memory that is in a state of constant evolution; her identity and the way she sees herself are in constant flux. Intrinsic to this state of "becoming" is the idea of ownership, of who owns Alice's past and future becomings. Its outcome is inextricably linked to imitation and mimesis, and this is increasingly apparent as the *Resident Evil* series progresses as power and control become focused on memory contained within biological and auratic reproduction. While power is largely centered on the acts of replication and reproduction, control is more and more upon surveillance and seeing: seeing, information, and control become almost synonymous within the *Resident Evil* series.

Not surprisingly then *Resident Evil: Extinction* is all about vision, not least in that—unusually for a zombie film—it is set in the wide open and well lit space of the desert. Where the underground hive and the abandoned city-scape of Raccoon City created a murkily dark gothic mise-en-scene in the first two films, *Extinction* is all about open spaces and light. Here the memories that clung to every surface of the ruined city are burned away under the heat of the sun, making the desert a memory-less space. Once again the film starts with Alice awakening in the shower in the mansion above the underground complex; fated to be reborn forever in the moment that originally created her. However, we quickly discover that this is not the Alice we have been following but a clone of her—yet unlike Ripley before her,[11] she does not have any iden-tifying marks to tell us which version she might be. We do discover though that she is not the first or the last, because we see the dead body dumped in a pit containing many previous versions of her, all wearing the distinctive red dress and black boots from the first film. As such, the Umbrella Corporation, and Dr. Isaacs in particular, are trying to replicate Alice, but not just any Alice, she has to be one that has gone through and survived the same memories that the original Alice has. It is the individuality of Alice's memories that uniquely characterize her and refute all the Corporation's attempts to control her. As such, she has the kind of "presence in time and space" that Walter Benjamin describes in his essay "The Work of Art in the Age of Mechanical Reproduc-tion" (1168). Such presence is described as "aura" which cannot be replicated. Copying the original can only, and inevitably, devalue the original, but also the reproduction. Umbrella's attempts to reproduce Alice are not only designed to "re-create" her but to control her as well—by copying the original you also make it less than it was. This is a motif that continues throughout the later films and again reappears in *Retribution* with not only copies of Alice but other characters from earlier installments in the series. A very similar situation is also seen in the continued use of surveillance cameras and video recorders throughout the film.[12] Their replicated images of Alice, particularly in the myriad monitors that show her location, are a way of diffusing her presence, making her somehow less and so more controllable. This theme is also used in *Diary of the Dead* (2007) by George Romero where the human characters use video cameras to not only record the ongoing zombie apocalypse but to gain some measure of control over the situation they find themselves in. More interestingly, the use of the camera within the film is shown to dehumanize those that use them, making them recorders of memory rather than actually taking part in the act of memory making itself.[13] As such, the surveillance cam-eras then further remove the Umbrella Corporation from both life and living memory.

This relates directly to the zombies that now infest the desert. They have become, almost, infinitely reproducible, all being as memory-less as the desert they now inhabit. The importance of memory to aura and uniqueness is then further shown by Dr. Isaacs himself. After conducting tests on the zombies to discover ways in which to manipulate them, he connects the effects of memory in controlling their appetites when he says, "giving back these creatures a measure of their intelligence ... their memories, thus curbing their hunger for flesh" (*Resident Evil: Extinction*, 2007). Consequently, the possession of aura, of memory, also becomes indicative of self-control but one that is beyond the authority of outside manipulation. This would seem to categorize the clones of Alice to be as dangerous, or mindless, as the zombies themselves, but unlike them they are not locked in the eternal moment of their creation. We see this at the end of *Extinction* and the start of *Resident Evil: Afterlife*, when Alice herself discovers the hundreds of clones that have been made of her, again diverging from Ripley's experience in *Alien Resurrection* where the evil of reproduction is shown when she discovers the mutated and monstrous clones that preceded her. Alice embraces these copies of herself, not because they all are made from the same memories as her but because they have the potential to change. As such, even though they choose to follow her in the battle against Umbrella, the choice was theirs and not imposed upon them by Alice. We see then, that Alice, the product of an ever-evolving memory, wishes the same for all those around her. Unlike the Umbrella Corporation, she does not try to impose a reified ideology or version of history. Although the zombies and the clones are similar in that they all come from one point of creation, the T-virus or Alice respectively, they do not all remain fixed in time. However, as the series develops the zombies themselves begin to change, and the mutations they undergo would seem to locate them alongside, not just as equal to the clones, but to Alice herself, and so it is time to consider the evolutions of Dr. Isaacs and Albert Wesker.

The Road to Nowhere

> Dr. Isaacs: "For so long I thought you were the future. I was wrong. I am the future."
> Alice: "No ... you're just another asshole!"—(*Resident Evil: Extinction*, 2007)

Mutation and evolution form a large part of the background story to the *Resident Evil* series. As described above, it begins as a simple division between mutation, as an evolutionary dead-end, and hybridity as a vision of future becomings. Simply put, the zombies are stuck in their moment forever, whereas Alice has the potential to continually become, and exactly what no one really knows. Within this memory plays a pivotal role because the zombies are stuck in their eternal present—they have no memory of anything else, while Alice is continually negotiating with her past, and the past inflicted on to her by the incorporation of the T-virus with her own DNA. This notion of memory being part of one's biological make up is useful here as it sees the battle between history and individual memory taking place within the very structure of the body. Marita Sturken, writing about the AIDS epidemic in America, interestingly describes the body's immune system as an archive of past encounters: "the image of immune system memory ... is similar to a traditional concept of history, in which the body keeps an 'official' record in a database" (Sturken 243). Vaccines then become ways to trick the body, providing, as Sturken observes, "'fake' memories that allow the body to produce antibodies to viruses stronger than those it has actually encountered" (ibid.). In this way we can see that the memories given to the zombies, and to Alice herself, can be viewed as fake ones that are designed to hold them in place forever, in the same way that fake memories are given to the replicas in Ridley Scott's *Blade Runner* (1982) as a means to control them. Alice then is trying to remember herself both before the introduction of the fake memories into her system but also what these new memories might be doing to who she is and what she may become.

This view of the effects of the T-virus on the human system has some interesting consequences for the different mutants we encounter in the various films. They roughly fall into two camps, being either mutated zombies or mutated humans. The mutated zombies offer little more than the original zombies themselves. So far we have the "super zombies" from *Extinction*, that, as described by Dr. Isaacs earlier, have been given some level of memory back, so that they are more controllable and it also allows them increased motor skills so that they can run. There is also the "Axeman" from *Afterlife*, a huge zombie that looks more like something from *Lord of the Rings* than a zombie film, but he is little more than a directed "weapon." *Afterlife* also boasts the "majini" zombies, which would seem to have the same level of motor skills as the "super" zombies, but also have extended mouths that open out, almost flower-like, when they attack their prey. They bear a comparison to the "Reapers" in *Blade II* (2002) by Guillermo del Toro. They too are the result of medical experiments, in this case mutated vampires, which have mouth parts which open up to create a much larger orifice. Like the "majini" here, rather than being an evolutionary step forward they in fact indicate a mutational dead-end, which is ultimately what all the mutant zombies do. To use Sturken's phraseology, the "fake" memories that have been used to create them lead nowhere other than being a means to subdue and control them. Once they have been turned into a "super" zombie or a "majini" that they are, they can evolve no further. In like fashion *Retribution* boasts the "Las Plagas" zombie which although is seen as an evolved and more intelligent version of the "majini" is actually created as an entirely separate species. This again sees them as moments fixed in time. Even more so, part of their mutation is that they all become the same, not individual but part of the many.

The virus itself, as a product of the Umbrella Corporation, bears the ideological stamp of that corporation; the history it puts into the genetic make-up of its creations, is its own history. Sturken's description of HIV perfectly fits the way that the T-virus is seen to work: "HIV is depicted as completely insinuating itself into the genetic makeup of the 'host' cell; it 'rewrites' the story of the immune system by substituting its own DNA narrative. The genetic identity of the cell has been altered, as has its memory" (Sturken 246). What this also intimates is that any trace of the T-virus in a system necessarily affects the memory of that system, changing it into one that contains the ideological intent of the Corporation. It is this idea which also underlies the human mutants in the films. Both Dr. Isaacs and Wesker, no matter how mutated or in control of themselves they appear to be, can never be in control, as all their cells inevitably bear the trademark, or memory, of the Umbrella Corporation. Within the context of the films, this unavoidably signals their decline, as they too can never evolve, or become more than the corporation allows them to.

This poses an interesting question to Alice herself, for although she manages to regain control of herself at the end of *Extinction*, she is still a product of the T-virus. Not surprisingly, this again links Alice to Ripley from *Alien Resurrection*. Ripley understands the nature of herself and the monster that lives within her, and she realizes that it cannot be allowed to live. Consequently, she destroys all the earlier clones of herself as well as the Alien Queen and its hybrid offspring, the "Newborn."[14] However, she does not destroy herself. When asked towards the end of the film, "How can you go on living, knowing what you are?" she replies "not much choice"—not exactly a rallying cry for existence but a recognition of continued life and the possibility of change in the future. This point is made at the end of the film when Ripley is asked, "what will you do now," and answers "I don't know ... I'm a stranger here myself."[15] Ripley can only go on living if she exiles herself from the rest of humanity. The self-awareness of the monster "living" inside her also includes her recognition of herself as a product of the company that made her; consequently, she is not safe to be around.

Alice can be viewed as having a similar awareness. At the end of *Extinction* her powers are increasing, she can now resist the control of Umbrella as well as manipulate matter around her, as we see in her "psionic" abilities, and she has defeated Dr. Isaacs, with the assistance of one of her clones—but these powers are still a result of the T-virus bonding with her own cells.[16] Although her own memory can be seen to be controlling the effects of the intruding "fake" memories they are still representative of an alien presence within her. Similarly, and in fact even more so, the clones of her are made with these fake memories as part of their original biological make-up; they have no memories that are not fake. This then begins to explain why they are all killed at the start of *Afterlife*—although they undertake the mission of their own volition, they still bear the mark of the corporation that they want to destroy. We can then read Alice's survival as a similar action to that of Ripley's in that the only safe way to contain the fake memories is to contain them inside herself and no one else. There is also an interesting restoration of aura in this process, where all the hundreds of parts of Alice that were disseminated throughout her clones are now re-concentrated back into her own body. Consequently, it is not surprising that once Alice's aura has been fully restored, she becomes human again. Because she is no longer anyone else she can now be truly herself. The effect of this is to reiterate the battle that has been continuing throughout the series—individual living memory against undead history, which could not have continued if Alice had remained infected with the virus. Now, as a human, her memories are fully her own and will change and evolve as she does. Wesker continues the undead history of the Umbrella Corporation, making him the embodiment of a "company" man but also an evolutionary dead-end.

The End of the Beginning?

Afterlife ends, not unlike many of the other installments, with a return, in this case that of Jill Valentine. The closing shots see her in charge of an Umbrella helicopter squadron that has come to capture Alice. But of course this is not really Valentine, as she is wearing a similar device to that we saw on Claire Redfield earlier in the film, which controls her mind but also takes away her memory. This once again shows how the Umbrella Corporation achieves power through the control of memory, just as it tried to do with the cellular fake memory it created in the T-virus to control and manipulate the zombies. *Retribution* opens in the moment after the previous installment ended, with Umbrella attempting to capture Alice. This ends with the destruction of the ship they are on, and Alice seemingly drowning. Once again she wakes to find herself in a different life, or at least it seems so until we realize that this is a different Alice. For a brief moment we are left with the possibility that this domestic suburban life we see Alice living is in fact the "real" one and that all that has gone before is a very bad dream.[17] However, not unlike the beginning of *Extinction*, it is revealed to be a test using a clone of the original Alice. Somewhat interestingly, it also contains clones of other characters from the previous films enacting the earlier notions of control through replication. Here though it is not just through replication of Alice herself but also the people and environment around her; it is as if by replicating the world you can somehow control it. After this episode ends, it is not surprising that we see Alice waking up, or being reborn once again, and once again this happens in an Umbrella facility. As usual this precedes another attempt by Alice to discover who she really is, with the most unexpected part of this being that she decides that she is a mother. Befitting the plot lines of the *Resident Evil* series as a whole, this is not as straightforward as it may seem, for her "daughter," Becky, is not actually her "real" offspring, but that of the cloned version of Alice we saw earlier in the film. As such, Alice's relationship to Becky is not that different from that of Ripley and Newt in the film *Aliens*, and indeed this is a point made by Anderson, the director of *Retribution*. The similarities between Alice and Ripley from the *Alien* series was mentioned above, not least in the amount of re-births each character experiences during the course of their respective narratives. However, I think Alice's experience here is slightly different from that of Ripley, for while Newt has no biological connection to her adoptive mother, in *Retribution*, Becky, possibly, does. In theory Becky's mother is a clone of Alice and so on some level they are biologically connected. Consequently, this then makes Becky an integral part of Alice's search for herself in the way that Newt never could for Ripley. Ripley's narrative within the *Alien* films is to discover that she is her own creation. She is then totally self contained and does not need the rest of humanity to become all that she can be, and this we see in the fact that she exiles herself from humankind at the end of the final film, *Alien Resurrection*. As a result this makes the disappearance of Newt between installments 2 and 3 of the series almost inevitable. For Alice, though, her becoming is one that is linked to the humanity around her and she will only realize what she was, and will be, through returning memory to the world around her. Becky then acts as a synecdoche of this, a signifier of the reciprocity of becoming that drives Alice onwards.

Ultimately, it is these constant re-births that are probably the biggest signifier of Alice as being in a state of constant becoming, revealing her to be constantly in a state of flux. More importantly, her re-births are never totally new, as in a beginning again, but are built upon all that has gone before, linking her to the kind of "entanglement" of memory that Sarah Nuttall describes in her book *Entanglement: Literary and Cultural Reflections on Post-Apartheid*. Here she explains how living memory is something that is never singular and discrete but complex and complicated; consequently, within memory "surface and depth exist in a set of relations in which each relies on the existence of the other, in which they are entwined or enfolded, suggestive each of the other, interpenetrating, and separating out at different points" (Nuttall 83). This is in stark contrast to the Umbrella Corporation, which remains static and unchanged. Whereas Alice is seen to grow and adapt in every situation she finds herself in, Umbrella treats each situation in which it finds itself exactly the same; that is, attempting control and assimilation.[18] As such, the zombification caused by the T-virus is a natural and inevitable expression of the ideology of the Umbrella Corporation, making everything identical and reproducing one moment of memory until all its aura has evaporated. Alice, on the other hand, reproduces not just herself, but the continuance of uniqueness, revealing that any one moment of memory is never singular but manifold. As such, Alice becomes the allegory of both living memory and possibility, and while she continues to change in the face of Corporate reification, as she says herself, "there is hope!" (*Resident Evil: Afterlife*).

Notes

1. Becoming here is meant in the way that Gilles Deleuze and Felix Guattari use the term in their book *A Thousand Plateaus: Captialism and Schizophrenia*. As such, it infers a state of change beyond normativity or what has already been seen but which does not have any known destination or ultimate goal.

2. Multi-directionality is a term used by memory theorist Michael Rothberg. In terms of the discrepancies and hierarchies between differing national histories and individual memories he sees "multidirectional memory ... [as an] ongoing negotiation, cross-referencing, and borrowing ... [producing an] interaction of different historical memories." (3)

3. As quoted in David Flint, *Zombie Holocaust: How the Living Dead Devoured Pop Culture*, London: Plexus, 2009, p. 75.

4. As well as changing the popular conception of what a zombie is Matheson also changed the vampire forever. After *I Am Legend* they were no longer solitary figures that took its victims one bite at a time and only "turned" a few into vampires, as in Bram Stoker's *Dracula*. Suddenly, they hunted in packs and infected everyone they fed upon. Further, vampirism didn't need to be spread by actual physical contact or the exchange of fluids anymore, but by an airborne contagion or some form of human scientific intervention.

5. See David Flint, *Zombie Apocalypse*.

6. The most obvious examples being the school children in *Apocalypse* and the gas station attendant in *Extinction*.

7. This point is of particular note in regard to Alice, not so much in relation to the zombies but the increasingly prevalent clones of herself that inhabit the *Resident Evil* universe.

8. A similar effect is seen in the film *Resident Evil: Extinction* with gas store man who is still wearing his uniform and seems unable to leave the station where he worked in life.

9. This scene has been used in various other zombie apocalypse films to show the protagonists' symbolic death and "re-birth" into the new world, most famously in *28 Days Later* (2002) by Danny Boyle and also at the start of the television series *The Walking Dead* (2010–present) by Frank Darabont. These representations, more often than not, evoke the trope of human medical intervention going wrong, hence the hospital setting. However, they also utilize the liminal status of hospitals as places of illness and death, but also birth.

10. This can be seen as her third birth if one takes her first one as being when she was actually born, and the second as when she awoke in the shower.

11. Ripley has the figure "8" tattooed on her arm denoting her as the 8th clone but also inferring the sign for infinity as well.

12. Linked to this is the notion of the image, or photo, replacing memory, as described by Marita Sturken in her book *Tangled Memories: The Vietnam War, the AIDS Epidemic and the Politics of Remembering*, Berkeley: California University Press, 1997. Here the image not only stands in for the memory of the event, but changes and replaces it. Sturken specifically cites how images and films of the Vietnam War have influenced and changed war veterans' remembrance of the events in which they actually took part.

13. Somewhat coincidentally, one of the central characters from *Diary of the Dead*, Tony Ravello, is played by the actor Shaun Roberts, who also plays Albert Wesker in *Afterlife* and *Retribution*.

14. The Newborn in *Alien Resurrection* is the mirror of the cloned Ripley in that it is the product of human DNA put into an Alien host. When born, it destroys its own mother, the Alien Queen, and only sees Ripley as being of the same order as itself.

15. This is at the end of the extended director's cut version as released on *The Ultimate Alien & Predator Collection*, Twentieth Century–Fox, 2007.

16. This "psionic" power is shown when she creates a huge blanket of fire in the sky to destroy a flock of zombie crows.

17. A very similar scenario was played out in "Normal Again" episode 17, season 6 of *Buffy the Vampire Slayer*, where we are given the possibility that none of what we have seen before is real and is only being acted out in the mind of an insane Buffy Summers, who is in fact locked up in a sanitarium.

18. Not dissimilar to the Borg in *Star Trek*, who assimilate many races and cultures but make them all look the same.

Works Cited

Anderson, Paul W.S., *Resident Evil*. Screen Gems, 2002.
_____. *Resident Evil: Afterlife*. Screen Gems, 2010.
_____. *Resident Evil: Retribution*. Screen Gems, 2012.
Bachelard, Gaston. *The Poetics of Space*. Trans. by Maria Jolas. Boston: Beacon Press, 1964.
Benjamin, Walter. "The Work of Art in the Age of Mechanical Reproduction," in *The Norton Anthology of Theory and Criticism*. New York: W.W. Norton, 2001.
Bishop, Kyle William. *American Zombie Gothic: The Rise and Fall (and Rise) of the Walking Dead in Popular Culture*. Jefferson: McFarland, 2012.
Botting, Fred. *Gothic*. London: Routledge, 1996.
Deleuze, Gilles, and Felix Guattari. *A Thousand Plateaues: Capitalism and Schizophrenia*. Trans. Brian Massumi. Minneapolis: University of Minnesota, 1987.
Gallardo-C, Ximena, and C. Jason Smith. *Alien Woman: The Making of Lt. Ellen Ripley*. New York: Continuum, 2004.
Jeunet, Jean-Pierre. *Alien Resurrection*. Twentieth Century–Fox, 1997.
Marx, Karl, *Capital Volume I*. Trans. Ben Fowkes. The Pelican Marx Library. Harmondsworth: Penguin, 1976.
Matheson, Richard. *I Am Legend*, 1954. London: Gollanz, 2007.
Mulcahy, Russell. *Resident Evil: Extinction*. Screen Gems, 2007.
Moretti, Franco. *Signs Taken for Wonders: Essays in the Sociology of Literary Forms*. Trans. Susan Fischer, David Forgacs and David Miller. London: Verso, 1988.
Nuttall, Sarah. *Entanglement: Literary and Cultural Reflections on Post-Apartheid*. Johannesburg: Witt University Press, 2009.

Romero, George. *Diary of the Dead*. Dimension Films, 2007.

Rothberg, Michael. *Multidirectional Memory: Remembering the Holocaust in the Age of Decolinisation*. Stanford: Stanford University Press, 2009.

Scott, Ridley. *Blade Runner*. Warner Bros. 1982.

Sturken, Marita. *Tangled Memories: The Vietnam War, the AIDS Epidemic and the Politics of Remembering*. Berkeley: California University Press, 1997.

Toro, Guillermo del. *Blade* II. New Line Cinema, 2002.

Warner, Marina. *Phantasmagoria: Spirit Visions, Metaphors, and Media into the Twenty-first Century*. Oxford: Oxford University Press, 2006.

Witt, Alexander. *Resident Evil: Apocalypse*. Screen Gems, 2004.

Wittgenstein, Ludwig. *Tractatus Logico-Philosophicus*, 1922. Trans. by D. F. Pears and B. F. McGuinness. London: Routledge, 1974.

About the Contributors

Suzan E. **Aiken** is an assistant professor of English at Saginaw Valley State University in Michigan. Her research is primarily concerned with rhetorical silence and listening, especially as silences are intentionally used, are connected to agency and identity, and have an effect on an audience, and often focuses on strong adolescent female characters.

Simon **Bacon** is an independent scholar based in Poznan, Poland. His research is focused on vampires and human memory in popular culture and he is editor of the inter-disciplinary journal *Monsters and the Monstrous.*

Stephen **Cadwell** received a Ph.D. from University College, Dublin. His research interests are horror, emotion, film and performance. He is an associate producer with the Galway Community Circus.

Margo **Collins** is a visiting assistant professor of English at DeVry University. She holds a Ph.D. in eighteenth-century British literature from the University of North Texas and in recent years has focused on Gothic literature, monstrosity and popular culture.

Adam M. **Crowley** is an assistant professor of English at Husson University in Bangor, Maine. His research is focused on the structural components of diverse works, from games such as *Tomb Raider* (2013) to *The Walking Dead* television series to the novels of Stephen King. His area of expertise is classical narratology.

Nadine **Farghaly** is a Ph.D. student at the University of Salzburg. She received an M.A. in English literature from Bowling Green State University in Ohio and a diploma in English and American studies from the University of Salzburg. Her research interests mainly focus on gender representations within popular culture.

Broc **Holmquest** is a graduate of the Department of Popular Culture Master's Program at Bowling Green State University. He has been a *Resident Evil* fan since 1996. While video games are his primary research focus, he also studies comic books and film, with an emphasis on popular genres and fandom.

Tanya Carinae Pell **Jones** holds a M.Ed. from Queens University of Charlotte and a B.S. in education from Slippery Rock University of Pennsylvania. Her scholarly interests lie in Gothicism, fairy tales, Celtic and Nordic folk tales and the paradox between science and the supernatural in literature.

Nicolas J. **Lalone** is working toward a Ph.D. in philosophy with a specialty in information science and technology at Penn State University. He is a long-time game enthusiast who began to study games as a means through which to examine ideology via procedure.

Kristine **Larsen** is a professor of astronomy at Central Connecticut State University. Her research focuses on the intersections between science and society, including astronomy education and issues of gender and science, astronomical allusions in the works of J.R.R. Tolkien and representations of science and scientists in zombie media.

Daniel **Müller** is a Ph.D. student at Heinrich Heine University, Düsseldorf. He is a research manager for FernUniversität in Hagen and lectures on film and literature. Among his research interests are the intersections of history, popular culture and social psychology, as well as film and cultural theory and psychoanalysis.

Jenny **Platz** is a Ph.D. candidate at the University of Rhode Island, focusing on film and popular culture. She earned an M.A. in cinema studies from San Francisco State University. Her research focuses on the aesthetics of the eating disorder body in television and film, as well as the use of popular music in anti-nostalgic television shows such as *Freaks and Geeks*.

Hannah **Priest** is a researcher based at the University of Manchester and Liverpool's John Moores University. Her doctoral studies explored the intersections of sex, violence and monstrosity in late medieval romance, and she is working on a cultural history of female werewolves and an exploration of Alice in Wonderland in popular culture. As Hannah Kate, she is a poet, short story writer and fiction editor.

JL **Schatz** is a professor of English and feminist evolutionary studies at Binghamton University, where he also serves as the director of the speech and debate team, which was ranked first in the nation in 2008. He has published essays on technology and apocalypse, environmental securitization and the influence of science fiction on reality.

James **Stone** is an assistant professor in the Department of Cinematic Arts at the University of New Mexico, Albuquerque, where he teaches several courses in film history. His primary interests are in apocalyptic imagery, gender studies and the aesthetics of violence.

Index